DEPARTMENT OF TRADE

Report of the
Committee of Inquiry
on
Industrial Democracy

Chairman
Lord Bullock

Presented to Parliament by the
Secretary of State for Trade
by Command of Her Majesty
January 1977

LONDON
HER MAJESTY'S STATIONERY OFFICE
£3 net

Cmnd. 6706

HD5660
G7
G74
1977

ISBN 0 10 167060 5

Contents

Preface

To the Rt Hon Edmund Dell MP, Secretary of State for Trade and President of the Board of Trade.

1. Your predecessor, the Rt Hon Peter Shore MP announced in the House of Commons on 5 August 1975 his intention to appoint a Committee of Inquiry, 'to advise on questions relating to representation at board level in the private sector' with the following terms of reference:

'Accepting the need for a radical extension of industrial democracy in the control of companies by means of representation on boards of directors, and accepting the essential role of trade union organisations in this process, to consider how such an extension can best be achieved, taking into account in particular the proposals of the Trades Union Congress report on industrial democracy as well as experience in Britain, the EEC and other countries. Having regard to the interests of the national economy, employees, investors and consumers, to analyse the implications of such representation for the efficient management of companies and for company law'.

2. Our membership was announced on 3 December 1975. Sir Alan (now Lord) Bullock, Master of St Catherine's College, Oxford, was appointed as Chairman. The members were as follows:

Professor George Bain ...	Director of the SSRC Industrial Relations Research Unit, University of Warwick.
Mr N P Biggs	Chairman of Williams & Glyn's Bank Ltd and former Chairman and Chief Executive of Esso Petroleum Co Ltd.
Sir Jack Callard	Former Chairman of Imperial Chemical Industries Ltd and (since 30 June 1976) Chairman of British Home Stores Ltd.
Mr Barrie Heath	Chairman of Guest, Keen and Nettlefolds Ltd.
Mr Clive Jenkins	General Secretary of the Association of Scientific, Technical and Managerial Staffs.
Mr Jack Jones	General Secretary of the Transport and General Workers Union.
Mr David Lea	Secretary, Economic Department, Trades Union Congress.
Mr John Methven ...	Director-General of Fair Trading.
Professor K W Wedderburn	Cassel Professor of Commercial Law in the University of London (London School of Economics).
Mr N S Wilson	Solicitor.

Mr John Methven resigned from the Committee on 15 July 1976, on taking up his appointment as Director-General of the Confederation of British Industry.

3. We were asked to report within 12 months and this we have done. We have not, however, reached a sufficient measure of agreement to present a single

report signed by all members of the Committee. Our report, therefore, is in three parts: the main report signed by the Chairman and six members of the Committee; a note of dissent on certain specific points in the main report by Mr N S Wilson; and a minority report signed by three members of the Committee.

4. We are greatly indebted to our Secretary, Mr Robin Hope of the Department of Trade, and to our Assistant Secretary, Mr David Normington of the Department of Employment, for their hard work and skill in organising the work of the Committee and in reducing many drafts to the final version of the report. We also wish to express our thanks for the valuable help we have received from the two other members of our secretariat, Mrs Muriel Sanders and Mrs Christine Hennessy.

Contents of the Main Report

CHAPTER 1

Introduction

1. We held our first meeting on 12 December 1975 and our last, to sign the report, on 14 December 1976. There were in all 29 meetings of the full Committee, including a two-day meeting in October at the Civil Service College, Sunningdale, during which we carried out a thorough review of the issues involved. In the later stages of our work, members of the majority group held 10 meetings to prepare the main report.

Written and oral evidence

2. We decided immediately to seek written evidence from all interested individuals and organisations. On 17 December 1975 we publicised in the press our terms of reference and asked to receive written submissions from anyone with views to put to us on the issues they raised. We repeated this invitation on 5 February 1976. In response we received 337 submissions.

3. We did not make a general request for oral evidence. We decided that it would not be valuable to go over ground which was already adequately covered in the written submissions. Our view was that oral evidence was an opportunity for us to clarify and pursue points which we considered were not sufficiently discussed in the written evidence. We therefore issued a number of specific invitations to individuals and organisations to meet the Committee. Eight sessions of oral evidence were held.

4. Many of the submissions made to us have already been published. Our report shows how helpful the evidence has been in clarifying some of the main issues before the Committee and in identifying some of the questions that have to be answered if board level representation is to be introduced. We list those who submitted evidence at Annex A. We are very grateful to them all. In addition to considering the written evidence, members of the Committee have read widely in the published literature on industrial democracy.

Terms of reference

5. Many witnesses were concerned that our terms of reference would restrict the scope of our inquiry to the single issue of board level representation and would exclude consideration of other forms of participation, seen as alternative or additional, particularly those at other levels in the enterprise. We agree that out terms of reference direct our attention to the issue of employee representation on company boards, on which we are particularly requested to report. To this extent, we believe that they were useful to us in providing a starting point for our studies; they have not however precluded us from considering the wider aspects of participation in decision-making. We could not have carried out our inquiry properly, if we had not examined other forms of participation or if we had ignored the relationship of board level representation to changes below that level. Nor were those who sent us written evidence constrained by our terms of reference. In addition to the submissions which dealt with aspects of employee representation on boards, we were sent

1

many descriptions of existing systems of participation at levels below the board and new proposals for the further extension of such participation. Our report shows that we have interpreted our terms of reference widely.

Study of European experience

6. We were asked in our terms of reference to consider the experience in the European Economic Community (EEC) and other European countries, and this was an important part of our work. Early in our discussions we decided to commission two reports on European experience of industrial democracy from Dr Eric Batstone of the Industrial Relations Research Unit established by the Social Science Research Council at the University of Warwick, and Mr P L Davies, Fellow and Tutor in Law of Balliol College, Oxford. Their task was to review the published material on experience of industrial democracy in Europe with particular reference to the representation of workers on boards of directors.

7. The two reports were presented to us in April 1976. We found their conclusions helpful in our evaluation of European experience. We refer to their findings at various points in our report. Since we felt that their research was of considerable general interest and that it filled a gap in the published material by providing an analytical, rather than simply descriptive, account of employee representation on boards in other countries, we decided that it should be published and this was done in July 1976[1].

8. We also decided that it would be beneficial to make two visits abroad to study the systems operating in the Federal Republic of Germany and in Sweden, at a time of important changes in both. We should like to thank all the people we met during our visits to both countries who gave so freely of their time and took such trouble to ensure that our discussions were fruitful and stimulating. A list of those we met is at Annex B. We should also like to thank the staffs of the British Embassies in Bonn and Stockholm, in particular Mr J S P Mackenzie, Labour Counsellor in Bonn and Mr C Marshall, First Secretary (Labour) in Stockholm who contributed in large measure to the success of these visits.

Organisation of our report

9. Our report has a number of elements. We begin in Chapter 2 with a brief statistical account of the private sector of industry, for which we are making recommendations. This includes information about the size of companies, the numbers of employees, investment in industry and the extent of unionisation, brought together from a number of sources. We are grateful to all those who have contributed to it. We found it necessary to supplement official statistics, particularly with regard to the number of employees in overseas subsidiaries of companies in the United Kingdom, by carrying out our own survey of the companies listed in *The Times 1,000 companies*[2].

---

[1]Eric Batstone and P L Davies, *Industrial Democracy: European Experience*. Two reports prepared for the Industrial Democracy Committee (HMSO 1976).
[2]Times Newspapers Ltd, *The Times 1,000, 1975-1976* (London 1976).

10. On the extent of unionisation Mr Robert Price, a lecturer in industrial relations at the University of Warwick, and Professor Bain, one of our Committee members, made available to us the results of their research into trade union organisation prior to its publication and much of our analysis on this subject at the end of Chapter 2 is based on their findings. Their research has since been published[1].

11. Following our analysis of the size and shape of the private sector, we go on to describe various aspects of the debate on industrial democracy. This includes a description of some specific objections to employee representation on boards, which were put to us in the evidence. We conclude this part of the report by considering some of the major issues which arise from points made in the written evidence, in particular the importance of participation below the board and the implications of board level representation for the efficient management of companies and for the interests of investors and consumers.

12. Having reached a conclusion in favour of employee representation on the board, we then turn to our proposals for the way in which it should be introduced. Chapters 7 and 8 discuss the structure of decision-making in companies in the United Kingdom, and how it will be affected by board level representation. The first of these chapters is largely descriptive of the boards of present companies in the United Kingdom and the duties of their directors, and includes our own analysis of the size and composition of boards of directors in *The Times 1,000 companies*. The second looks at the changes which will be necessary to ensure effective employee representation on boards and the continuing efficiency of companies, and considers the arguments for and against the introduction of a two-tier board system.

13. Chapter 9 contains the core of our proposals on the proportion of employee representatives who should sit on the board, and on the reconstitution of the board which we believe is necessary to create a workable system. Chapter 10 discusses how employee representatives should be selected, the role of trade unions, and the relationship between board level representation and collective bargaining. In Chapter 11 we consider the size of companies to which our proposals should apply, and the special problems posed by groups of companies and multinationals. Chapter 12 contains some consequential proposals, namely the setting-up of an Industrial Democracy Commission and the establishment of training programmes.

---

[1] R Price and G S Bain, *Union growth revisited: 1948–1974 in perspective*. British Journal of Industrial Relations Vol XIV No 3 (November 1976) pages 339–355.

CHAPTER 2

Size and shape of the private sector

1. At an early stage in our deliberations we decided that it would be necessary to have as clear an understanding as possible of the size and shape of the private sector of the British economy. We needed to know how many people worked for how many large, medium-sized and small enterprises; who owned or controlled the enterprises; what trends could be observed; the extent to which workers in the private sector were organised in trade unions. This chapter seeks to present a simplified statistical profile of the enterprises to which our recommendations refer. They include all companies subject to the Companies Acts—whether limited by shares or by guarantee, unlimited, public or private, quoted or unquoted—irrespective of ownership; but exclude the nationalised industries incorporated under their own statutes as well as building societies, cooperative societies and other bodies such as partnerships which are not companies. Our more general conclusions may apply to some of these excluded enterprises, but our recommendations refer only to companies as defined above.

2. Difficulties in collation and interpretation of statistical data spring from the variety of purposes for which official records are kept; from problems of definition (eg of what constitutes a company); from the timelag between the collection of raw data and production of comprehensible results; from the constantly changing nature and structure of the economy; and from other causes familiar both to statisticians and to laymen who seek answers to statistical questions. These difficulties mean that the data presented in this chapter cannot be complete and that the statistical portrait of the private sector is painted with a broad brush, but despite this shortcoming we believe it is essential for those who discuss industrial democracy to know at least approximately how many companies and how many employees they are talking about.

Enterprises and employment

3. Table 1 shows the number of enterprises employing 200 or more people in the United Kingdom, broadly divided into nine economic sectors and into six size groups, by reference to the numbers of employees in the United Kingdom. The figures are taken from accounts published in 1973–74. Where the accounts of subsidiary companies are consolidated with those of their United Kingdom holding companies, those subsidiaries are not counted as separate enterprises, and the United Kingdom employees of all consolidated subsidiaries in the group are counted together. But where the accounts of partly-owned subsidiaries or associated companies are not consolidated with those of the group, those subsidiaries are counted as separate enterprises, and their United Kingdom employees are not counted as employees of the group. For example, Imperial Metal Industries Ltd (although a quoted company) is consolidated in the accounts of its parent, Imperial Chemical Industries Ltd (ICI) and therefore does not count as a separate enterprise; but Carrington Viyella Ltd and Tioxide Group Ltd (although associated companies of ICI) are counted as separate enterprises, and their United Kingdom employees are counted separately. The number of enterprises controlled from overseas is given in brackets after each figure. The population in the table consisted originally of enterprises with

4

TABLE 1

United Kingdom enterprises with over 200 employees in the United Kingdom

ANALYSIS BY INDUSTRY AND NUMBER OF EMPLOYEES

Standard Industrial Classification order	Sector	201–500	501–1,000	1,001–2,000	2,001–5,000	5,001–10,000	Over 10,000	Total over 2,000	TOTAL
		Number of enterprises (of which controlled from overseas)							
I-III	Food, drink and tobacco	21 (3)	30 (7)	28 (4)	20 (4)	9 (3)	22 (1)	51 (8)	130 (22)
IV-V	Petroleum products etc. and chemicals etc.	34 (18)	31 (19)	24 (11)	21 (9)	8 (3)	7 (1)	36 (13)	125 (61)
VI-XII	Metal manufacturing, engineering, shipbuilding, vehicles	55 (17)	140 (30)	138 (31)	125 (34)	45 (9)	48 (10)	218 (53)	551 (131)
XIII-XV	Textiles and clothing	11 (1)	44 (4)	44 (2)	37 (3)	8 (—)	10 (—)	55 (3)	154 (10)
XVI-XIX	Other manufacturing	32 (5)	78 (5)	62 (8)	57 (7)	35 (1)	17 (3)	109 (11)	281 (29)
XX and XXII	Construction, transport and communications	32 (2)	44 (3)	55 (2)	40 (1)	16 (—)	11 (—)	67 (1)	198 (8)
XXIII	Wholesale and retail distribution ...	43 (10)	65 (4)	55 (7)	59 (5)	17 (1)	22 (3)	98 (9)	261 (30)
XXIV	Insurance, banking, finance and business services	124 (19)	73 (6)	37 (1)	32 (1)	18 (—)	11 (—)	61 (1)	295 (27)
XXVI	Miscellaneous services	17 (6)	21 (6)	18 (4)	22 (1)	12 (—)	9 (—)	43 (1)	99 (17)
	TOTAL	369 (81)	526 (84)	461 (70)	413 (65)	168 (17)	157 (18)	738 (100)	2,094 (335)

Note: See text (paragraph 3) for definitions and methodology.
Source: Department of Industry

5

net assets in 1968 of £2 million or more, or with gross income in 1968 of £200,000 or more. Enterprises whose separate existence ceased between 1968 and 1973–74 have been removed. Certain sectors (eg agriculture, banking and petroleum) and United Kingdom enterprises whose main interests were overseas were excluded from the original population. But the sectors known to include enterprises employing large numbers of people in the United Kingdom have been analysed individually, and such enterprises have been added to the population. Enterprises included in *The Times 1,000, 1975–76* and *The Top Private Companies 1974–75* have also been added, if not already present. The figures in the two left-hand columns of the table may therefore be understated, but it is unlikely that any enterprises employing 1,000 or more people in the United Kingdom have been excluded.

4. The table shows that enterprises employing 200 or more people in the United Kingdom number approximately 2,100; 57 per cent of them are employers of 1,000 or more people and about one third of them, 738 enterprises, employ 2,000 or more people in the United Kingdom. But this count does not include all the *companies* employing 2,000 or more people in the United Kingdom, since virtually all these enterprises are in fact groups of companies, organised in pyramids of holding and subsidiary companies. Within each enterprise there may be one or more subsidiaries employing 2,000 or more people. It is difficult to estimate their number, since the internal organisation of groups of companies is so various, but consideration of a few examples shows that there are probably over 1,000 of them. The question of groups of companies is treated in detail in Chapter 11. The enterprises controlled from overseas form a substantial minority, more significant in some economic sectors than in others, but generally accounting for about one enterprise in six or seven. The largest group (about 70 per cent) of enterprises controlled from overseas consists of subsidiaries of United States enterprises; some 10 per cent are controlled by enterprises incorporated in other member states of the European Economic Community (EEC).

5. Table 2 shows that the enterprises whose turnover is greatest—*The Times, 1,000*—are predominantly very large employers; only one in five of them employs under 1,000 people; nearly two thirds of them employ 2,000 or more people; and there are 155 enterprises with 10,000 or more United Kingdom employees. This high degree of economic concentration means that over 7 million people in this country, more than one quarter of the total workforce, are employed by large enterprises in the private sector. This may be compared with the figures of 18 million for the private sector as a whole; nearly 2 million employed in public corporations (nationalised industries); rather less than 3 million employed by local authorities (including education); and 2 million employed in central government (including the National Health Service and the Post Office).

6. This concentration of industry in larger units has been a steady trend in the British economy since World War II. The increasing share of output accounted for by the 100 largest manufacturing enterprises is paralleled by the growing proportion of the workforce employed by large enterprises. The phenomenon appears to be more pronounced in Britain than in other industrial countries:

6

TABLE 2

Large United Kingdom enterprises by number of employees in United Kingdom and overseas

UK employees		Number of enterprises	Total number of UK employees[1] (thousands)	Total number of overseas employees[2] (thousands)
Not disclosed ...	...	18	n.a.	n.a.
Under 1,000 ...	...	184	91	60
1,000– 2,000 ...	...	174	264	43
2,000– 3,000 ...	...	157	394	26
3,000– 4,000 ...	...	100	351	147
4,000– 5,000 ...	...	67	297	42
5,000– 7,500 ...	...	94	567	154
7,500–10,000 ...	...	51	444	105
10,000–20,000 ...	...	73	985	354
20,000–50,000 ...	...	56	1,674	675
Over 50,000 ...	...	26	2,093	635
TOTAL ...	...	1,000	7,160	2,241

Notes:
(1) Possibly overstated, since a few companies only gave figures for all employees, and these are assumed to be in the UK.
(2) Understated—see text, paragraph 8.
Source: *The Times 1,000, 1975–76* and the Committee's own survey.

in the unpublished *EEC Economic Survey 1970,* figures for share of total output and share of total employment accounted for by enterprises with over 1,000 employees are consistently higher for the United Kingdom than those for other countries of the EEC, for Sweden and for the United States of America.

7. Large and powerful though these enterprises are, they are owned and controlled (at least in law) by their shareholders. It is pertinent therefore to ask who the shareholders are. An examination of the pattern of ownership of quoted ordinary shares in United Kingdom companies between 1963 and 1973 shows that the shares owned by persons, executors and trustees resident in the United Kingdom account for a decreasing, though still substantial proportion of the total: 59 per cent in 1963, 42 per cent in 1973. By contrast the shares owned by British financial institutions (insurance companies, pension funds, banks, unit and investment trusts, etc) account for a smaller but increasing proportion: 28 per cent in 1963, 42 per cent in 1973. Charities, non-financial companies, the public sector and overseas holders account for the remainder[1]. Having noted this changing pattern of share ownership, we then considered the sources of new funds. Table 3 shows that since 1950 larger quoted British companies in manufacturing, distribution and other services have depended for funds primarily on internal sources—retained profits and provisions for depreciation. The next most important sources of funds were bank and other borrowings. The role played by the issue of new equity appears to be comparatively modest. The Diamond Commission noted:

'Over the period we studied (1950–72) internal funds accounted on average for 76 per cent of the total funds raised, about 40 per cent being retained profits and 36 per cent provisions for depreciation. Equity capital raised for cash accounted for 6·5 per cent of total funds during the period 1950–72, this figure falling from an average of 10·4 per cent in 1950–61 to 4·6 per cent over the period 1962–72'.[2]

It will be seen from Table 3 that bank borrowing played an exceptionally important part in 1973 and 1974, whereas 1975 saw a very large number of rights issues, which increased the figure for funds from the new equity source to 13 per cent in that year. In 1976 it appears that the pattern is nearer the average for the whole post-war period.

8. The part played in British industry by enterprises controlled from overseas has been mentioned. But to have a clear picture of large British enterprises and of those who work for them, we must consider not only the United Kingdom employees but the large numbers of people overseas that these enterprises employ. Unfortunately the Companies Acts do not require any statement as to their numbers in annual reports. We therefore wrote to some 700 companies in *The Times 1,000, 1975–76,* asking them how many people they employed overseas. We are grateful for the response (66 per cent), and have added this information to that which other enterprises provide in their annual reports, in order to make up the right-hand column of Table 2. Although these figures are understated, because some companies did not reply, it can be seen that the group of large

[1]Royal Commission on the Distribution of Income and Wealth (Diamond Commission) Report No 2, *Income from Companies and its Distribution* (HMSO 1975), Table 10, page 17.
[2]Diamond Commission *op cit* paragraph 326.

8

TABLE 3

Sources of funds of larger quoted companies in manufacturing, distribution and other services 1950-75

Percentage of total sources

	Average 1950-54	Average 1955-59	Average 1960-64	Average 1965-69	1970	1971	1972	1973	1974	Average 1970-74	Provisional 1975
Retained profits ...	56	44	36	32	25	39	51	44	38	39	47
Depreciation	25	32	37	40	45	47	32	26	30	36	36
Total internal funds ...	81	76	73	72	70	86	83	70	68	75	83
Bank borrowing ...	3	5	8	11	19	−4	7	21	29	15	−1
Ordinary shares issued for cash	6	10	10	5	2	4	4	1	1	2	13
Preference and long term loans issued for cash	10	9	9	12	8	15	6	8	2	8	5
Total external funds ...	19	24	27	28	30	14	17	30	32	25	17
Total sources of funds	100	100	100	100	100	100	100	100	100	100	100

Source: Department of Industry, *Business Monitor M3.*

9

enterprises as a whole employs over 2 million people overseas, in addition to their United Kingdom workforce of over 7 million. Of the 624 enterprises in this table employing more than 2,000 people in the United Kingdom, at least 320 (51 per cent) have some overseas employees, and at least 35 (6 per cent) actually have more employees overseas than in the United Kingdom.

Trade union membership

9. The representation of overseas employees raises problems to which we shall refer in Chapter 11. But the question of how United Kingdom workers may be represented at board level is central to our inquiry, and we have therefore been particularly interested in the extent to which they already speak with a collective voice, in negotiation with management through trade union representatives.

10. The remainder of this chapter is drawn from a paper published in the November 1976 issue of the *British Journal of Industrial Relations, Union Growth Revisited: 1948-1974 In Perspective* by Robert Price (Lecturer in Industrial Relations, University of Warwick) and George Sayers Bain (Director, SSRC Industrial Relations Research Unit, University of Warwick). Professor Bain is also a member of this Committee. Table 4, which is derived from that

TABLE 4

Total Trade Union membership and density in the United Kingdom Selected years, 1948–74

Year	Labour force (000s)	Annual % change in Labour force	Total Union membership (000s)	Annual % change in Union membership	Density of Union membership (%)
1948	20,732	..	9,362	..	45·2
1958	22,290	n.a.	9,639	n.a.	43·2
1963	23,558	n.a.	10,067	n.a.	42·7
1968	23,667	n.a.	10,193	n.a.	43·1
1969	23,603	−0·3	10,472	+2·7	44·4
1970	23,446	−0·7	11,179	+6·8	47·7
1971	23,231	−0·9	11,127	−0·5	47·9
1972	22,959	+0·3	11,349	+2·0	49·4
1973	23,244	+1·2	11,444	+0·8	49·2
1974	23,339	+0·4	11,755	+2·7	50·4

Source: Price and Bain.

paper, demonstrates that total trade union membership in the United Kingdom now stands at 11.8 million and that the figure is almost exactly half the total labour force. Table 5 gives the labour force, union membership and union density between 1948 and 1974 by industry. It can be seen from this table that the overall increase in union density which has occurred since World War II has taken place in an environment which has been basically unfavourable to trade union growth. On the one hand, there has been a substantial decline in the numbers employed in industries with a long tradition of unionism and very high membership densities—notably, in mining, railways and cotton textiles. On the other hand, sectors in which unions have historically been much weaker and less well established have grown extremely rapidly—for example, professional services, insurance, banking and finance, and distribution.

11. This shift towards the less well unionised service sector is mirrored in the steady growth in white-collar employment over the same period. Price and Bain show that the proportion of the labour force in white-collar employment rose from 31 per cent to 43 per cent between 1951 and 1971, while manual employment declined commensurately from 64 per cent to 55 per cent. The growth of non-manual jobs is doubly unfavourable to the maintenance of aggregate union density, since it reflects not only the shift noted above towards service industries, but also an internal shift within the manufacturing and public sectors towards a higher proportion of white-collar employment. Price and Bain calculate that the density of white-collar unionisation in 1974 stood at slightly over 39 per cent compared with a manual union density of nearly 58 per cent. Nevertheless, despite this steady shift towards white-collar occupations which are less well unionised than manual occupations, British unions have been able to increase their total membership by some $2\frac{1}{2}$ million over the post-war period and to increase their level of representation within the labour force to over 50 per cent. In only three sectors identified in Table 5 has there been a decline in union density since 1948, while Table 6 shows that the aggregate white-collar and manual groups have both made substantial density gains since that year—from 30 to 39 per cent in the first case, and from 51 to 58 per cent in the second case.

Unionisation in relation to size of establishments and enterprises

12. Available union membership data are insufficiently detailed to permit a precise analysis of union density by establishment size. But Price and Bain refer to evidence from a wide range of countries which supports the proposition that the larger the establishment the more likely it is to be unionised. They also demonstrate the way in which density levels in the United Kingdom are affected by making a number of assumptions about the pattern of unionisation by establishment size. Table 7 is based on the assumption that union membership in manufacturing establishments of less than 100 and 200 employees is negligible so that the exclusion of employment in establishments of these sizes from the density calculations in manufacturing does not seriously overstate the resulting union density figures for larger firms. When employment in establishments with less than 100 workers is excluded, the density figure for manufacturing rises from about 62 per cent to 77 per cent; and when employment in establishments with less than 200 workers is excluded, the density figure rises to about

TABLE 5

Union membership and density by industry in the United Kingdom, 1948 and 1974

Industry[1]	1948			1974		
	Labour force (000s)	Union membership (000s)	Density (%)	Labour force (000s)	Union membership (000s)	Density (%)
Agriculture and Forestry ...	785·9	215·7	27·4	415·5	92·3	22·2
Fishing	37·7	14·9	39·6	12·2	7·4	60·5
Coal mining ...	802·7	675·3	84·1	314·0	302·1	96·2
Other mining ...	81·4	37·0	45·5	50·6	26·2	51·8
Food and drink ...	597·4	227·4	38·1	783·9	401·1	51·2
Tobacco	49·1	26·1	53·1			
Chemicals... ...	426·8	127·3	29·8	483·6	247·4	51·2
Metals and engineering	3,676·1	1,837·5	50·0	4,118·0	2,862·7	69·4
Cotton and man-made fibres ...	395·2	276·6	70·0	596·7	243·8	40·9
Other textiles ...	533·3	180·4	33·8			
Leather	79·0	24·7	31·2	44·0	20·5	46·6
Clothing	429·1	145·5	33·9	345·8	207·7	60·0
Footwear	139·5	92·8	66·6	87·1	68·8	79·0
Bricks and building materials	172·2	70·1	40·8	171·9	69·4	40·4
Pottery	75·3	31·3	41·5	60·5	56·8	93·8
Glass	68·1	28·2	41·3	74·5	58·5	78·5
Wood and furniture	279·8	122·0	43·6	289·6	102·0	35·2
Paper, printing and publishing ...	455·5	264·1	58·0	596·1	426·6	71·6
Rubber	97·9	48·5	49·6	127·2	71·1	55·9
Construction ...	1,353·7	613·2	45·3	1,428·8	388·1	27·2
Gas, electricity and water	322·9	218·3	67·6	352·3	324·0	92·0

TABLE 5 (*cont.*)
Union membership and density by industry in the United Kingdom, 1948 and 1974

Industry[1]	1948			1974		
	Labour force (000s)	Union member-ship (000s)	Density (%)	Labour force (000s)	Union member-ship (000s)	Density (%)
Railways	694·9	612·1	88·1	224·0	217·0	96·9
Road transport ...	490·6	295·0[2]	60·1[2]	468·3	445·4[2]	95·1[2]
Sea transport ...	120·8	108·0	89·3	90·6	90·3	99·6
Port and inland water transport	155·7	123·2	79·1	81·5	77·2	94·7
Air transport ...	32·1	13·0	40·5	79·8	74·7	93·6
Post Office and tele-communications	353·2	283·4	80·2	509·7	448·1	87·9
Distribution ...	2,167·9	325·3	15·0	2,810·1	321·8	11·4
Insurance, banking and finance ...	425·9	137·1	32·2	680·5	305·1	44·8
Entertainment and media services ...	238·4	95·7	40·1	189·6	123·0	64·9
Health	525·9	204·6	38·9	1,175·2	715·8	60·9
Hotels and catering	708·1	n.a.	—	824·2	42·5	5·2
Other professional services	276·8	n.a.	—	470·2	17·6	3·7
Education and Local Government	1,280·5	792·2	61·9	2,752·4	2,356·0	85·6
National Govern-ment	724·1	480·6	66·4	623·7	564·5	90·5

Notes:

[1]The following industries are not included in this table: miscellaneous transport services, other manufacturing (less rubber), business services (property owning, advertising and market research, other business services, central offices not allocable elsewhere), other miscellaneous services (betting and gambling, hairdressing and manicure, laundries, dry-cleaning, motor repairers, distributors, garages and filling stations, repair of boots and shoes, and other services). Union density in this heterogeneous group of industries was less than 3 per cent in 1974; total employment was 2·4 million.

[2]These figures are substantially overstated since it has not been possible to disaggregate the membership of the Commercial Trade Group of the Transport and General Workers' Union into those employed by haulage firms and those employed by manufacturing concerns. Union membership among the latter group should be classified to the relevant manufacturing industry

Source: Price and Bain.

TABLE 6

The growth of white-collar and manual unionism in the United Kingdom, 1948–1974

	Union membership (000s)				% Increase	
	1948	1964	1970	1974	1948–74	1970–74
White-collar ...	1,964	2,684	3,592	4,263	+117·1	+18·7
Manual	7,398	7,534	7,587	7,491	+ 0·1	− 1·3

	Union density (%)				Increase	
	1948	1964	1970	1974	1948–74	1970–74
White-collar ...	30·2	29·6	35·2	39·4	+9·2	+4·2
Manual	50·7	52·9	56·0	57·9	+7·2	+1·9

Source: Price and Bain.

TABLE 7

Unionisation in larger manufacturing establishments in the United Kingdom, 1948 and 1974

	1948		1974	
	Labour force (000s)	Density (%)	Labour force (000s)	Density (%)
All manufacturing	6,709·3	52·2	7,778·9	62·2
Excluding employment in establishments with less than 100 workers	5,193·9	67·4	6,292·4	76·9
Excluding employment in establishments with less than 200 workers	4,268·4	82·1	5,422·5	89·2

Source: Price and Bain.

89 per cent. To the extent that there are nnion members in manufacturing establishments of less than 100 employees and of less than 200 employees, however, these density figures are overstated. But even if we make an assumption that generously overstates the likely number of union members in small establishments—that the average density in manufacturing establishments with less than 100 employees is 20 per cent and the average density in manufacturing establishments with between 100 and 200 employees is 40 per cent—and if the union members given by these assumptions are excluded from the calculations, the union density figure for manufacturing still rises to 71 per cent and 78 per cent respectively.

13. Comprehensive and systematic employment data by establishment size exist only for manufacturing industries, and hence the above analysis cannot be extended to the economy as a whole. But it is well known that construction, agriculture, and private sector services are dominated by small undertakings[1]. Table 8 shows aggregate employment, union membership, and union density levels for the private sector based on the cumulative exclusion of the industries which are dominated by small establishments and on the more generous assumptions in respect of union membership in small manufacturing establishments made in Table 7. When these exclusions are made, the overall density figure for the private sector of the economy reaches about 72 per cent.

14. For reasons which will be clear from later chapters of this report, we are particularly concerned to assess the likely extent of trade union organisation in those enterprises employing 2,000 or more people in the private sector; taking the 624 enterprises in *The Times 1,000* which employ 2,000 or more people in the United Kingdom, these in total employ 6.8 million as compared with 10.4 million employees in the smaller companies which comprise the rest of the private sector (excluding self-employed people). No data are available which can give a precise figure for union density in large enterprises, but the data set out in the two preceding paragraphs, deriving from information about establishments, create a strong presumption that in enterprises employing 2,000 or more people in the private sector, average trade union membership is of the order of 70 per cent. This hypothesis may be tested against what it implies for the relative density of the membership in smaller enterprises. Beginning with the overall figure of 6.7 million trade union members in the private sector (1974), a 70 per cent density in the larger enterprises (ie those with 2,000 or more employees) implies a figure of 4.7 million trade union members in those enterprises, leaving 2·0 million for the smaller enterprises; this gives a density for the smaller enterprises of the order of 20 per cent. This figure for enterprises with less than 2,000 employees is consistent with the evidence from Table 5, which shows that union density is extremely low in the industries which are dominated by smaller enterprises—eg agriculture and forestry, distribution, hotels and catering, professional services; it therefore tends to confirm that it is reasonable to assume a union density figure of around 70 per cent for larger enterprises.

---

[1]In distribution, for example, which dominates the private services sector, the 1971 Census of Distribution shows that there were 1·8 million employees in the 460,000 retail establishments with less than 20 workers. See *Census of Distribution 1971, Part I*, Business Monitor SD 10 (HMSO 1975), Table 8.

TABLE 8

Unionisation by industrial sector and by establishment([1]) size in the United Kingdom 1974

	Labour force (000s)	Union membership (000s)	Density (%)
Total	23,339	11,755	50·4
less Public sector	6,113	5,079	
	17,226	6,676	38·8
less Agriculture, fishing and forestry	428	100	
	16,798	6,576	39·1
less Distribution	2,810	322	
	13,988	6,254	44·7
less Construction	1,429	388	
	12,559	5,866	46·7
less Miscellaneous services([2])	1,622	([4])	
	10,937	5,866	53·6
less Other private sector services([3])	1,294	([4])	
	9,643	5,866	60·8
less Manufacturing establishments with less than 100 workers	1,487	297	
	8,156	5,569	68·3
less Manufacturing establishments with less than 200 workers	870	348	
	7,286	5,221	71·7

Notes:
([1]) As defined in the Standard Industrial Classification.
([2]) Comprises property owning and managing; advertising and market research; other business services; hairdressing; laundries; dry-cleaning; motor-repairers; boot and shoe repair; other miscellaneous services and storage.
([3]) Comprises law; accountancy; religion; hotels and catering.
([4]) Union membership negligible.
Source: Price and Bain.

Number and size of unions

15. There has been a marked trend in recent years towards the concentration of union membership into fewer and larger unions. Table 9 shows that there were 488 trade unions recorded by the Department of Employment in 1974, compared with 664 in 1960 and 1,323 at the beginning of this century. The

TABLE 9

Numbers and size of Trade Unions in the United Kingdom and affiliation to TUC

Number of trade unions	1960	1965	1970	1973	1974
Analysis by number of members					
Under 1,000 members	362	333	291	253	258
1,000– 10,000 „	209	193	152	157	142
10,000– 50,000 „	55	59	69	47	48
50,000–100,000 „	21	20	17	14	15
100,000–250,000 „	10	8	14	13	14
Over 250,000 „	7	10	9	11	11
Total all trade unions	664	623	552	495	488
Total organisations affiliated to TUC	183	170	142	109	111
Membership (thousands)					
Analysis by size of unions					
Under 1,000 members	91	86	76	70	74
1,000– 10,000 „	646	602	517	507	452
10,000– 50,000 „	1,102	1,306	1,037	1,088	1,120
50,000–100,000 „	1,405	1,394	1,202	997	1,045
100,000–250,000 „	1,742	1,189	2,188	1,810	1,995
Over 250,000 „	4,848	5,746	6,155	7,035	7,264
Total membership of all trade unions	9,834	10,323	11,175	11,507	11,950
Total membership of organisations affiliated to TUC	8,299	8,868	10,002	10,022	10,364

Source: Department of Employment Gazette, November 1976 and TUC.

Department includes in its figures, 'all organisations of employees—including those of salaried and professional workers as well as those of wage earners—which are known to include in their objects that of negotiating with employers with a view to regulating the wages and conditions of their members'. The effect of this definition is that the official series tends to overstate the real number of trade unions; it records separately the sections of certain trade unions such as the National Union of Insurance Workers and the National Union of Textile and Allied Workers which are organised on a semi-autonomous basis but which

17

TABLE 10

Proportion of United Kingdom Trade Union membership in larger and smaller unions

Year	1960			1970			1974		
	No of unions	No of members (000s)	% of total membership	No of unions	No of members (000s)	% of total membership	No of unions	No of members (000s)	% of total membership
Unions with 100,000 members or more	17	6,590	67·0	23	8,343	74·7	25	9,259	77·5
Unions with 50,000 members or more	38	7,995	81·3	40	9,545	85·4	40	10,304	86·2
Unions with 10,000 members or more	93	9,097	92·5	109	10,582	94·7	88	11,424	95·6
Unions with less than 10,000 members	571	737	7·5	443	593	5·3	400	526	4·4
Unions with less than 1,000 members	362	91	0·9	291	76	0·7	258	74	0·6

Source: Department of Employment Gazette, November 1976.

effectively operate as single unions; it also includes a substantial number of small organisations in the education, local government and health fields which have very limited representational functions and which effectively operate for collective bargaining purposes via the major trade unions in these fields. A more precise idea of the number of trade unions can be gained from the fact that 226 trade unions had applied to the Certification Officer by September 1976 for certificates of independence; of these applications, 161 have been approved, one has been withdrawn, six have been refused, and the remainder are awaiting decision.

16. Table 9 shows that while TUC-affiliated unions accounted for only 25 per cent of the total number of trade unions recorded by the Department of Employment in 1974 their combined membership amounted to 87 per cent of aggregate trade union membership. Data for 1975 indicate that TUC-affiliated membership now accounts for over 93 per cent of total union membership. In Western Europe, only Britain, Austria and the Republic of Ireland have single trade union federations to which all major unions are affiliated and which embrace a very high proportion of the total unionised workforce.

17. The growing concentration of union membership into a few large organisations is shown in Table 10. In 1960, the 17 unions with 100,000 members or more accounted for 67 per cent of total unionisation; by 1974, there were 25 unions of this size with a greatly increased membership which accounted for 77·5 per cent of all union members. At the other end of the size spectrum, the Department of Employment recorded 362 unions with less than 1,000 members in 1960, accounting for 0·9 per cent of the total unionised workforce; by 1974 there were only 258 of these very small unions and their aggregate membership had fallen to 0·6 per cent of the total unionised workforce. Thus, while multi-unionism remains the norm in most British industries and firms, the trend is clearly towards a rapid reduction in the number of small unions and an increased concentration of members into a handful of large unions. Of particular significance is the fact that an overwhelming majority of the unionised workforce are now members of the relatively small number of organisations affiliated to the TUC.

CHAPTER 3

The pressures for change

1. One of the earliest uses of the term 'industrial democracy' was by Sidney and Beatrice Webb in 1897, as the title of their book on the structure and functions of trade unions[1]. Since then there has been a shift of emphasis in the use of the term. With changes in the structure of the economy and the nature of society since World War II, it has come to focus increasingly on the need to involve employees to a greater extent in company decision-making. In this and the following chapter, we look at how the debate has reached its present state, at the economic and social changes since World War II and at the proposals for greater participation which they have produced.

Industrial and economic changes

2. The last 20 years have seen the growth of the giant industrial enterprise, and the concentration of economic power in the hands of fewer and fewer such companies. For example, in 1953 the 100 largest manufacturing enterprises in the UK accounted for 25 per cent of the total net output; in 1971 the corresponding figure was 40 per cent. In Chapter 2 we showed how many people now work in firms whose total workforce is counted in thousands. There has been a growing recognition of the influence of such companies on many aspects of people's lives at home as well as at work. As companies have grown in size and complexity, they have also tended to become remote from the communities in which they operate and from the people whom they employ. Major decisions about the nature of a company's or plant's organisation, affecting closely the future of the local community or the jobs of the employees, may often be taken far away from the site by the directors of a parent or holding company, sometimes by the management of a parent company overseas.

3. The power and complexity of the industrial enterprise and the remoteness of decision-making have led to demands for large companies to be more responsive to the needs of society in general and of their employees in particular. Industry has come under pressure to consider the wider effects of the decisions it takes in pursuit of profitability, and companies now explicitly or implicitly accept that they have responsibilities not just to shareholders, but also to employees, customers, creditors, suppliers, the local community and to society at large. The Confederation of British Industry (CBI), has accepted the special duty of companies to take into account the interests of employees and argued strongly that companies should develop effective systems of employee participation to channel the energies and abilities of its workforce to constructive ends:

'The responsibilities of the board to its employees are today different from but no less important than those which it must accept to its shareholders. It might be said that they are even more important, at least in the

---

[1]Sidney and Beatrice Webb, *Industrial Democracy* (London 1902).

short term, as failure to achieve satisfactory working relationships with employees can put a board in a position where it will have great difficulty in fulfilling its obligations to its shareholders'.[1]

This is, of course, partly a recognition of the reality of the increased and increasing influence of employees, through their trade unions, on company decision-making, but it is also an acceptance of the principle that a socially responsible company in a democratic society cannot operate without taking account of the interests of its employees.

4. At the same time, the effect of the 'managerial revolution' in large companies has been to concentrate power in the hands of boards of directors. Although in theory, and in law, directors are appointed by shareholders, the shareholders are too numerous to act effectively as a body, and have largely acquiesced in effective control by the board of directors. It is only when there is a financial crisis or dissension within the board that shareholders are called upon to exercise power and take decisions. Except in such circumstances the members of the board are free to run the company and secure the appointment of the directors they wish.

5. During recent decades the directors and senior executives of large companies have as a result of the speed of technological change and rapid fluctuations in the economic climate become increasingly aware of the need to be more responsive to change, if they are to remain profitable. They are faced more often with important investment decisions about the introduction of new technology, the re-equipment of a plant or the transfer of production to a new locality. Often their decisions closely affect the lives of thousands of employees, and in such cases it becomes increasingly difficult for employers to deny the right of these employees, not only to have their interests taken into account by management, but also to have an opportunity for active involvement in the decision-making process. Such responses on the part of companies may in part be a recognition of social responsibility or of democratic principles, but they are also evidence of the practical reality that if a company neglects to make provision for such involvement, employees are now in a position, through the strengthening of trade union organisation and power, to resist the implementation of changes that threaten their livelihood and security. Such resistance may appear shortsighted, but it is understandable that individual workers or groups may interpret the universally accepted goal of full employment as meaning job security for themselves. The EEC Green Paper, *Employee participation and company structure*[2], has pointed out that there is a potential contradiction between the needs of companies to respond to change quickly and the need to involve employees in those changes, because of the inherent and understandable reluctance of employees to accept changes which seem to threaten their work and livelihood. But the Green Paper goes on to argue that, in the long term, conflicts between unions and management and frustrations arising from failure to involve the employees in such changes from the outset are liable to prove much more damaging than any delays and inconvenience caused by the participation of employees in the decision-making process.

---

[1]The Confederation of British Industry, *The responsibilities of the British public company*. Final Report of the Company Affairs Committee (1973), page 19.
[2]Commission of the European Communities, *Employee participation and company structure*, Bulletin of the European Communities. Supplement 8/75, page 9.

6. More recently a recognition, shared by Government, management and trade unions, of the urgent need for British industry to be more responsive to change if there is to be any hope of reversing the relative decline of this country's industrial performance, has led to the development of a tripartite industrial strategy. This is founded on the assumption that Britain's industrial problems can only be successfully remedied by concerted action to improve the performance of industry. The strategy takes account of the trends in size and concentration mentioned earlier and aims to develop effective mechanisms for ensuring that the plans of large companies are in harmony with national needs and objectives. Trade union involvement is seen as fundamental to the strategy, not simply because such involvement is necessary to forestall negative resistance to change, but also because employees through their trade unions have a positive role to play in combating industrial stagnation and in stimulating much needed changes in industrial structure and performance. This tripartite industrial strategy is likely to act as a catalyst to the further development of joint regulation of forward planning decisions at company level.

Social changes

7. New concepts of the role of employees in decision-making at company level are not just reactions to economic trends. They also derive from social changes which have taken place since the war, especially rising standards of education and higher standards of living. The significance of the educational developments is not just that more people have received a basic education; it is the nature of that education which has changed. There is now less concentration on formal authoritarian teaching methods and more encouragement to children to adopt independent and questioning approaches in order to develop individual initiative and ability. It is only since World War II that we have seen the end of the deferential society, in which working people rarely aspired to positions of power or authority in local or national life. The coming of age of democracy in our society is a process that inevitably affects the whole of people's lives; it cannot be excluded from the workplace. The parallel increase in standards of living has also been important. Most people now live in more comfortable homes and have more money and leisure to enjoy them. They have come to expect a higher and rising standard of material comfort and are therefore naturally less tolerant of low standards, discomfort, boredom and lack of proper provisions for safety and health in their working environment, as well as less prepared to accept the prospect of redundancy and unemployment. The EEC Green Paper quoted above recognised these social changes in Western Europe in the following paragraph:

'Furthermore, the current economic situation, with its reduced possibilities for growth, has emphasised the need for mechanisms which will adequately ensure the pursuit of goals other than economic growth, such as the improvement of the quality of life and working conditions, the protection of the environment and the interests of the consumer. The pursuit of such goals can probably be secured only by the existence of decision-making processes in enterprises which have a broader, more democratic base than such processes often have at present'.[1]

---

[1]EEC Commission, *op cit* page 11.

22

8. The effect of those social changes has been an increasing desire among employees to control their working environment and to have a say in decisions which affect their working lives. They have become less prepared to accept unquestioningly unilateral decisions by management, and have shown a readiness to challenge a decision if it seems to have ignored their point of view or to affect them adversely. Traditional management prerogatives have therefore come under attack, and the modern manager has had to develop a style of participative management, which has recognised the necessity and the benefits of involving employees in decision-making, rather than imposing decisions upon them without consultation.

Trade union and legislative developments

9. The trade unions have harnessed the desire of employees both to be protected and to have a voice in decision-making and have strengthened the position of employees in many large companies by expressing their hopes and fears collectively. The extension of trade unions' influence on the economy and on industry has been one of the more marked changes in the last decade, and it is through the trade unions that a large measure of employee participation has already been achieved. This participation has developed mainly at two levels. We have already referred to developments at national level whereby the trade union movement, through the TUC, has accepted its share of responsibility for the development of industrial strategies and in the regulation of the economy. Second, at local level the growth of the shop steward and equivalent union representative systems, chronicled in the report of the Donovan Commission in 1968[1], has strengthened the voice of employees at local level through collective bargaining over issues which are of immediate importance to the shopfloor. But the *scope* of collective bargaining is also widening. Trade unions are no longer concentrating exclusively on questions of pay and conditions, but are pressing for an extension of collective bargaining to cover decisions which were traditionally the prerogative of management. In its evidence to us, the TUC identified a number of areas apart from wages where some unions are already in substantive negotiations with management. These areas include provision of facilities for lay trade union representatives, such as office services and time off for union duties; manpower planning; job and income security; and disclosure of information. This gradual, albeit uneven, extension of the scope of collective bargaining is evidence of the shopfloor pressures for greater industrial democracy.

10. Recent legislation such as the Employment Protection Act 1975 and the Health and Safety at Work Act 1974, which give legislative backing to specific extensions of collective bargaining, reflect and may be expected to give added stimulus to such pressures. The Employment Protection Act provides for the extension of joint regulation into areas that were previously managerial prerogatives, and contains important provisions on the disclosure of information and advance consultation on redundancy. The provisions of the Health and Safety at Work Act providing for safety representatives and safety committees will inevitably bring a whole range of issues associated with health

---

[1]*Report of the Royal Commission on Trade Unions and Employers' Associations 1965–1968* (Chairman: The Rt Hon Lord Donovan). Cmnd 3623 (HMSO 1968; reprinted 1971).

and safety into the sphere of joint regulation. It can be argued indeed that the basis for a legislative framework designed to encourage extensions to industrial democracy at shopfloor level already exists. At the same time the emphasis of the industrial strategy on union involvement in company level planning, together with new concepts like planning agreements, are creating new pressures for the extension of joint regulation to higher levels of company decision-making. Such pressures inevitably raise the question whether existing institutions can be developed to provide for employee involvement at this level or whether new institutions are needed.

11. This is one reason, together with the other pressures for change described above, why recently the debate has extended to encompass the idea of employee representation on company boards responsible for the making of strategic decisions. The development of participation at national and local level has left a gap at company level, which some would argue can only be filled by employee representation on the company board. This is the TUC's position, stated clearly in its report on industrial democracy. While reiterating its belief in collective bargaining as an important method of extending employee influence at local level, it argues that there is a range of important decisions which collective bargaining alone cannot reach.

'It is clear that this leaves a wide range of fundamental managerial decisions affecting workpeople that are beyond the control—and very largely beyond the influence—of workpeople and trade unions. . . . Major decisions on investment, location, closures, and take-overs and mergers, and product specialisation of the organisation are generally taken at levels where collective bargaining does not take place, and indeed are subject matter not readily covered by collective bargaining. New forms of control are needed'.[1]

12. The TUC's belief that employee representation on the board could be an appropriate means of achieving this aim was first set out in 1966 in the TUC's written evidence to the Donovan Commission[2]. At that time the TUC only spoke of the need for legislation which would allow companies to make such provision. By 1974 it saw board level representation as a right that should be available to organised workers and in the report of that year called for legislation to provide for that right to be exercised. The publication of the TUC's Report and its endorsement by Congress in September 1974, albeit qualified in a number of ways and now re-formulated in the TUC's supplementary evidence[3], were clearly important events in the current debate. They provided a stimulus to many other organisations to reconsider their views on industrial democracy and to argue the case for and against employee representation on the board.

Developments in Europe

13. Another fact which has had considerable influence on the debate has been the experience of Britain's neighbours in Europe. As part of a general movement to involve employees more effectively in decision-making, some eight countries

---

[1]Trades Union Congress, *Industrial Democracy* (TUC 1974), page 35.
[2]Trades Union Congress, *Trade Unionism* (TUC 1966).
[3]For TUC's supplementary evidence, see Industrial Relations Review and Report, No 126 (April 1976). The evidence is also reprinted in the new edition of the TUC's *Industrial Democracy*.

in Western Europe now have schemes of one kind or another in operation which secure or at least make possible the representation of employees on company boards. It is now 25 years since *Mitbestimmung* (co-determination) was introduced in the Federal Republic of Germany. This year has seen further steps to increase the proportion of employee representatives on the supervisory boards of companies employing more than 2,000 people. In Sweden, 1976 has also seen confirmation of the three-year experiment in putting employee representatives on company boards. The fact that the West German and Swedish economies, despite differences between the social philosophies of the two countries, have been among the most successful in the world—not least in avoiding the industrial conflict which has cost Britain so dear—has not escaped notice.

14. As long ago as 1972 the EEC Commission published draft proposals for a Fifth Directive on company law, proposing employee representation on the supervisory boards of all companies in the Community with over 500 employees[1]. The Directive is being revised in an attempt to find a more flexible approach which can accommodate more easily the various systems of company law in the nine member states. To help this, the Commission published at the end of 1975 the Green Paper[2], the discussions and comments on which are to be the basis of a revised Fifth Directive. During 1975 the Commission also published its amended proposals for a European Company Statute, which will permit the creation of 'European Companies'[3]. These will have to meet certain requirements regarding employee participation, including the establishment of a European Works Council and the representation of employees on a supervisory board of the Company. Thus, even without the current interest in board level representation in the United Kingdom, the British Government as a member of the EEC would have found itself involved in the debate about its merits and demerits.

Conclusion

15. Our conclusions from the foregoing discussions are two-fold. First, we believe that there is a widespread recognition in this country of what the EEC Green Paper has called 'the democratic imperative' for employee participation, described in that document as follows: 'those who will be substantially affected by decisions made by social and political institutions must be involved in the making of those decisions'[4]. We believe this is an important agreed basis on which the debate on the extent and method of participation can take place. Second, there is already a great deal of participation through the trade unions, particularly at local level in collective bargaining and at national level through discussions between the TUC and the Government and in such tripartite institutions as the National Economic Development Council. The concern of this Committee has been to consider how these existing forms of participation can best be complemented, extended and developed, in response to the pressures for change documented in this chapter.

---

[1]Proposal for a Fifth Directive to co-ordinate the laws of Member States as regards the structure of *societes anonymes*. Bulletin of the European Communities. Supplement 10/72.
[2]EEC Commission, *op cit*.
[3]Commission of the European Communities, *Statute for European companies*. Amended proposal for a regulation. Bulletin of the European Communities, Supplement 4/75.
[4]EEC Commission, *op cit* page 9.

CHAPTER 4

The main proposals before the Committee

1. In this chapter we examine in more detail the TUC proposals contained in the 1974 Report *Industrial Democracy* and modified by their supplementary evidence to us[1]; the EEC proposals contained in the Green Paper *Employee participation and Company structure*[2] and the Draft Statute for European Companies[3]; and the CBI proposal[4] for an extension of industrial democracy by means of 'participation agreements'—a scheme advocated or supported in slightly modified form by a number of other witnesses. We concentrate on these three because they were the most detailed proposals before the Committee and because taken together they introduce many of the principal issues in the debate on methods of extending industrial democracy with which we shall be concerned in later chapters.

The TUC position

2. The explicit mention in our terms of reference of the TUC's proposals for extending industrial democracy has been criticised in some submissions to this Committee on the grounds that it would bias our inquiry towards the trade unions. The view of this Committee is that the TUC Report would have played a significant role in our inquiry whether or not it was mentioned in the terms of reference. Although a small number of unions have themselves given evidence to us, and this evidence, as we shall see below, does not always follow the TUC lines, we know that the TUC is speaking for a large number of affiliated unions who have not felt it necessary to submit evidence on their own account. The evolution of current TUC policy on industrial democracy has been of considerable importance in contributing to the pressures for change referred to in the last chapter and much of the evidence we received took the form of reactions to the TUC's Report. However, this has not been the only set of proposals before us. Many other proposals were discussed, and while we viewed the TUC proposal as an important factor in the debate, the same could be said of the European developments also mentioned in our terms of reference. It is in the context of the catalytic effect the TUC proposals have had in stimulating the current debate on industrial democracy that we feel it is fruitful to begin by drawing out some of the main features of the TUC argument.

3. The main TUC proposals are as follows:

(a) worker representation on the board to be a legal right which a recognised and independent trade union may demand;

(b) selection of representatives to be through trade union machinery;

(c) half the seats on the board to be occupied by worker representatives;

---

[1]Both the 1974 report and the supplementary evidence are available in the latest edition of the TUC's *Industrial Democracy op cit.*

[2]EEC Commission, *op cit*; see also recent expansion of Commission's view in *Worker Participation: EEC Commission Expands on Earlier Views*, The European Industrial Relations Review, No 35 (November 1976), page 6.

[3]Statute for European Companies *op cit.*

[4]Confederation of British Industry, Evidence to the Bullock Committee.

(d) the provisions to apply (at least initially) to all companies and groups employing 2,000 or more people;

(e) the responsibilities of worker representatives to be analogous rather than identical to those of shareholder directors, and their accountability and reporting back to their constituents to be safeguarded.

4. The key to the TUC proposals is the view implicit in the 1974 Report that capital and labour are in some respects equal partners in the modern enterprise. The TUC's policy recommendations for the extension of joint regulation stem from a desire, inherent in the concept of trade unionism, to redress what they see as the current imbalance in control between the representatives of capital and labour. In their emphasis on joint regulation, the TUC are making certain assumptions about the form extensions to industrial democracy must take in modern large-scale industry—namely, as they spell out in their supplementary evidence, 'that relations between workpeople and employers are most effectively regulated on the basis of collective representation which, on the employee side, takes the form of representation by independent trade unions . . .'[1]. They therefore advocate a single channel of representation for employees, based on trade union machinery. If collective bargaining and board level representation are to be compatible with each other, it follows, they argue, that the basis of board representation, and the functions carried out by employee representatives on the board, must be such as to minimise any problem of demarcation between the two. Thus, the TUC conclude that the channel for the appointment of employee representatives to the board, and for them to report back to their constituents, should be the same machinery or substructure as is established for collective bargaining, ie the joint machinery of the recognised trade unions operating within the company or group.

5. The TUC recommend both the revision of company law and new legislation on employee representation on company boards. Their view is that present company law reflects a conception of management's responsibilities to capital and labour that is outdated and inappropriate in the prevailing economic and social climate. The law defines 'interests of the company' as the interests of the shareholders as a whole in the long term. The TUC Report argued, as indeed did many other submissions of evidence, that the law should be altered to reflect the essentially joint interest of labour and capital in the enterprise by placing a statutory obligation on companies to have regard to the interests of employees as well as shareholders.

6. Where the TUC goes much further than some submissions proposing a statutory basis for representation of employees on boards of directors is in demanding that the way in which policy is formed in an enterprise be altered to reflect *equality* between labour and capital in the running of an enterprise. They argue that this equality should be expressed by allotting 50 per cent of the places on a reconstituted policy board to representatives of employees and 50 per cent to representatives of shareholders. A further argument in support of parity is that the employee representatives would have little credibility if the shareholder representatives could outvote them on every issue. Such built-in

---

[1]TUC supplementary evidence, paragraph 5.

inequality would make it impossible for the employee representatives to accept equal responsibility with the shareholder representatives. This was summed up by the TUC General Secretary in oral evidence in the phrase 'equality of responsibility means equality of representation'.

7. In their 1974 Report the TUC suggested a two-tier structure with representation on the top board of the company, whose function would be to establish the broad policy framework to be implemented by the second-tier management board. In their supplementary and oral evidence however they modified their view on board structure, indicating that their basic objectives could also be achieved in the context of a reconstituted form of the unitary board which presently exists in the United Kingdom. The TUC view is that such a reconstituted policy board should be the supreme organ of the company, with the ultimate right to overrule the general meeting of shareholders on certain specified issues. This issue of board structure and the relationship with the shareholders' meeting is examined further in Chapter 8.

8. The benefits in terms of the effective management of companies accruing from such a reconstituted policy-making board would, in the TUC's view, be considerable. By establishing a forum for agreement on a framework of policy within which management could act, the existence of such a board with parity employee and shareholder representation could provide a new legitimacy for the exercise of the management function. Given the increasing tendency, referred to in the last chapter, for employees to question more traditional bases of managerial authority, this could be a key factor in making possible the fruitful co-operation between management and labour needed to tackle and overcome our current industrial problems. The urgency of achieving such a new basis of consent in industry was also stressed by the Fabian Society in support of the TUC proposals:

'. . . if it is true, as we believe, that our prospects of economic recovery depend largely on industry, then the need for a new basis of consent becomes even more vital. In many companies and industries, it will not be possible to carry through the necessary investment and reorganisation programmes unless the employees themselves are involved'[1].

9. The TUC are clear in their evidence that employee representation on boards is no substitute for extension of industrial democracy at other levels. Its function is rather to complement joint regulation through collective bargaining at lower levels of the enterprise. And indeed it is implicit in the TUC's evidence that the success of board level representation will depend on the strength of industrial democracy at lower levels and on the effectiveness of the links between the various levels.

EEC policy

10. The view that social and economic changes require a new relationship between capital and labour has clearly played a major role in the development of industrial democracy in the EEC. The Green Paper said that 'employees are

---

[1]The Fabian Society, *Workers in the Boardroom*, Fabian Tract No 441 (1976).

increasingly seen to have interests in the functioning of enterprises which can be as substantial as those of shareholders, and sometimes more so'[1], and concluded that decision-making structures need to reflect this fact. Strong emphasis is put by the EEC Commission on representation of employees at the level of company boards as an integral part of a system of employee participation at all levels of the enterprise. The Green Paper puts forward no single blueprint for the form employee representation on boards might take, preferring a more flexible approach that might accommodate the different systems of member states. However, in the form of the Draft Statute for European Companies[2], a specific EEC Commission proposal for such representation does exist, and has stimulated comment in the evidence submitted to us.

11. The Draft Statute provides for an optional, new form of incorporation which companies with activities in two or more member states might adopt. The main provisions relating to industrial democracy in the Draft Statute are as follows:

(a) a two-tier system with a management board appointed and monitored by a supervisory board;

(b) the supervisory board to consist of one third shareholder representatives, one third employee representatives and one third members co-opted by the other two groups to represent general interests;

(c) the supervisory board to have rights of access to all management information and powers of veto over all proposals for closure or transfer of activities; curtailment, extension or modification of activities; major organisational changes and long-term co-operation with other enterprises;

(d) appointment of employee representatives to the supervisory board to be by a uniform system of indirect elections in all member states, with voting by all employees whether trade union members or not;

(e) a European Works Council on which all establishments within the company would be represented, with no functions overriding established collective bargaining machinery but with certain rights in relation to the management board: co-determination on matters of company employment policies and working conditions; prior consultation on matters subject to veto by the supervisory board; and information on a wide range of other matters.

12. The scheme can be viewed as an alternative proposal for achieving equal representation of labour and capital on the boards of companies. Where it differs from TUC policy is in advocating a role for a third group of 'independent' members on the board; in its elaboration of complex statutory procedures for the indirect election of employee representatives in all member states, rather than leaving such procedures to the agreement of the parties involved; and in stipulating that voting should be by all employees, whether union members or not. At the same time, the EEC Commission takes a similar view to the TUC on the question of the beneficial consequences for industrial management and

---

[1]EEC Commission, *op cit*, page 9.
[2]Statute for European companies *op cit*.

performance of such extensions to industrial democracy. In oral evidence to us, Commissioner Gundelach expressed the view that where more advanced types of industrial democracy had been implemented, the relationship between industry and the labour force had improved considerably and wasteful confrontation had been minimised. He also said that when the Fifth Directive on harmonisation of company law came into force it would undoubtedly include a mandatory requirement for all member states to provide for employee representation on the boards of companies.

The CBI proposal

13. The third proposal examined in this chapter, that of the CBI, is different from those of the TUC and EEC Commission; in written and oral evidence to us the CBI was strongly critical of employee representation on the board based on any form of compulsion. The essence of the CBI's evidence, echoed in a number of other submissions, was a plea for flexibility in developing alternative forms of participation and for building on what had already been developed, free of any statutory right or obligation for employees to be represented on boards of directors:

'It is vital that employers and employees retain freedom of action to develop a form of participation which can reflect their wishes and the structure of their particular organisation. A standard system applied to all companies, large or small, centralised or decentralised, could not possibly be suitable to meet the needs of employees and companies'.[1]

14. Many individual companies and industry associations have echoed this view. Some have emphasised some special feature of their organisation or industry—the complexity of their company group, the diversity of their product range, the size of their overseas activities—to argue for an approach which recognises their special difficulties. Others have described in detail the progress they have made in developing participation below board level and have expressed concern that a sudden legal requirement to take a new course could damage what has already been achieved.

15. Reflecting their concern with the different needs of companies, the CBI laid strong emphasis on the value of voluntary participation schemes.

'A fundamental principle, therefore, on which proposals for greater employee involvement in company affairs must be based, is that participative arrangements must be designed to fit a company structure, and not vice versa. Moreover, such participative arrangements must be sufficiently flexible to accommodate the various forms of participation already in operation successfully, and to the satisfaction of all parties, in a number of companies'.[2]

'Many large and small companies already successfully operate formal, but voluntary consultative arrangements. The CBI favours this approach, and therefore proposes that the establishment of deliberative bodies representative of all employees should be actively encouraged in all firms of a size where they would be practicable and where the need for increased participation is felt.[3]'

[1]CBI evidence, paragraph 9.
[2]*ibid*, paragraph 13.
[3]*ibid*, paragraph 19.

30

'The CBI recognises, however, that in larger firms where even over a reasonable span of time it might not be possible, for whatever reason, for voluntary agreement on the form of participation to be reached, it would be necessary for there to be a requirement of law to provide compulsory arbitration by an independent third party. This form of legislation would afford the maximum degree of flexibility possible, while providing considerable safeguards for the interests of industrial efficiency, as well as those of employees. The provision of an individual solution suited to the needs of the individual enterprise is essential'.[1]

16. Thus, the CBI evidence leads to the conclusion that some legislation is desirable. The proposal for 'participation agreements' is the core of their evidence. Companies with more than 2,000 employees in the UK would be obliged to conclude such agreements with their employees within a four-year period. These, to be valid, would require affirmation in a secret ballot by a majority of employees. The parties to an agreement would have maximum flexibility to determine the scope and contents of an agreement, provided it accorded with certain very general criteria which include safeguards for collective bargaining, for minority groups of employees, for profitability, confidentiality, and the executive function of management. The range of options envisaged as falling within the scope of such agreements is spelled out in the following list:

'. . . company councils; plant or subsidiary councils, with or without a company council, for multi-plant or groups of companies; non-executive directors to whom employee representatives have special access; trustee advisory "boards"; direct employee representation on either unitary or supervisory boards, with a suitable representative structure beneath this level; and other variations and combinations'.[2]

17. The CBI believe that the main focus of attention at present should be below board level participation. What is needed in their view is a gradual, organic development of industrial democracy from the shopfloor upwards. It is pointed out that the willingness of employees to participate needs to be nurtured at lower levels, where their interest and attention can be captured by discussion of ideas of immediate, direct import. The CBI evidence states clearly that in their view at the present time 'employee representation at board level will not usually be a suitable form of participation'[3]. But they do not rule out the possibility that voluntary agreement on such representation might be reached between management and employees in a particular company. Nevertheless the CBI argue that any such agreement must conform to the following standards: not more than one third of the directors should be elected by employees; they must be elected by secret ballot; the legal rights of shareholders should not be impaired; and the full responsibilities of all directors for the whole enterprise should not be diluted.

18. The proposal for participation agreements aims to provide the greatest possible flexibility, within a framework of enforceable legal obligations. In the event of a failure to agree after four years, and the failure of conciliation, an

[1]*ibid*, paragraph 21.
[2]*ibid*, paragraph 24.
[3]*ibid*, paragraph 28.

independent agency should, it is proposed, have the power to impose a participation agreement on a company, and (subject again to approval by a ballot of the workforce) this agreement would then be legally binding. Employee representation on the board is specifically excluded, however, from the range of options that could form part of an arbitrated agreement, reflecting once more the CBI feeling that the main focus at present should be below board level. In their oral evidence the CBI representatives said that the arbitration board should not impose employee representatives on a company's board, because such an imposed solution simply would not work.

19. The British Institute of Management (BIM) also suggested in its written evidence that, in the event of failure to conclude a participation agreement, an independent government agency should in the last resort be obliged to make recommendations that would be legally binding on all parties. The submission adds:

'The procedure for ensuring implementation is similar in many respects to those available under the Employment Protection Act for independent trade unions seeking recognition or disclosure of information and could be adapted to be in accordance with these procedures'.[1]

20. A different approach to sanctions was put to us by the Industrial Participation Association (IPA) in the context of similar proposals for participation agreements. Starting from the premise that:

'. . . participation on a voluntary basis will always be more effective and satisfying than participation by legislation, and legislation should therefore encourage voluntary arrangements as far as possible'[2],

the IPA suggests that if there is no voluntary agreement and the employees are not satisfied with the *status quo*, their representatives should be able (subject to a ballot of the workforce) to invoke a statutory fallback provision, which would impose on the company a supervisory board with one third employee representation, separate from the management board and with a limited mandate similar to that proposed in the EEC Fifth Directive on employee participation. This solution would:

'. . . (a) be specific, so that everyone knows in advance what may be invoked if there is no agreement on alternatives;

(b) not be so attractive to either management or trade unions that either party would try to avoid agreement on other forms of participation in order to gain advantage by waiting until the statutory provisions could be invoked'.[3]

It would also have the advantage of enforceability, since the sanction for failure to agree would be the establishment of a body with legal powers and duties and rules about its membership.

---

[1]BIM evidence, paragraph 25.
[2]Industrial Participation Association, *Industrial Democracy—the way forward*. (March 1976). Paragraph 39(4).
[3]*ibid*, paragraph 42.

21. The implication of the proposals put forward by bodies such as the CBI BIM and IPA is that employee representation on boards has little positive to contribute at present to the extension of industrial democracy. At best it is a sanction of last resort designed (as in the IPA proposal) to be so unattractive to all parties that alternative solutions will be actively sought. This contrasts with the positive advantages claimed by the TUC and the EEC Commission for employee representation at board level.

CHAPTER 5

Objections and difficulties raised by the evidence in regard to board level representation

1. The last chapter set out in some detail three proposals before the Committee, which serve, when taken together, to raise many of the principal issues in the debate on methods of extending industrial democracy. The aim of this chapter is to outline the main problems of board level representation which were put to us in evidence, before moving on to express our views on the main issues which arise.

2. Some of the criticisms made had a strongly ideological basis. There were those who stated that any current proposal for board level representation of employees would be no more than a compromise with the capitalist system. From the other end of the political spectrum some witnesses asserted the inviolable rights of ownership in relation to limited companies. They took the view that any diminution of shareholders' ultimate right of control would constitute a fundamental political and economic change which was totally unacceptable. Some other critics, while not opposed to some evolution in the economic system, nevertheless believed that it would be wrong to blur the lines of responsibility between labour and capital.

3. The majority of the points raised in evidence were concerned with more pragmatic questions associated with board level representation. One concern running through much of the evidence from companies, industry and trade associations, and professional and managerial groups was whether legislative provision for employee representation on boards might not be premature at the present time and conflict with or hinder the development of other forms of participation. Another major area of concern was with the problems of implementation that could be raised by a statutory commitment to some form of employee representation on boards. The problems envisaged included such matters as the channel of representation, responsibilities of directors, confidentiality and effects on the role of management.

Substructure

4. As we have said, our attention was often drawn to the relationship of board level representation with existing participative structures below the board. The British Institute of Management (BIM) dealt with this subject in their evidence to us as follows:

'The British Institute of Management considers it a narrow approach to look at an extension of industrial democracy only in respect of the "extension of representation on boards of directors" .... BIM ... [advocates] a greater involvement of employees in both the longer term policy decisions and in the day-to-day decisions and it is particularly concerned to ensure that this is achieved without:

(a) relieving the management of the business from the ultimate responsibility, or

34

(b) creating a structure which gives the appearance of industrial democracy without genuine involvement and corresponding responsibility by those involved in the process.

Accepting the terms "industrial democracy" and "employee participation" as synonymous, we would define industrial democracy as the practice in which employees take a part in management decisions. The decisions on day-to-day operations have a direct and fairly immediate impact on employees at their place of work . . . . For the Committee to omit consideration of this type of employee participation would, we consider, be overlooking a major area where employees can influence the decisions that affect their working lives. The BIM . . . strongly recommends an open style of management with a regular flow of information and ideas between the management and the employees of an enterprise which, it considers, essential to an improvement in industrial relations. If employee participation is not effective at this level, it is unlikely that any imposed change in the board structure or its composition is going to achieve the mutually co-operative approach that we believe is necessary for constructive involvement in policy decisions'.[1]

5. Almost all the evidence agreed that a well-developed structure of participation below board level would be essential to the success of board level representation. Where differences did emerge was on the question, whether there is at present in large companies a sufficiently well-developed substructure of participation to support immediate moves, backed by legislation, towards board level representation. A number of management organisations and other groups put forward the view that the substructure was not sufficiently well-developed at the present time. Many linked their arguments with the question of timing. They were not against the principle of employee representation on the board: they thought that companies should allow or encourage the system of board level representation to evolve naturally in its own good time.

6. This argument has a number of facets, but essentially it is that companies must be allowed to build up their participative systems from the bottom, thus gradually fostering the will to participate among employees, and that there must not be a sudden jump to representation on the board. The Engineering Employers' Federation (EEF) was one of many organisations which wrote to us expressing this view:

' . . . joint involvement must grow organically from the combined will and determination of those who manage and work within an enterprise to develop and operate participatory practices which best satisfy their needs and circumstances'.[2]

Some of those who wrote to us concluded from this that there was therefore no need to set a time limit for the introduction of board level representation. Others felt that there should be a finite period for evolution and experiment, after which some form of board level representation might be enforced.

7. The case for a gradual build-up of participative systems from the bottom upwards was frequently justified by the argument that the majority of employees

---

[1]BIM evidence, paragraphs 1–4.
[2]EEF evidence, paragraph 10.

were not interested in being represented on the board, being more concerned with the immediate problems of the shop floor or office. The dangers of trying to impose board level representation on an uninterested or hostile workforce were frequently pointed out to us. There was, however, little hard evidence of opinion. A few companies described to us in detail the apathy they had found among their workforce for schemes of participation below board level and concluded that the same would be true of representation on the board. The question of how the desire of a particular workforce to be represented on the board may be tested is treated in Chapter 10.

8. In support of the argument that the main focus of attention at present should be participation systems below board level, some companies described to us the kinds of experiments they were making at this level. Some of the evidence concentrated on direct relationships within the hierarchy of line management, eg between the supervisor and the foreman or between a senior manager and his immediate subordinate. Moves to abandon traditional methods of management in favour of a participative style, and to involve those who will be directly affected by decisions in the process of making them, are seen by many people with experience of management as ways of improving the quality of decisions and increasing job satisfaction at all levels. We received evidence from employers and especially from management consultants about methods of decision-making that increased the involvement and sense of responsibility of those whose job is to implement the decisions and those who are affected by them. Job enrichment and work restructuring schemes and achievements both at home and abroad were brought to our attention.

9. At the same time we cannot ignore the many submissions which asserted or conceded that the present substructure for joint regulation below board level was imperfect. A major concern was with the inadequacy of joint trade union machinery at company level. The General and Municipal Workers Union (GMWU) stated:

'There . . . has to be a significant development of trade union machinery in the private sector towards the creation of *company level* machinery, involving both officials and lay members at the point where strategic decisions are really made . . . . At present, in most instances, there is a gap in trade union machinery and collective bargaining machinery between the plant level and the national (JIC) level. Yet it is at company level that the major decisions are made. The creation of collective bargaining machinery at company level is a necessary prerequisite to any further institutional development on industrial democracy . . . .

In most cases this machinery does not, at present, exist'.[1]

The GMWU supports the TUC proposal for a statutory right to 50 per cent trade union representation on the main policy boards of companies where recognised trade unions wish to take up that right, but lays emphasis on the need, whether or not that statutory right is established, for a mandatory general obligation on company management and directors to consult and negotiate with trade unions on all major decisions involving investment, closures, mergers, organisational changes and re-deployment.

---

[1]GMWU evidence, paragraph 6.

36

10. Many submissions emphasised the importance of a flexible approach to the extension of industrial democracy, in order to complement rather than disrupt the wide range of existing practices in industrial relations that have developed over time in particular companies. Flexibility in the method of putting employee representatives on the board was urged both by proponents of the idea and by those who, having recorded their opposition, have gone on to consider how, nevertheless, it might best be carried out. From quite different sides there was considerable opposition to the idea that a law might try to define too closely the method of selection, the constituencies and the standard of eligibility or the structure of boards. Many submissions warned the Committee against copying continental systems, particularly the West German system where the law defines these matters very closely. Several submissions focussed in particular on the West German system of two-tier boards, which they argued was too rigid a structure to be imported into the United Kingdom. It was felt that for the law to be too specific in such areas would constitute a serious threat to the tradition of British industrial relations, which has been to give trade unions and management maximum freedom, within a basic legal framework, to reach agreement on their own procedures and institutions.

11. It was argued that the attitudes of management were of special importance to the success of board level representation; there was a danger that managers would feel threatened by their subordinates being elevated to the board, and thus, theoretically at least, placed above them in the managerial hierarchy. Proponents of the evolution argument believed that time—in some cases a considerable time—was needed to prepare the managers of a company for a change in the structure of decision-making. Some said that special training would be necessary for managers to respond to the new demands that would be made of them by board level representation of employees.

12. Many organisations went on to refer to the special role of a manager in the running of a company. The BIM in its written and oral evidence to us described the unique position of managers as both executors and representatives of employer policy and as employees in their own right, and a number of other bodies representing management wrote to us in a similar vein. Some submissions proposed a special seat on the board for representatives of management, on the lines of the seat set aside for senior executives in the West German Co-Determination Act 1976. The BIM in their oral evidence to us opposed the principle of representation on the board but concluded that if other parts of the workforce were to be represented, then management must have its own seat. We return to this matter in Chapter 10.

Channel of representation

13. The TUC proposals for election through trade union machinery have been severely criticised. Several alternative methods of election—universal suffrage, nomination by the trade unions but election by the whole workforce, electoral colleges, elections from a works council—have been proposed. Arguments for the representation of non-unionised employees have taken a number of different forms. Some have argued that it is unjust to exclude an employee from representation just because he is not a member of a union. Others have argued the case

37

for non-unionised but distinctive groups. Some companies, for example, described situations where, though the company group is highly unionised, one industrial sector or a significant subsidiary of it is non-unionised. Others have pointed out the reverse situation, where one sector is highly unionised but the rest of the company is not. We have also had described to us cases where the workforce is represented through a company staff association or a works council. Several staff councils, among them the head office staff committee of BOC and BOC International Ltd and the staff council of the Shell London Service Companies, pleaded the case for representation of non-unionised, but organised, employees. We acknowledge that all these points require careful consideration, and they are taken up again in detail in Chapter 10.

14. Those submissions which specifically dealt with the TUC proposals saw two main difficulties. Some thought that the main problem was that the unions were basically undemocratic and needed to review their own internal procedures for election before claiming an exclusive right to represent the employees on the board. Others, particularly individual companies, feared arguments between recognised unions over who should take the board seats. Those companies with a large number of recognised unions pointed out the difficulties of achieving fair representation of them all, without a cumbersome extension to the size of the board. On the other hand, it has been argued that the problem of implementation arising from situations where there are several unions has been exaggerated. The TUC pointed out in its supplementary evidence that joint negotiating bodies in the various industries have long been accustomed to reaching accommodation between the (sometimes numerous) trade unions involved.

Responsibility of Directors

15. Both sides of industry were also concerned about how the employee representatives would behave once they had been appointed to the board. Employers were insistent that all members should accept the same duties to act for the good of the company and the same responsibility for decisions taken at board level. There should be no question of employee representatives being mandated by their trade unions. Every director should be individually and personally responsible for the views he expressed and the votes he cast in the boardroom—a representative, not a delegate. There was particular alarm at the TUC Report's comment[1] that it was no use giving workpeople the legal rights to involvement in decision-making by representation on the board, 'and then requiring that worker-directors should behave like any other directors'. We asked the TUC for clarification on this point when they gave oral evidence to us, and this is discussed in the next chapter.

16. Much attention focussed on the question of confidential information which employee representatives would receive as members of the board, and here again considerable anxiety was aroused by the TUC's comment that employee representatives 'should not be unnecessarily hampered and restricted in reporting back to their constituents by narrow requirements of confidentiality'[1]. Many submissions emphasised the importance of preventing commercially confidential information from falling into the hands of competitors.

[1]TUC *op cit*, page 37.

They were not claiming that employee representatives would be any more likely to leak information than any other director. But they did see problems in employee representatives being required to report back freely to their constituents, as the TUC evidence insisted that they should do, thus possibly disseminating confidential information widely throughout the company or even beyond. Only a few went further than this to argue that employee representation on the board opened the way for those who wished to destroy the company, and that leaking confidential information was one way of achieving this. Many submissions linked these arguments with the proposal that, if there were to be employee representatives, they should come from inside the firm, since there was thought to be a greater danger of confidential information leaking if it fell into the hands of those without a personal stake in the company.

17. The counterpart to these arguments from employers about responsibilities is the trade union fear that in some way their independence will be compromised by having seats on the board. Eric Batstone in his report for this Committee on European experience pointed out the employee representative's essential dilemma: on the one hand to be effective he must become involved in the company's decision-making process; on the other if he is effective he may lose the confidence of his constituents by becoming too closely identified with management[1]. Some of those who wrote to us feared that employee representatives would have to participate in unpopular decisions, affecting employment prospects, thus alienating themselves from the workforce. Others thought that the ability to influence decisions would be illusory because management would try to bypass the board, and that in this way there might be a danger of the trade unions accepting responsibility without power. Chapters 9 and 10 take up this important issue.

Possible conflict with collective bargaining

18. Another source of concern was that board representation might conflict with the traditional role of trade unions, which is seen as one of opposing management in collective bargaining, not collaborating with it on the board. The objectives of board level representation and collective bargaining may therefore be incompatible. The sharpest expression of this view came from the Electrical, Electronic, Telecommunication and Plumbing Union (EETPU), who thought that there was a fundamental and irreconcilable incompatibility between board representation and the collective bargaining function of trade unions. In their evidence to us, the EETPU describes two interrelated aspects of the problem:

'First, there is the institutional impossibility of separating the boardroom consultation from the potential negotiating implications behind the issues under discussion. Second, there is the irreconcilable split loyalties of the worker directors themselves. They will find it immensely difficult to separate their boardroom responsibilities dictated by business priorities from their representative functions derived from their relationship with the workforce. The pursuit of trade union objectives will not then be helped by the disunity created in such an atmosphere. And this ignores the crude disagreements that must occur on occasion with worker directors, in possession of all the

---

[1]Batstone and Davies *op cit*, pages 23–24.

information, being party to a decision or a policy that is opposed by the collective bargainers. Far better in the interests of those affected by a managerial decision that the responsibility for that decision is firmly laid at the management's door; then the collective bargaining machinery can oppose and moderate the impact of the decision when necessary'[1].

In the next chapter and in Chapter 10 below we discuss this question of compatability between board level representation and collective bargaining.

Diversity and complexity of the private sector

19. Another group of practical difficulties put to us concerned the application of board level representation to small companies, to groups of companies and to multinationals. Many submissions argued for the exemption or special treatment of small companies because of the informality of their decision-making structures and the flexibility of their participative arrangements. Descriptions of 'small companies' ranged from those with under 2,000 employees to those with under 200. Bodies representing a number of industrial and commercial sectors, such as shipping, banking, construction and hotels, argued that the special circumstances of their industries made it inappropriate for legislative provisions on board level representation to apply to them.

20. The basic question about groups of companies is where the representation of employees should be implemented: on the main board of the group, on the board of a sizeable subsidiary, on both, or on neither. Many companies have argued to us that it is essential to maintain the effectiveness of the group as an economic unit and that it would be increasingly difficult to do so, if the parent company lost control of the appointments to the subsidiary board. Others have pointed out in contrast the difficulties of achieving some meaningful form of representation on the top board of a large and diverse group, which may have over 100,000 employees.

21. These problems are aggravated in the case of multinational companies. Most people are agreed that it is impossible in the absence of transnational legislation to put employee representatives on the board of a foreign-owned company overseas, and that the foreign-owned company can only be influenced through its United Kingdom subsidiaries. The problem with the British-based multinational is different: here the question is how far representatives of the company's United Kingdom employees should be able to influence decisions affecting unrepresented employees overseas. A number of companies, including Reckitt and Colman Ltd, Consolidated Goldfields Ltd and Gestetner Holdings Ltd, have written to us to say that the majority of their employees are overseas and that they consider it unjust for their employees in the United Kingdom, who are in a minority, to have a say in decisions affecting the whole group. Chapter 11 deals with the application of our proposals to companies whose size, sector of activity or international character may suggest that they are special cases.

---

[1]EETPU evidence, paragraphs 29 and 30.

CHAPTER 6

A review of some major issues

1. The last chapter raised a number of issues that require serious consideration in the context of any recommendation to implement some form of employee representation on company boards in the United Kingdom. We consider these questions here and give the reasons for our conclusion that legislation is desirable. The remainder of the Report is chiefly concerned with the provisions that the legislation should contain.

2. Before we turn to the issues themselves, it may be helpful to narrow the ground by setting out our position on the views we described as strongly ideological at the beginning of the last chapter. On the one hand, given the existence of a sizeable private sector in the United Kingdom economy in which private capital plays and is likely to play an essential role, we did not discuss industrial democracy in terms of enterprises managed solely for the benefit of employees. Nor are we called upon to express any view on arguments that the private sector should be diminished by an extension of public ownership. On the other hand, it seems to us (as it did to most witnesses) that to regard the company as solely the property of shareholders is to be out of touch with the reality of the present-day company as a complex social and economic entity, subject to a variety of internal and external pressures, in which the powers of control have passed from the legal owners to professional management.

Participation below board level

3. Despite some of the fears expressed that our terms of reference would cause participation below board level to be ignored, we have devoted serious consideration to it. We agree wholeheartedly with the view expressed in submissions both favourable and opposed to employee representation on boards that changes at board level are not by themselves sufficient to ensure an extension of industrial democracy. What is needed is an inter-related structure of participation or joint regulation at all levels of the enterprise, and a sufficiently well developed structure of participation below the board is clearly vital.

4. Should action therefore be concentrated, for the present at least, on strengthening and extending forms of participation below board level, allowing developments at board level to evolve naturally in their own time? In many respects the sequential process of working upwards from the bottom appears logically desirable: not only does participation begin with issues close to the daily concerns of employees and progress gradually from these to longer-range, more complex questions, but the people who represent their fellow employees begin by contributing to the solution of day-to-day problems and thereby gain experience and skill that can be progressively applied to more difficult questions. Thus in a large company over a period of years there will develop a group of employee representatives with increasing ability to contribute to decision-making at higher levels.

5. The evidence we received convinced us that the process of development is in fact already advanced, particularly in larger companies, and that a wide

41

range of participation already exists below board level. Employee participation may take many forms, from improved communication to joint responsibility for decisions, to experiments in job enrichment and participative management, and it may range from unwritten but accepted codes of practice within companies to formal structures such as representative councils with constitutions, officers, etc. It is impossible in the confines of this report to do justice to all the information on such forms of participation contained in the evidence we received. But a brief review of some of the main developments may serve to give weight to the view that the structure of participation which already exists is sufficiently developed to make employee representation on boards a realistic consideration.

6. Some submissions to us regarded the question of provision of information as central to the discussion of industrial democracy. Both sides of industry increasingly appreciate that availability of information to employees or their representatives can increase mutual understanding and involvement. Such information may relate to operating budgets and costs, departmental trading results, manpower policies, market analysis, future prospects, strategic plans, productivity, product changes or any other aspect of the business on which management needs to be informed in order to formulate policy and monitor the implementation of it. The usefulness of such information to employee representatives in collective bargaining is obvious. Legal provisions for disclosure of information to bargaining agents, in the Employment Protection Act 1975 and to a lesser extent the Industry Act 1975 have therefore commanded strong support from trade unions; they have been resisted by employers' organisations, because such legal provisions are seen as erosion of the management prerogative to decide what information should be released to the workforce or their representatives and what should remain confidential. There was strong support however in the evidence submitted to us by companies for full and clear provision of information by management to employees. Efforts are being made by many companies (and the CBI itself has issued guidance to its members on how this can be achieved) to provide their employees with relevant company information and to present it clearly, so that a generally improved appreciation of the relation between turnover, productivity, wages, overheads, profits, dividends and capital investment may enable employees to understand the inter-dependence of their own interests and those of the enterprise. These attitudes and initiatives on the part of management often fail, however, to face an important issue of principle about access to information: whether it should be granted by management *ex gratia*, or alternatively claimed by employees as a right.

7. In our view, full provision of information, important though it is, cannot by itself ensure real involvement, any more than 'open government' can guarantee political democracy. Many submissions to the Committee gave detailed descriptions of the kind of consultative machinery that had been developed to foster communication between management and employees. Today the overwhelming majority of larger British companies have some formal system of consultation between the management and the workforce. It has been customary to draw a distinction between consultation on the one hand and negotiation or collective bargaining on the other, but in practice the distinction is blurred and there has

been a gradual trend in recent years towards the fusion of consultative and negotiating machinery. The purely consultative system, where it is clearly understood that, however much influence those consulted may have, any decisions taken are those of management, is becoming less common. Consultation is being developed to the point where those consulted acquire a *de facto* power of veto over certain actions of management. The term has indeed become so stretched that its usefulness must be doubted, as must the neat categorisation of participation into *communication*, *consultation* and *co-determination* which some witnesses suggested we should adopt.

8. Perhaps the most important development below board level has been the extension of the scope of collective bargaining, already touched on in Chapter 3. Collective bargaining is central to British industrial relations. The trade union advocates of employee representation at board level see the continued development of collective bargaining, and especially the extension of its scope to cover subjects and issues going far beyond pay and conditions at work, as the principal means whereby employees may increase their say in company decision-making. The TUC report is unequivocal on this point: '. . . collective bargaining is and will continue to be the central method of joint regulation in industry and the public services'[1]. Forms of joint regulation below board level are by no means perfect, but what is clear is that they are in a continual process of development.

9. We mentioned in the last chapter the fears expressed by some trade unionists and others that there might be conflict between collective bargaining and board level representation. It is right that these fears should be recognised and discussed. We noted the cautious tone adopted by the Labour Party in its report *The Community and the Company*, which was part of their evidence to us:

'We consider that behind the TUC conditions (for putting workers on the board) is a rationale of fundamental importance . . . namely that trade union participation at board level must be a supplement to, and not in any way detract from, the trade unions' position in collective bargaining'[2].

The view taken by the TUC was that, as long as board representation was based on the single channel of trade union machinery, it was not only compatible with, but a natural extension of, the role of trade unions in encouraging their members to be involved in all aspects of policy formulation and in the management of industrial change. In their oral evidence to the Committee the TUC reiterated this view, indicating that as long as any system of employee representation on boards made the employee directors truly representative and properly accountable, then there would be no reason for such a system to undermine existing joint machinery. It was the failure to incorporate these principles in the British Steel Corporation worker director scheme, the TUC argued, that accounted for the relative lack of success of that experiment.

10. We have taken serious note of the inadequacies in present structures of joint regulation to which a number of submissions pointed. Although there

---

[1]TUC *op cit*, page 7.
[2]The Labour Party, *The Community and the Company* (London 1974), page 12.

43

is extensive collective bargaining machinery at company level, in addition to plant and national level, we agree fully that the further development of joint union machinery will be vital to the successful functioning of board level representation. In our view, however, there is nothing inherent in the structure of trade union organisation in large companies to prevent such developments; indeed, a number of trade unions in large enterprises are increasingly concerned to establish forms of combine organisation that link together representatives of the various trade unions recognised in different parts of the company or group. But developments in trade union organisation are dependent on management's responses and attitudes, and the present inadequacy of recognised joint structures at company level is a reflection not only of British trade union structure but also of current management attitudes. The view was expressed in evidence that legislation on employee representation on boards might in fact be an effective way of stimulating managements and trade unions to devise the necessary joint machinery at company level to support such developments.

11. It has been strongly argued to us that changes in board structure can act as a catalyst to developments at other levels of the enterprise. To suggest that we have to make a choice between *either* legislation *or* evolution is, in our view, not true. There need not be any incompatability between extensions to industrial democracy based on the natural development of existing forms of joint regulation below the board and a parallel extension of industrial democracy based on legislation providing for employee representation on boards. Indeed representation at board level may be the guarantee and catalyst for effective participation at lower levels. There are three ways in which we believe the essential interdependence of the two may operate; the following paragraphs describe them.

12. In the first place, where large numbers of people are involved, a working structure of employee representation is necessary to any form of industrial democracy such as collective bargaining or board level representation. The employees must know how their representatives are to be selected and how they can communicate with those who represent them, and the representatives must know who their constituents are and how they can report back to them. If employees are represented at the highest level in the company, on the board itself, then a company-wide structure of some sort must exist or be created. In Chapter 10 we discuss channels of representation and methods of selection of representatives. In this more general discussion we are concerned to establish that, where no representative structure exists, the principle or possibility of board level representation will help to create it, and where it is inadequate the fact of representation will tend to improve the structure so that it can survive and become effective as a two-way channel. The more strongly this structure is established, the more its function as an electoral mechanism and channel for reporting back will be extended to embrace the representation of employees' interests at all levels in the company.

13. Second, if representatives of shareholders and employees meet on the board, but communication, participation and collective bargaining at lower levels are inadequate, the tendency will be for matters of concern to both sides to work their way up through the separate channels of employee representation and management hierarchy to the board itself. It will then be evident to the

board that many of these matters should be settled lower down. There will therefore be joint pressure from above on representatives of management and the workforce to meet each other at appropriate levels and to consult or negotiate there. Such pressure for the creation of joint consultation machinery and for its effective use would be much weaker if it came from a board on which employees had no representation.

14. Third, the nature as well as the extent of participation below board level is influenced by the composition of the board. As long as top policy decisions are taken by a body with no employee representation, representatives of the workforce at lower levels are at a disadvantage compared to their opposite numbers representing management, in terms of reference upwards through the decision-making structure. If the board is also a joint body, where the employees' point of view can be directly represented, a mere knowledge of this fact may produce at lower levels a shift towards greater participation, more genuine commitment and co-operation in order to produce joint solutions.

15. Finally, if there is no joint representative structure at the top, any decision by the board that participative structures should be established or strengthened at lower levels will be a unilateral decision by management alone. The force of such decision will be far less than that of an equivalent decision reached by the top level representatives of both parties in the enterprise.

16. The greatest enemy of participation is said to be apathy. Management's willingness to forego all or part of the prerogative to decide and to command will lead to increased participation only in so far as employees are willing to listen, to contribute and to accept responsibility. A satisfactory degree of participation may therefore be achieved when the wish for it is equal on both sides, and ways are found of putting this into practice. But the enthusiasm of employees is liable to suffer when they perceive that the joint procedures stop short of major decisions, which are taken behind the closed doors of the boardroom.

17. The evidence of how employees behave when they are collectively represented by trade unions does not, in our view, support the contention (which was strongly put to us in evidence) that employees generally want to be consulted in advance about decisions which affect them, but equally want the decisions themselves and the responsibility for them to belong exclusively and unambiguously to management. We accept that participative management is desirable, not only for its mobilisation of mental and social abilities that might otherwise be wasted, and thus for its contribution to greater fulfilment at work, but also for the enhanced efficiency that it may bring to companies. But we do not believe that the whole answer to the demand for greater industrial democracy can lie in changed attitudes and practices in the exercise of line management functions, however valuable and necessary such changes may be.

18. For a similar reason we do not consider that the evidence we received about job enrichment and work restructuring meets the point of substance central to this discussion. By this we do not wish to detract from the important work which is going on to find ways of improving the quality of working life,

45

or the practical efforts described to us in the written evidence and during our visit to Sweden to increase job satisfaction. Such forms of direct participation as job rotation, job enlargement, job enrichment, autonomous work groups, work restructuring, and participative management styles aim to increase job satisfaction and labour productivity by giving employees greater discretion in defining the scope of their jobs and in deciding how these will be performed. Their potential for increasing employee participation and decision-making, however, is extremely limited. At worst, they are merely techniques for persuading employees to accept decisions which have already been made. At best, they give employees some control over job content and task performance. But they do nothing to enable employees to participate in decision-making which occurs at organisational levels above the shop floor or to democratise the overall authority structure of a firm. In short, the area of decision-making in which they allow employee participation is extremely narrow.

19. It may well be that, for most people working in the private sector, developments in participation below board level during the next few years will have more impact, in terms of change in their working lives, than representation at board level. In our view, however, each depends upon the other for its effectiveness. Each company will have to work out its own programme for the extension of participation at all levels. The question will not be whether to build upwards from the bottom or to work downwards from the top. The task will rather be to use existing structures where they are available and to create new ones where they are needed, so that a complete system evolves, fitted to the particular needs of the company and introduced on a timescale that corresponds to the desires of the employees.

20. The main argument therefore for choosing legislation on employee representation on boards as a major method of extending industrial democracy is that it is likely simultaneously to strengthen existing forms of industrial democracy below board level and to extend these structures to the highest levels of decision-making within the company. We do not believe that the legislative alternative put forward by the CBI would lead to anything like the same result, and it would certainly not make the major policy decisions of companies the subject of joint regulation.

21. A particular problem raised by the CBI proposals is that of sanctions. Whatever may be said about pressure on employers and trade unions to reach agreement voluntarily, both before and after referral to arbitration, the strength of these pressures depends at least partially on the nature of the ultimate sanction. Participation agreements, whether reached voluntarily or imposed through arbitration by the proposed independent agency, would be legally binding. They might contain detailed provisions on the machinery for consultation, lay down rules for the membership of committee or councils, stipulate what information was to be provided by management to employee representatives and specify the subjects to be discussed. In the case of arbitrated agreements, however, they could not in the CBI's view include employee representation on the board. Thus, if goodwill were not present on both sides—and the law must face up to the possibility of such cases—a participation agreement might prove unsatisfactory because one party to it failed to respect what would amount to an obligation to consult in good faith, or because the other party believed that

the necessary good faith was lacking. In disputed cases courts of law inevitably and understandably find it difficult to decide whether such an obligation has been observed or not. It would therefore be difficult to determine whether the parties to a participation agreement, perhaps especially an arbitrated agreement, were observing it. Each dispute would have to be judged on its facts, and case law would establish few if any principles of general application. Moreover, if it was found that an obligation had been breached, what penalty would be appropriate? The efficacy of injunctions, fines or other penalties that a court might impose on companies, trade unions or individuals who failed to observe the court's orders must be doubtful.

22. It may be objected that it is unrealistic to suppose that ill-will and disagreement between management and trade unions on the issue of participation would be so intense that court action would be necessary. Unfortunately, the history of British industrial relations does not justify such optimism that the possibility of severe conflict can be dismissed as insignificant. It is all too possible that management and trade unions in particular companies may have sharply opposed views on industrial democracy. Legislation must therefore provide more than an obligation to agree which is ultimately unenforceable. Moreover, the virtue of an effective sanction is that it reduces the chances of resort to court action. We saw in Chapter 4 that the BIM envisaged sanctions on employers analogous to those specified in the Employment Protection Act 1975 for failure to recognise a trade union or to provide it with information, when an award by the Central Arbitration Committee (CAC) has been made in the trade union's favour. But Section 16 of that Act shows clearly that the sanction relates to the terms and conditions of employment—eg wages—of the employees concerned. The CAC can order the employer to observe the terms demanded by the union, or other 'appropriate' terms. This sanction may prove an effective stimulus to the employer to recognise the union and negotiate with it. But it is hard to see that a dispute about the extent of participation by employees in the formulation of a company's policies has anything to do with terms and conditions of employment. Such a sanction would in our view be inappropriate, and for this reason we do not find the analogy helpful.

23. The need for a clear and appropriate sanction that would discourage litigation was evidently borne in mind by the Industrial Participation Association when it proposed that the alternative to a voluntary participation agreement should be the imposition on a company of a supervisory board with one-third employee representation. While this sanction is ingenious and has the virtue of enforceability, it is doubtful whether the alternative of board level representation—as a sanction—would act as a clear and adequate incentive to management and trade unions to negotiate a participation agreement satisfactory to both sides. Moreover, to taint the concept of board level representation with the label of a 'sanction' would be to frustrate much of the positive potential inherent in it. We consider that none of those who proposed a legal obligation on management and unions to negotiate about participation or to enter into participation agreements was able to suggest an effective and workable legal sanction for breach of such an obligation, or of any obligation stemming from arbitration where that was part of the proposal.

24. The Committee is aware that other countries have favoured a statutory approach to developments in industrial democracy below board level, either in terms of statutory works councils as in West Germany (which are further discussed in Chapter 10 or in terms of legal obligations on managements to negotiate on all issues of enterprise organisation, as in Sweden. At first sight the Swedish approach of statutory backing to the extension of collective bargaining might seem more appropriate to the British context. It has certain similarities with the policies advocated by unions like the GMWU. But the reasons behind the recent legislation relate to specific aspects of Swedish law as it has existed hitherto. There were obstacles in Swedish labour law (eg the so-called peace obligation and its relationships to management prerogative) which hindered the extension of workplace bargaining on issues other than wages and conditions of employment. The recent legislation was designed, as the Swedish Labour Attache informed us in oral evidence, to remove these obstacles and to enable national level wage bargaining and local level negotiations about other issues to be separated.

25. No such obstacle to the extension of collective bargaining exists in this country. Indeed, as this chapter has indicated, a number of developments are currently taking place in this sphere. Recent labour legislation imposes only a very limited 'obligation to bargain', with indirect sanctions, and is designed to support and encourage the strengthening of trade union organisations and the extension of collective bargaining. In the United Kingdom it is only at the level of representation on boards that there is a legal impediment to the extension of industrial democracy. Changes at this level require alterations to company law, and this is one of the reasons why legislation is necessary. As far as possible we feel that developments should take the form of natural evolution in harmony with existing practices and institutions. But, because our company law, like that of other countries, has traditionally given to shareholders the exclusive right to appoint directors, the extension of industrial democracy to give to employees the right to board representation necessarily requires legislation.

The efficient management of companies

26. A major preoccupation of much of the evidence submitted to us was the likely impact of employee representation on boards on the efficiency of companies and on the ability of companies to meet their obligations to their customers and to the community. In view of the request in our terms of reference that consideration be given to the effects of employee representation on boards on the efficient management of companies, we seek in the following paragraphs to indicate and evaluate the comments we received on this aspect of the debate.

27. The predictions about the effects on efficient management ranged from those who thought that employee representation would enhance the efficiency of firms, to those who thought it would have no more than a nuisance value and those who believed that it would disrupt the management of the company. At one end of the spectrum there were those who said that employee directors would be out of their depth, inexperienced, and therefore unable to make any effective contribution to board level decisions. Such people believed that the board should continue to be composed of those who had worked their way up

through the company and proved their ability, with the judicious addition of outsiders with particular experience of expertise. To some of them employee representatives seem an irrelevance. Another group of industrialists felt that a major effect would be a slowing-up in decision-taking. Management would have to spend more time explaining policies to the employee representatives and through them to their constituents; though not all thought that this would necessarily be a bad result. Decision-taking might also be slowed up because the employee representatives felt the need to report back and consult their constituents before committing themselves.

28. At the other end of the spectrum is the view that employee representation on boards would not only improve efficiency but was indeed essential to developing new forms of co-operation between labour and capital and a new legitimacy for the exercise of the management function, which are needed if Britain is to overcome its current industrial and economic difficulties. Examples of such views were cited in the last chapter. Closely related to such arguments is the view that employee representation on boards will have beneficial effects by providing better mechanisms for the resolution of conflicting interests at crucial stages in policy formation. The real benefits, it is argued, will come from the opportunity provided for employee representatives to be involved from the start in the formulation of policy. They will be able to express their concerns before a decision is taken, to point out the implications of a proposal for the interests of employees, to question management on what they are proposing and to suggest alternatives. This will lead to increased commitment to the company on the part of the workforce. For their part, many managers will have to rethink their method and style of working in order to take more account of employees' interests. It will no longer be sufficient for them to go through the motions of consultation after a policy has been decided. It will not always be easy to reach an agreed policy on the board, and no one is suggesting that conflicts between capital and labour ending in industrial action will be eliminated. But the hope is that, if decisions are taken jointly, they will be more often implemented without costly industrial disputes and loss of production. Some have put the alternative bluntly: if, in an increasingly complex industrial society, we do not develop a new basis of consent for decision-taking, the result will be worsening industrial strife, making it increasingly difficult for companies to respond to the changing demands of technology and the marketplace.

29. On the question of its effect on the speed of decision-making, many supporters of board level representation agreed with the critics that it may take longer to reach decisions, and that management may have to spend more time in explaining and justifying their proposals to employees. But they argued that once the consent of employees has been obtained decisions will be easier and quicker to implement. The TUC in its supplementary evidence had little doubt that ultimately those companies with employee representatives on the board would be more efficient than those without:

'This point cannot be proved, but in the view of the TUC the major gain in efficiency would derive from the creation of a new approach to policy-making in companies, particularly in relation to new products and new methods of work . . . . Although initially the length of time taken to consider future policy might be extended, the acceptance and implementation would undoubtedly be assisted, given the greater confidence in the work of the policy board and the systematic reporting-back to established stewards and office committees of the board's work.[1]

30. Many employers seem to fear that the single channel approach which we are advocating will extend collective bargaining and conflict to the board-room. In our view, conflicts of interest and views are already not unknown in the boardroom, as must be the case in any forum in which a number of different interests have to be reconciled before agreement can be reached. Nevertheless, we accept that the introduction of employee representatives will change the nature of board meetings. We believe, however, that the board will often become a more active force in policy-making to the benefit of all those with an interest in the good of the company. Indeed, we hope that many British companies will have the experience of one Swedish managing director we met, who said that since employee representatives had come on to his board the meetings had become not only more lively but also more useful, and of a senior executive of a major German bank who expressed the view that the presence of employee representatives on his board created greater precision of thought in its consideration of policy options.

31. Another fear frequently expressed to us was that parity representation on the board could lead to conflict between the two sides, and on occasion even to deadlock, with the result that decisions would be postponed or inade-quate and weak compromises would be negotiated. This was described as bring-ing confrontation into the boardroom. At its worst, it was said, it would result in the demoralisation of management and the inability of the company to respond to the needs of the marketplace. These fears were reflected in a recurrent theme in the written evidence that employee representatives on the board should not be involved in executive management. Several submissions argued that it was possible to divide the board's functions into supervision, in which the employee representatives should be involved, and executive management, which should remain the preserve of the managers. A few companies believed that, if there was to be employee representation, then the separation of functions should be recognised by the legal creation of a two-tier board structure on the grounds that it would prevent employee representatives from being involved in executive management. But at the same time there were as many others who felt that it was not possible to divide the board's functions in this way and that to attempt to do so would be a hindrance rather than a help to efficient manage-ment.

32. On this general question of the effect of employee representation on boards on the efficiency of industry, we tend to agree with those who argue that board level representation will have beneficial effects on the performance of British companies. Our belief is that at present it is sometimes difficult to im-plement policies because it is believed that they have been devised without the involvement of the workforce. The reaction therefore to new policies proposed by management is sometimes suspicion and hostility from the workforce and

---

[1]TUC supplementary evidence, paragraph 14.

trade unions, which can be reflected in conflict with management over their introduction. In the worst cases the implementation of proposals can be delayed or even abandoned as a result of costly industrial disputes. Such problems would not disappear with the introduction of board level representation. But, since employee representatives would be involved in the taking of the decision before any attempt was made to implement it, they would have a significant influence on the decision that was reached, and because of this would share responsibility for what the board decided. Managers would no longer have to begin negotiating with the trade unions in an atmosphere of suspicion about an unfamiliar policy agreed by a board representing only the shareholders; they would be implementing a policy already agreed between the representatives of employees and shareholders jointly at board level.

The interests of investors

33. In discussing the impact of employee representation on boards on the interests of investors, we have interpreted the term 'investors' widely to include all providers of outside funds to companies. This definition encompasses individual investors who directly or indirectly own shares, institutional investors like pension funds and investment companies, and the providers of short and longer term loan facilities of all kinds. These sources of outside capital have provided between 15 and 30 per cent of new capital for British companies over the last 25 years[1] to enable them to finance new projects, invest in new plant and machinery and generally extend their operations. The rest of the capital for new investment has been generated internally by companies from undistributed profits including provisions for depreciation. Many of those who gave evidence to us feared that parity employee representation on the board would damage the confidence of the investor in British industry, and therefore make it more difficult for companies to raise capital. We felt this was a serious concern, but one that was too often unspecified and unsubstantiated. We therefore invited experts in different aspects of investment to give us their views, not about the philosophy of employee representation on the board, but about its practical effects on investment in British industry.

34. Our discussions with them concentrated on three aspects of the provision of capital: short term lending, mainly the provision of overdraft facilities; medium and long term lending against notes and loan stock; and institutional investment in equities. Though there are differences of emphasis, particularly with regard to the short and long term view of a company's prospects, it is possible to distinguish a number of basic common interests, which we believe are applicable to all providers of capital. The lender wishes to ensure that the company is able to service the debt and ultimately repay it. The equity investor is concerned that he should be paid an adequate dividend on his investment and that the value of his investment should grow. All providers of capital therefore are interested to varying degrees in the performance of the company in the short and long term—in its ability to generate profits and to expand.

35. The witnesses from the City felt that the difficulties they foresaw would be at their most acute during the period when employee representation on the

---

[1] See Table 3.

board was being introduced and was unproven. Confidence might be damaged by the investors' perception of what might happen as a result of board level representation—the possibility of interference with the efficiency of management, leading to a reduction in the profitability of companies. A major source of concern, it was felt, would be that the objectives of employee representatives would be different from those of shareholder representatives. In consequence, lenders of capital would tighten their controls over existing loans and be wary of lending money afresh to companies with employee representatives on their boards, and investors would look elsewhere for safe investment—to government stock, to property, to companies without employee representation on their boards, or overseas.

36. Proponents of employee representation on the board believe, on the other hand, that it will lead to better industrial relations, to more efficient management of companies and because of this eventually to the revitalisation of British industry. Thus, fears about the detrimental effects for investors are thought to be misplaced. The result, they conclude, is more likely to be a strengthening of the private sector, from which investors as well as employees can benefit. It was also put to us by those less fearful of the effects on investment of employee representation on boards that such representation is only one of many economic and political forces which affect confidence, and taken with these forces its actual effect on investment in the short term will be marginal and almost impossible to measure.

37. The effects of board level representation on direct investment are particularly important in the context of foreign investors. Most foreign capital is put into British industry by foreign companies developing and expanding the operations of their subsidiaries in the United Kingdom, and foreign portfolio investment in equities overall is relatively unimportant. We note in Chapter 2 that 100 of the 738 enterprises employing 2,000 or more people in the United Kingdom are foreign-controlled. A number of submissions expressed the view that loss of confidence among investors in the United Kingdom, if it occurred, might be compounded among foreign investors in British industry, either because alternative investment destinations are available to them, or because the fact that they are foreign makes them react more nervously to conditions here. Some foreign investment might therefore be withheld, they concluded, at least until employee representation had proved itself. The effect of our detailed proposals on foreign-based multinational companies is discussed in Chapter 11.

38. Few were prepared to claim that damage to the interests of investors was the inevitable consequence of board level representation. What was at issue was more the form and proportions such representation took and the manner in which it was introduced. Moreover, those submissions taking the view that employee representation on boards would have a beneficial influence on the efficiency and viability of companies concluded that in the long term the interests of investors would be enhanced. Their willingness to provide capital would at worst be unaffected, and at best increased, leading to a positive desire to invest in companies with the new board structure, and to a wish on the part of the overseas investors to expand their operations in this country to take

52

advantage of the improved industrial relations. Such a view was implicit in the remarks made to us during our visit to Germany, by the Federal Chancellor, Dr Helmut Schmidt, amongst others, who expressed the belief that the implementation of employee representation on company boards would have a positive influence on the whole British economy and would not be inimical to foreign investment in the United Kingdom.

39. It is not only in the context of foreign-owned multinational companies that some groups feel employee representation on boards would affect investment *by companies* as well as investment *in companies*. Much investment is internally financed from undistributed profits and provisions for depreciation, and in 1970–1975 these internal sources accounted for 75 per cent of all new funds[1]. This raises the question whether employee representation on boards will affect the willingness of companies to reinvest profits. It has been suggested that employee representatives on the board, unlike other directors, will not recognise the need for growth and expansion to ensure the continued prosperity of their company. Even if the company's policy on distribution of profits to shareholders remains unchanged, the use of undistributed profits for financing capital investment may be questioned by the employee representatives. The tendency may be for the company's wage and employment policies to become more generous, thus depressing profits within a short time. However, the argument that employee representatives on the board, regardless of particular circumstances, will tend to push the company towards a high wages and high employment policy rests on the assumption that short term benefits to their constituents —higher wages or more jobs now—will seem more important than the long term benefits to the same constituents represented by profitable growth, ie secure or expanding employment in the future. The reasonableness of making such an assumption has received strong criticism in a number of submissions.

40. We do not see why a board comprising employee as well as shareholder representatives should be unable to strike an adequate balance between short term and long term interests. A board consisting of shareholder representatives is said to be able to strike the correct balance between the short and the long term interests of equity investors in determining, for example, the size of dividends. If employee representatives are unable to strike a similar balance on wage and employment policies, it must either be because they or their constituents are more short-sighted than shareholders and their representatives, or because the real economic interests of employees lie, relatively speaking, in the short term and those of shareholders in the long term. Neither proposition is self-evident, let alone proved. To put it no higher, there does not seem any reason to believe that employee representatives will not have as clear a perception of where their constituents' best interests lie, or that the stake held by employees in the long term health of the company is less than that of the shareholders.

41. We recognise that in the long term it is only experience over many years that will vindicate our belief that the involvement of employees in decision-making through representation at board level will increase the efficiency of companies and ultimately make them more profitable. In the short term clearly confidence could be affected by sudden changes in the control structure of

---

[1]See Table 3.

British companies, and it is for this reason that we point out in Chapter 9 the period of time over which the reconstitution of boards of directors to include employee representatives will take place. The multiplicity of factors that influence the complex behaviour of investors in a modern industrial market economy—and on occasion the apparent irrationality of the causes and effects involved—lead us to the conclusion that any attempt to predict, let alone to quantify the implications for investors of employee representation on the boards of large British enterprises is difficult. On the question of foreign confidence, it is worth emphasising that the United Kingdom is not stepping out of line with other European countries in introducing board level representation. Large multinational enterprises have adapted to the requirements of legislation on employee representation in Scandinavia, in West Germany and in some cases even in Yugoslavia. We see no reason to doubt that they will adapt here also.

The interests of consumers

42. Two main concerns were expressed in evidence to us on behalf of consumers. The first was that there would be a conspiracy at board level between the representatives of capital and labour to pursue the twin aims of higher profits and wages without due regard to the consumer. As the National Consumer Council (NCC) commented in their written evidence:

'We cannot but fear that if labour and capital were locked together into one organisational combine the push for security would become strongly underpinned and the tendency to monopolistic limitation of new entrants to a trade enhanced. Since the interests of consumers are served best by competition (even with all its weaknesses), such tendency would not be to their advantage'[1].

43. The second source of concern was that the introduction of parity representation on the lines proposed by the TUC and the extension of trade union power involved could only reduce the efficiency of companies, making for higher prices and poorer service to the consumer. The NCC emphasised the importance of efficiency to the consumer as follows:

'The more efficiency, the better the prospects of consumers getting goods and services which are better value for money—reasonably priced, safer, more durable, more reliable, better serviced and delivered on time'[2].

The NCC concluded by opposing employee representation on the board, but it added that if the concept was accepted then the interests of consumers should also be specifically represented.

44. Others took the view that the interests of consumers would be furthered, not damaged, by the introduction of employee representation on the boards of companies, because of the positive influence this would have on productivity, efficiency and the avoidance of wasteful confrontation. Given our persuasion that board level representation will have a positive impact on efficiency, we naturally incline to the view that such developments will enhance rather than

---

[1]National Consumer Council, *Industrial Democracy and Consumer Democracy: Seven reasons the TUC is wrong!* (NCC 1976), page 3.
[2]*ibid*, page 1.

54

damage consumer interests. Moreover, fears of adverse effects on consumer interests appear to be based at least partly on a misunderstanding of how boards reach decisions and how companies operate. We do not believe that boards representing labour and capital could, even if they wanted, pursue profit without regard to the interests of consumers. The constraints of competition in the marketplace, however imperfect, oblige companies which by definition depend absolutely for their existence on customers for the goods or services they produce, to be constantly aware of and responsive to the needs and preferences of consumers. These constraints will not change simply because the composition of the board is altered. The economic relationship between the company and its customers remains constant. Whatever interests or instinct to 'exploit the market' a company may have, the addition of employee representatives to its board will not enhance its capability of so doing.

45. A separate question is whether the predisposition of companies to act contrary to the interests of consumers may be increased or decreased by representation of employees on company boards. The NCC foresees a greater propensity to anti-consumer behaviour, operating for example through the monopolistic or at least oligopolistic powers of large companies to raise prices or to limit new entrants to a trade or industry. Assuming that such powers exist, and that they are not fully used by companies with their present boards of directors, we may still ask why boards of directors including employee representatives would be more inclined than existing boards to make use of them. The NCC gives as the reason an increased 'push for security'. In contrast to this hypothesis of a conspiracy by the representatives of capital and labour to exploit the consumer, some British trade unionists have asserted that employee representation on boards will lead to monopolistic or anti-consumer policies being modified or abandoned, because they will be subject to the scrutiny of people in closer touch with the interests of consumers in general than the predominantly middle-class group of existing directors of large companies. We find both arguments speculative and therefore unconvincing.

46. We do not accept the view put forward by the NCC that if there was to be employee representation on company boards (to which it was opposed in principle) then there must also be representation of consumer interests. We do not agree that there is a need for the latter, partly because we do not accept the thesis that board level representation of employees will damage the consumer interests. Consumer interests must continue to be protected, as they are now, against the actions of industrial enterprises, but the way to do this is through legislation and through the existing consumer organisations, rather than by involving consumers in the running of companies. The involvement of employees and shareholders in a company is different in kind from that of consumers. Furthermore, we see serious practical difficulties in achieving satisfactory representation of consumers on boards. Generally speaking there is no recognisable consumer constituency equivalent to that of employees and shareholders and therefore no way in which a guardian of consumer interests could be appointed to the board through representative machinery. In certain cases a company may have as the single or dominant customer for its products another company —a corporate consumer. The right or duty to appoint a 'consumer director' would therefore have to be given to consumer organisations, to some other

company, to the Secretary of State for Prices and Consumer Protection (the solution which the Chairman of NCC suggested in answer to our questions when he gave oral evidence), or to the companies themselves. Problems would arise, such as the undesirable and unwelcome extension of Ministers' powers of patronage, amounting to a power to appoint Government directors to the boards of all large companies. Whilst these problems might not be insoluble, they must weigh in the balance against this proposal.

47. There are other ways as well in which the consumer interest is protected. The Monopolies Commission, for example, exists to ensure that the abuses of a monopoly position, where one company dominates and in consequence can manipulate a market, are curbed. Recent years have seen the growth of the consumer movement, reflected in the establishment of bodies like the NCC itself, to identify and represent the consumer interest, and in the increasing amount of legislation like the Fair Trading Act 1973 and Consumer Credit Act 1974 to protect various aspects of the consumer interest. We are not saying that such protection is perfect. Our point is that none of these forms of protection will be affected by employee representation on boards. The many different pressures within the economy which require companies to take into account the interests of consumers will continue to exist. In our view, the effect on consumers of employee representation on company boards will be marginal. For this reason, and because of the problems mentioned above, we do not recommend that the law should provide for consumer representation on boards of directors in the private sector.

European experience

48. In conclusion it is worth pointing out that experience in other European countries suggests that employee representation on the board can have some of the benefits claimed for it. Comparison between different countries can be dangerous, and there is no way of knowing whether the same benefits will accrue here if board level representation is introduced. Nevertheless the evidence of the successful operation of employee representation in several advanced industrial countries with strong trade union movements cannot be ignored. At least, it is clear that nowhere has board level representation had the disastrous effects on industry that were often feared before its introduction. Indeed, in both Sweden and West Germany we heard strong support for the principle of board level representation from both sides of industry.

49. At the end of the three-year experiment with employee directors on company boards, Swedish industrialists and trade unionists both expressed the view that board level representation had made a positive contribution to the performance of Swedish industry. Industrialists admitted that though they had had initial doubts they would now not want to go back to a system where there were no employee representatives on the board. Employee representation had led to a better understanding of the board's activities and to more commitment from the trade unions to the policies adopted by the board. In some cases managers agreed that they had to spend more time explaining policies to employee directors and to the trade unions, but the longer-term benefit was seen in a better appreciation of management's problems and in better industrial

relations. Trade unionists whom we met emphasised that their aims in putting employee representatives on the board had been modest. They had sought insight into the workings of the board and more financial information about the company; although the results varied from company to company, they had achieved both. They had no illusions about the influence that could be wielded at board level when the employee representatives were in a minority, but they did feel that their position in collective bargaining was strengthened by the insight into the company's affairs that board level representation gave them.

50. In the Federal Republic of Germany many of those we met saw a strong and direct connection between the success of the West German economy since World War II and the presence of employee representatives on supervisory boards. West German industrialists, though opposed to parity representation, were largely in agreement that board level representation provided a system of legally enforced communication between managers and employees which led to an earlier identification of problems involving changes for employees and to a more thoughtful and far-sighted style of management. West German trade unionists were in broad agreement with the employers about the benefits of *Mitbestimmung*, but expressed their dissatisfaction with minority representation as provided up to 1976 on the supervisory boards of all companies except those in the coal, iron and steel industries, and with the provisions of the Co-determination Act 1976, which come closer to parity but still tip the balance in the shareholders' favour. We shall return to the much disputed question of proportions on the board in Chapter 9.

Conclusion

51. While the evidence submitted to us raised a formidable number of difficulties that might be associated with the implementation of employee representation on boards, we are confident that none of these is insurmountable. Clearly, careful consideration needs to be given to questions of timing, proportions, methods of election, confidentiality, application to groups of companies, and so on, if some of the worries expressed in evidence are to be allayed. It is to such questions that the remainder of this Report is devoted.

52. We have dealt at some length with what seem to us the main issues in the debate about the difficulties and possible adverse effects that could arise in introducing employee representation on company boards because we do not wish to minimise these difficulties, especially those that may arise in the first few years. In drawing up our proposals we have taken careful account of the points that have been put to us in evidence. We have been constantly aware of the pleas for flexibility and we believe that our proposals embody a flexible and workable approach. In Chapter 8 our proposals about directors' duties and responsibilities reflect to a large extent the criticisms which were put to us, and in that chapter we also return to the question of confidential information. In Chapter 9 we take up some of the arguments about an evolutionary approach, discussing the controversial questions of proportions and timing. Chapter 10 is about the role of trade unions. There we have taken careful note of the claim that employees are not interested in representation on the board, building into our proposals a method of testing opinion before a scheme is implemented.

We also discuss there how far trade unions should be involved in the procedures for selection and reporting back, taking into account the points put to us about non-unionised employees. In Chapter 11 we tackle the difficulties of applying our proposals to small companies, to groups and to multinationals. And in Chapter 12 we make proposals for an independent agency and for the training of those involved in the new structure, designed to make board level representation work as effectively as possible.

CHAPTER 7

Present law and practice in the structure and function of company boards

1. Before considering how employee representation on boards might be introduced, it is important to examine the present structure of companies in the United Kingdom and in particular the composition and role of their boards of directors. In this chapter therefore we begin by looking at the requirements of company law concerning the relationship between the board of directors and shareholders, and the duties and functions of directors. We then consider how within this legal framework company boards have developed and what part they play in the process of decision-making in large companies. This is an essential preliminary to our discussion in Chapter 8 about the changes needed in company law and company practice to allow the introduction of effective employee representation on company boards.

The shareholders and the board

2. Company law is largely based on the concept of ownership. The ultimate control of the company is seen in law as residing with its owners or shareholders. They have the right initially to draw up, and subsequently to amend, the memorandum and articles of association, in which it is stated what the company shall do and how it shall be organised to do it. They may, and almost invariably do, delegate the management of the company to appointed officers. They may revoke the delegation at any time by changing the articles of association or dismissing those they have appointed. In addition the shareholders' ultimate authority cannot be delegated or overriden in a number of specified areas. These include: appointing the auditors (otherwise than in respect of a casual vacancy); requiring a Department of Trade investigation of the company's affairs; ratifying acts carried out by directors who have exceeded their delegated authority (eg exceeding their borrowing powers); approving certain payments to directors for compensation for loss of office; agreeing to changes in the capital structure; and putting the company into voluntary liquidation. In some of these instances a special resolution (ie one passed by a three-quarters majority vote at a general meeting) is required.

3. In practice of course, particularly in large public companies, the shareholders are often a passive force, exercising their powers on the advice and initiative of the board of directors and rarely initiating action themselves. This is not to say that the shareholders' powers are not important in a few unusual cases, nor to imply that the shareholders are in some way manipulated or bypassed by their directors. It is inevitable that where the shareholders are numerous and diverse, they will in many cases be insufficiently organised and interested to do more than leave the detailed business of the company to a board of directors and to professional managers.

4. The law allows considerable freedom to companies to devise a constitution and an organisational structure best suited to their needs. The statutes lay down certain minimum conditions that must be fulfilled but within this framework there is great flexibility. The Companies Act 1948, for example, requires that all public companies should have at least two directors, and all private companies at least one, but it is left to the individual company to state in its articles of

association, if it wishes, a maximum number of directors. The statute is particularly flexible in respect of limited liability companies, which are by far the most important category in United Kingdom company law. Table A of Schedule 1 to the Companies Act 1948 provides a model set of articles which companies limited by shares may adopt in whole or in part. Table A is deemed to apply, if a company fails to register alternative articles.

5. It can be seen from Table A how much is left for the company to settle for itself. The articles will usually deal with the role of directors in some detail. They will state for example how much authority is to be delegated to them. Regulation 80 of Table A gives an example of how this might be and almost invariably is done.

'The business of the company shall be managed by the directors, who may pay all expenses incurred in promoting and registering the company, and may exercise all such powers of the company as are not, by the Act or by these regulations, required to be exercised by the company in general meeting . . .'

The articles also deal with procedures to be followed by the board, the powers and duties of directors in addition to those specified by the law, and with how directors' remuneration is to be determined.

6. It seems clear from this brief description that the chief characteristic of this flexibility of company law lies in its non-interference in the organisation of companies. Though it sets the legal framework within which companies must operate, company law does not try to dictate a single structure which all limited liability companies must follow. We shall see later in this chapter the practical diversity in the functions of company boards and the way in which companies reach decisions which has been the result of this company law system.

Directors' legal duties

7. In addition to any powers and duties conferred on directors by a company's articles of association directors have a number of legal duties and responsibilities. Some of these are in the Companies Acts themselves but many more, as the Jenkins' Committee report said in 1962, 'are still determined by extensive and complex case law which does not find expression in the Act'[1]. For the purposes of this report it is sufficient to have an understanding of the main principles involved rather than the whole complex picture.

8. The common law duties of directors fall into two distinct parts: the fiduciary duties of loyalty and good faith and the duties of care and skill. The fiduciary duties require the director to act in what he believes to be the best interests of the company and to exercise his powers for the particular purposes for which they were conferred. He must not put himself in a position where his ability to do so is restricted or where there is a conflict between his duty and some personal interest. Of the many facets of this fiduciary duty the following seem to us of particular relevance. First, the director must not have *outside interests* which prevent compliance with his duty as a director of a company to act in its best interests, although so far this has not been applied to prohibit a director from being a member of a board of two competing companies. Second, the director must not make any *secret profit* (ie one not approved by the company) out of the execution of his office as director. Third, there is the problem of *insider trading* (ie a director making profits from dealing in shares or debentures on the basis of information known to him as a director). The Companies

---

[1] Report of the Company Law Committee, Cmnd 1749 (HMSO 1962), paragraph 86.

Act 1967 requires disclosure of a director's interests and those of his immediate family in his company's securities or the securities of its holding or any subsidiary company. Fourth, there is the question of *confidential information*. The exact ambit of the law of confidence is not clear; but there can be no doubt that in respect of companies' plans, projects, 'know-how', the director is under a duty not to reveal confidential information to outsiders.

9. By contrast to these fiduciary duties the degree of care and skill to be shown by a director is not high and the Courts have had difficulty in deciding how much care and skill should be displayed by a director in carrying out his functions. A number of principles can be distinguished. A director is not obliged, in the absence of a contractual obligation, to give continuous attention to his company's affairs and he is, generally speaking, entitled to leave matters to properly delegated officers of the company so long as nothing 'puts him on enquiry' that something improper has been done. His liability for negligence is measured by a subjective duty of care, ie by the standard of what is reasonable for a person of his knowledge and his experience, although his conduct must not fall below what is considered to be the reasonable behaviour of an ordinary man. There is scarcely any modern case in which a director has been held liable for mere negligence.

10. Two other important aspects of the director's duty should be mentioned here in connection with *misfeasance* and *fraudulent trading*. If a company is in liquidation, any director, manager or officer of the company is liable in misfeasance proceedings for actual loss suffered by the company if he has misapplied, retained or become accountable for, any property of the company, or been guilty of any misfeasance or breach of trust in relation to the company. The word 'misfeasance' does not include ordinary negligence nor, it has been said, does it involve moral turpitude. For such breach of duty the director must repay money misapplied or pay compensation. The term 'fraudulent trading' is somewhat misleading. It occurs if, in the course of the liquidation of a company, it is shown that the business is being carried on with intent to defraud creditors or for any fraudulent purpose. In such circumstances, the liquidator or any creditor, shareholder or the Official Receiver can apply to the Court to have any persons who were knowingly a party to the fraud made personally liable for all or any of the debts or liabilities of the company, without limit on their liability. Any person guilty of being party to such fraudulent trading commits a criminal offence, punishable by a fine of up to £500 and/or imprisonment of up to two years. The cases show however that the burden of proving fraud is not easy to discharge. One case suggests that it is committed by carrying on business 'when there is, to the knowledge of the directors, no reasonable prospect of the creditors ever receiving payment of their debts'. But the same judge also said that 'fraud' means: 'real dishonesty involving, according to the current notions of fair trading among commercial men, real moral blame'. The Jenkins' Committee in 1962 recommended that for civil (but not criminal) liability for fraud, it should be enough that the directors were reckless in continuing to trade; but the Companies Bill 1973 did not include this proposal. The Bill did, however, propose that criminal liability for fraudulent trading should arise whether or not the company is being wound up.

11. We shall be discussing in the next chapter how the duties of directors might be clarified and defined in the law, if employee representatives are on the board. One problem, however, arises here immediately in connection with the

fiduciary duties of directors described above. We have seen that directors have a duty to act in what they consider to be the best interests of the company. This has been very narrowly interpreted by the Courts to mean the best interests of the shareholders both present and future, and to include the interests of other groups like employees, creditors and customers, only insofar as they coincide with those of the shareholders. In practice this does not normally matter as the interests of the shareholders and other groups do coincide. However, the principle was tested in 1962 in the case of *Parke v The Daily News Limited* which arose out of the sale of the ailing *News Chronicle and Star*. Professor Gower described the case and the decision as follows:

'The Cadbury family, who controlled the selling company wished to distribute the whole of the purchase price among the employees who would become redundant. At the suit of one shareholder they were restrained from doing so. To the argument that "the prime duty must be to the shareholders; but boards of directors must take into consideration their duties to employees in these days", Plowman J answered tersely: "but no authority to support that proposition as a proposition of law was cited to me; I know of none and in my judgment such is not the law".'[1]

12. We have found wide acceptance of the view—which we share—that a reform in the law in this area is long overdue, whether or not employee representatives are put on boards. The matter becomes pressing however in the context of representation on the board, as it is unrealistic to expect employee representatives to pay sole regard to the interests of shareholders. A number of formulations have been suggested for extending the duties of directors to take into account the interests of all employees, notably in the Companies Bill of 1973 and again in the Industrial Democracy Bill, the Private Members Bill introduced by Giles Radice MP in 1975. In the next chapter we consider how far these were adequate, and whether some new formula is necessary to *require*, rather than simply *entitle*, directors to have regard to the interests of employees. The question must be considered in connection with the issue of how far directors' duties should be set down in law. The Jenkins' Committee as long ago as 1962 thought that such a codification would be useful both to directors and to company management in trying to find their way through the complexities of case law. Again, we return to this matter in the next chapter.

Company boards: composition

13. We examine in this and the next two sections how within the framework of the law we have described, companies have developed their boards and decision-making structures to suit the particular needs and demands of their business. It is not surprising in view of the foregoing paragraphs that great diversity exists both in the composition and functions of boards and in how companies reach decisions.

14. As we have seen, the law requires companies to have a minimum number of directors, but does not prescribe a maximum. The size and composition of company boards therefore varies according to the needs of the individual company. We have analysed the boards of *The Times 1,000 companies*. Our aim is to get an idea of the size range of company boards and to see how many of them have non-executive directors and in what proportions. The results of the analysis are shown in Table 11.

---

[1] L C B Gower, *The Principles of Modern Company Law* (third edition, 1969), page 522.

TABLE 11

Number of directors and non-executive directors by size of company

UK employees	Total number of companies	Number of directors					Number of non-executive directors			
		2–5	6–10	11–15	16–20	Over 20	None	1–2	3–5	Over 5
Under 1,000	184	60	109	12	2	1	58	66	46	14
1,000– 2,000 ...	173	35	123	11	3	1	34	85	43	11
2,000– 3,000 ...	158	32	107	18	1	—	35	67	41	15
3,000– 4,000 ...	100	14	71	13	2	—	26	38	29	7
4,000– 5,000 ...	67	8	54	5	—	—	17	25	20	5
5,000– 7,500 ...	94	2	56	33	2	1	26	28	29	11
7,500–10,000 ...	51	2	24	17	5	3	10	16	13	12
10,000–20,000 ...	73	6	34	25	3	5	18	25	21	9
20,000–50,000 ...	56	—	15	33	5	2	14	22	12	8
Over 50,000 ...	26	1	1	14	6	4	5	10	7	4
Total	982 (a)	160	595	181	29	17	243	382	261	96

Note: (a) excludes 18 companies who did not disclose total number of employees (see Table 2).
Source: The Times 1,000, 1975–76 and the Committee's own survey.

15. This shows that very few companies, only 46 of those studied, have more than 15 directors, and that over two-thirds (755) have ten or less. The analysis also provides some confirmation of the generalisation that small companies tend to have small boards of directors and large companies large ones. Of the 184 companies analysed with under 1,000 employees, only 15 had a board with more than ten directors and only three a board with more than 15. At the other extreme over half (97) of the 155 companies with over 10,000 employees had a board with more than ten directors and 25 had boards of over 15.

16. On the appointment of non-executive directors, there was little difference between the smaller and larger companies in our sample which admittedly consisted of the largest companies in the United Kingdom. Nearly 25 per cent of the companies (243) had no non-executive directors at all, and a little under 10 per cent had more than five. The overwhelming proportion of the companies had between one and five non-executive directors.

17. A survey of directors in 200 large companies, carried out by the British Institute of Management in 1972, provided some interesting information on the origins and backgrounds of company directors[1]. It found that over 70 per cent of the executive directors had worked in the company before being appointed to the board. Median length of service before appointment was 13 years. Over 60 per cent of the companies had made their most recent board appointments after recommendations from the chairman and chief executive and about 12 per cent had formed a committee of the board to do the selection. Of the 466 non-executive directors in the BIM sample, 82 were retired executive directors of the company and another 66 had family or historical connections with it. Thirty-five were substantial shareholders, 26 were politicians and the rest, 253, were specialists: mainly, accountants, bankers, barristers and solicitors.

18. Various surveys have been done into the educational background of directors, but as the Royal Commission on the Distribution of Incomes and Wealth commented, differences in their coverage, in the questions asked and the levels of response make it difficult to draw any reliable conclusions about changes in the underlying situation[2]. A 1972 survey of directors in 200 companies which appeared in *Management Today* and had a response rate of 55 per cent demonstrated that only 29 per cent of respondents had received a state education, a figure which contrasts with the fact that between the wars about 90 per cent of people received a state education. This proportion of 29 per cent had not altered significantly from earlier surveys in 1964 and 1968[2].

The role of the board

19. What then is the role of a typical board of directors? It is impossible to generalise, either about what matters are discussed at board level or how far the board is involved in actual decision-making. The role of a board varies from

---

[1]British Institute of Management, *The Board of Directors*, Management Survey Report No 10 (BIM 1972).
[2]Royal Commission on Distribution of Income and Wealth Report No 3, *Higher Income from Employment*, Cmnd 6383 (HMSO 1976), pages 120–233.

company to company and is constantly changing with the requirements of business. It may be related to the size, complexity and nature of the company's operation and therefore to the organisational structure which has been developed over many years. It may depend on the philosophy of management in the company or on the personality of the chief executive.

20. Many different kinds of boards were described to us in the written evidence. The Industrial Participation Association distinguished at least nine different company structures: from the small company with a board of executive managers closely involved in every aspect of a company's affairs, to the decentralised group with a holding company board appointing senior managers and allocating resources, but leaving operating policy to its subsidiary boards[1]. We heard of companies where equally there was little delegation of authority to subsidiary boards, so that though they were boards of separately incorporated companies they were no more than legal entities which had no powers and rarely met. We also heard of companies which had boards of directors, who were not directors at all in the strict legal sense but who nevertheless exercised considerable powers. A clear example of this is where a company is organised into divisions, each one controlled by a committee or board of senior executives who are referred to in the company as 'divisional directors'. Such a divisional board may have considerable delegated authority to draw up a strategic policy for the division and allocate resources between subsidiaries or operating units. It may look and act very much like the board of a separately incorporated subsidiary: it may indeed have more power. But in legal terms its directors may have no legal standing as such and, if so, may not be subject to the requirements of company law concerning directors.

21. Considerable diversity exists even within large companies. To illustrate this, it may be useful to examine the organisations of five companies, as they were described to us in the written evidence. Guest Keen and Nettlefolds Ltd (GKN) provided us with an example of a decentralised group, organised to encourage local autonomy with the minimum direction from the centre. It described to us what it called 'a four-tier board structure' encompassing 143 boards in the UK and 583 directors. At the top is the holding company board of GKN Ltd; below that the two boards of GKN (Overseas) Ltd and GKN (UK) Ltd; below those are 13 sub-group boards in the United Kingdom and below those 137 United Kingdom company and division boards[2]. In contrast, the main business of Imperial Chemical Industries Ltd (ICI) in the United Kingdom is carried out through nine manufacturing divisions each of which is managed by a divisional chairman and a number of divisional directors. There are subsidiary and sub-subsidiary companies within these divisions but the divisional structure forms the organisational hierarchy. 'Some matters are reserved to the centre, but subject to this, there is a wide delegation of authority to Division Chairmen and the Division is a key unit in the Company's procedures for the implementation of industrial democracy'[3]. Electrical and Musical Industries Ltd (EMI) gave us a detailed list of the functions of its top board: ensuring the executive functions are properly performed through monthly meetings to review the results; undertaking an annual review of the budget for the forthcoming

---

[1]Industrial Participation Association, *op cit*, pages 29–31.
[2]GKN evidence, page 7.
[3]ICI evidence, paragraph 1.3.

year; devising the five year plan; formulating group policy with regard to government relations, public relations and international affairs; taking investment or divestment decisions; approving half-yearly and annual accounts and the reports to shareholders; and appointing and reviewing the remuneration of executive directors. Below this level however there is an enormous complexity and variety within a group based on both divisions and subsidiaries;

'Generally speaking the legal corporate organisation—that is, the conduct of businesses by subsidiary limited companies—does not necessarily correspond with the substantive businesses or management structure. Thus one business may include the activities of several companies; alternatively, a business may not be represented as a separate company at all; only as a division of a company whether the parent company or a subsidiary of the parent. The Boards of Directors of wholly-owned subsidiary companies within the EMI Group do not therefore have the same functions as the parent Board: some of these Boards do function as a management committee, but others have no more than purely legal functions'[1].

The building and construction firm John Laing & Son Ltd is a smaller decentralised group, based much more on the separately incorporated subsidiary. The group board's functions include establishing aims and policy, approving divisional plans and budgets, and reviewing performance. It operates through a number of divisions, each of which may be made up of wholly or jointly owned subsidiaries. Each division is virtually a self-contained business or group of businesses, 'with full accountability and freedom of action within centrally approved budgets and plans'[2]. Finally, Bass Charrington Ltd described to us another decentralised group employing over 62,000 in both manufacturing and retailing[3]. The main board of the group appoints top management and sets the constraints of budgets and capital expenditure within which the four main operating subsidiaries, the ten regional companies concerned in marketing and the 3,600 managed outlets (mainly public houses and off-licences) operate.

22. Whatever we say therefore about the nature and role of boards is inevitably a generalisation. We believe however that the real diversity exists below the top board level in large companies and among smaller companies, and that it may therefore be possible to make some useful general comments about the main boards of large companies and company groups. We have tried on the basis of the evidence we have received and the experience of individual members of the Committee to draw up a list of the matters for which such boards usually have ultimate responsibility:

(a) appointing senior managers, reviewing their performance and fixing their remuneration;

(b) setting the company's objectives and strategic plans and ensuring that adequate machinery exists in the company for planning;

(c) controlling the financial affairs of the company including the approval of capital programmes and capital expenditure, and allocating resources between operations;

---

[1] EMI evidence, paragraph 9.
[2] John Laing & Son Ltd evidence, paragraph 1.2.
[3] Bass Charrington evidence, paragraph 1.

(d) agreeing the company's organisation to meet the objectives and delegating authority for certain functions within the company;

(e) considering policy on take-overs and mergers;

(f) monitoring and evaluating performance;

(g) setting overall guidelines for employment and personnel policies.

23. Though it may have overall responsibility in these areas, the extent to which a main board exercises detailed control of policy is inevitably limited. In most companies it is the apex of the decision-making hierarchy and the focus of managerial authority. It cannot exercise detailed influence over every aspect of the company's affairs and it is largely reliant on the proposals and policies put to it by management, Equally, it retains the power to question, to check, to approve, to monitor and even in some cases to initiate policy. It sets the guidelines within which the company can operate and at critical points where major decisions are at stake its approval of management policy is not always a foregone conclusion. Above all it has the potential to make virtually any decision taken within the company subject to its approval. Two sociologists who have investigated the working of company boards felt that the ability of the board to formulate policy was limited but they recognised its importance as a 'legitimating institution':

'To be sure, the final yea or nay at a board meeting may be seen as the decision point, and may so appear in corporate histories . . . . But the board actions we have observed are better interpreted we feel, merely as ratifications of decisions made earlier and elsewhere, sometimes by much more junior men, about which the board had no practical alternative. The distinction between "making" and "taking" decisions is relevant. Boards of directors are, we feel, best conceived as decision taking institutions, that is, as legitimating institutions, rather than as decision-making ones'[1].

24. While boards themselves may have a limited role in the decision-making process, this cannot be said of individual directors. The majority of large company boards are composed of the company's senior managers, sometimes the heads of operating divisions, sometimes the chief executives of subsidiaries, who have an active role in the running of the company and in the preparation of policies for approval at board level. Many companies have formal management committees composed perhaps of executive directors and senior managers to which the board may delegate considerable responsibility for the formulation and execution of policy. The BIM survey found that 70 per cent of the companies studied had some sort of management committee 'to look at the overall affairs of the company':

'The pattern varied enormously, but a broadly typical situation would be for the full board to meet monthly and for a committee of the senior executives to meet more frequently . . . . Sometimes, junior executive directors and senior managers would attend the management committee, occasionally a non-executive director would be a member or be asked to attend'[2].

25. In short the structure of decision-making in large companies is extremely complex. It is often not possible to say that one man or one body of people

---

[1]R E Pahl and J J Winkler, 'The Economic Elite: Theory and Practice' in *Elites and Power in British Society*, page 110. P Stansworth and A Giddens (eds).
[2]BIM, *op cit*, page 3.

has responsibility for a decision or policy. The process of formulating policy can begin at top level with a group of senior managers or the board itself; it can then involve the whole of the managerial hierarchy, or in a group of companies, subsidiary boards and their managers; it might then work its way back up to board level for a final decision or for the seal of approval. Many internal and external pressures may affect those involved in devising a policy and taking a decision. They may be influenced by the expert advice of bankers, accountants and solicitors. They may have to alter their policy to suit their customers or providers of capital. In the best companies special attention will be paid to the interests of employees and policies will only be devised after thorough discussions with the trade unions. The decision may be affected by government policies, economic situations, the availability of credit and many other outside influences. Ultimately therefore it is difficult to assess the power of the board, but easy to exaggerate its ineffectiveness.

26. A good deal of attention has been given in recent years to the role of non-executive directors in the decision-making process. The BIM survey found, and this was confirmed in some of the evidence to us, that most large companies saw their role as being two-fold:

'First, as a guarantor to the shareholders that the company is being run in a reputable and competent fashion and, second, as an objective force able to offer the board independent advice and criticism on general policy and specific subjects such as senior salaries'[1].

Some who gave evidence to us were critical of present non-executive directors because of their inability to have real influence on company policy and because they are drawn generally from a very restricted social group. Lord Wilfred Brown combined both approaches in his evidence[2], criticising present non-executive directors and arguing that they should play a more positive role in supervising the performance of senior management.

The present structure of company boards

27. This analysis of British company structure leads us to agree with Paul Davies that 'once one begins to take account of corporate practice as well as corporate law, it no longer is clear that the UK system should be regarded as a one-tier rather than a two-tier system'[3]. Of course there is no British equivalent to the requirement in West German law that companies should have a supervisory and a management board, each with carefully defined powers. But in practice many large British companies and company groups operate a system where the functions of supervision and management are roughly divided between different levels of the organisation. As we have seen, the top boards of large companies often play a mainly supervisory role, with overall responsibility for strategic policy, allocating resources and monitoring performance, and delegate authority for the detailed formulation and implementation of policy to a lower level: to specified senior executives, to a formal management committee, to a group of managers sitting as a divisional board or committee, or even to the board of a separately incorporated subsidiary. But such boards of course, retain a power of initiative over decision-making which the German style supervisory board does not possess.

[1]BIM, *op cit*, summary of survey, paragraph 6.
[2]Lord Wilfred Brown's evidence, *Proposals for improving the means of keeping the performance of chief executives under more effective scrutiny . . . passim.*
[3]Batstone and Davies, *op cit*, page 56.

28. In some senses this can be represented as a *de facto* two-tier system, but in view of the diversity of company structure in the United Kingdom such categorisation is largely unfruitful. The advantage of the British system is, we believe, that it *cannot* be easily categorised. Within the framework of law, companies may mould their organisations to suit their individual needs and a one-tier, two-tier or many tiered system only operates where a company decides that such is the best form of structure for its efficient operation and management.

29. We shall be discussing further the relative merits of a one-tier or two-tier system in the next chapter. In our view it is important in such a discussion to concentrate on the functions rather than on the structure of company boards, on what boards do rather than on what they are called. In other words it seems to us to matter less whether employee representation is on a board which is called a supervisory, a management, or a unitary board, than that it should be clear that the functions of that board are sufficient to enable the employee representatives to have a real say in the important decisions about the future of the company. Paul Davies in his analysis of European experience expressed a similar view:

'... the important questions concern the distribution of decision-making functions in the company and ... these questions arise whether the company law of a country requires the creation of only one or of two boards.'[1]

Conclusions

30. In the next chapter we consider the changes in company law that would be necessary to introduce employee representation on boards, and how that will affect the diversity of practice which exists at the moment. Our analysis of company law and practice in this chapter has led us to the view that, as far as it is consistent with the introduction of effective board level representation, we must try to build upon the flexibility of the present system. We do not believe that it would be helpful to the efficient management of companies or to the success of employee representation on boards to impose a rigid or inappropriate legal formula, which restricted the ability of companies to devise a company structure which they considered most suitable for the management of their business.

31. We do think however that the law must be more precise about the role of the company board and about its relationship both to the shareholders' meeting and the management of the company. This is important for two reasons. First, we must try to ensure that the boards on which employees have representation have an opportunity to influence decision-making and carry ultimate responsibility for the control of the company's strategic policy. We are concerned that if the present system remains unaltered, employee representatives could find themselves sitting on a board with the illusion of influence, on the one hand overruled by the shareholders and on the other bypassed by management. Second, we think that management themselves will benefit from a clearer definition of the board's role and functions. As we shall argue in the next chapter we do not think it is possible or useful to draw a strict dividing line

[1] Batstone and Davies, *op cit*, page 53.

between the functions of a board to formulate policy and the functions of management to implement it. But it does seem to us important that if employee representatives are to have seats on the board, the managers responsible to that board should have a clearer definition of the limits of their discretion to take executive action within the policy guidelines laid down by the board. The next chapter discusses how this fine dividing line between continuing flexibility and more precision might be drawn.

CHAPTER 8

The implications of employee representation for the structure and function of company boards

1. Employee representation on company boards will involve fundamental changes both in the company law and the practice which we described in the previous chapter. Some of those who sent evidence to us suggested that employee interests could be adequately represented at board level with the minimum of change in the present system, by making employee directors directly accountable to the shareholders. The Stock Exchange, for example, in its evidence to us was '. . . concerned to show that the legitimate claims for a greater degree of involvement by employees in their companies can be met without making fundamental changes to the structure of company law', and accepted an employee presence at board level only 'provided that the appointment of such worker directors is always subject to the overriding right of shareholders as owners of the company to remove any director at any time'[1]. We cannot agree with this view. We believe that real involvement of employees in decision-making and the practical benefits for companies which will result from such involvement cannot be achieved by adding employee directors to the present system, so that they are in the last resort accountable only to the shareholders and can be overruled or dismissed by them whenever the shareholders so decide. The extension of industrial democracy, to which our terms of reference refer, can only be achieved in our view if there is direct *representation* of employees on company boards in just the same way as there is direct representation of shareholders on boards at present. It is that essential representational element which necessitates major changes in company law, and in consequence in the way companies operate.

2. We devote a large part of this chapter therefore to considering the company law changes which are essential to the introduction of employee representation on the board. Those changes are particularly important in the extent to which they encourage the development of a new partnership between capital and labour in the control of companies and improve their efficient operation. In making our proposals we have had two main aims: first, to balance the interests of employees and shareholders so that on the one hand employees have a real say in decision-making at board level and on the other the shareholders retain some control over how their investment in the company is managed; second, to ensure that in achieving the first aim companies are not constrained in how they are organised to take decisions at top level by rigid and inflexible legal requirements.

Board structure and functions

3. What then should be the powers and functions of the boards on which employees are to be represented? The debate has centred on two main alternatives: the creation of a two-tier board system with employee representation on the top or supervisory board or the modification and development of the existing United Kingdom unitary board system. We argued in the previous

---

[1]The Stock Exchange evidence, section 14.

71

chapter that in practice the distinction between a one-tier and a two-tier system is blurred and that there are senses in which many United Kingdom companies have developed a *de facto* two-tier system, delegating responsibility for the formulation and implementation of policy from the main board perhaps to a management committee or a lower board. The distinguishing feature of a statutory two-tier system is that the *law* establishes two levels of control in companies —usually the board and executive management—and defines in detail the functions of each. Its aim is to separate the responsibilities of the board for the supervision and appointment of management from the job of senior managers to run the company within the constraints set by the board. In the eyes of many of its proponents the advantages of such a system in relation to employee representation on boards, is that it enables employees to be involved in the job of supervision of the company's affairs, but leaves management free to manage.

4. The best known example of a statutory two-tier system is provided by the Federal Republic of Germany, where the law stipulates a strict division of function and personnel between a supervisory board on which employees are represented and a management board on which they are not. The EEC Green Paper describes the system as follows:

'The division of function and responsibility established by the law is clear and establishes that the board of management directs and is responsible for the management of the company, while the supervisory council supervises the management. Thus, while the board of management is responsible for the management of the company and normally represents it in and out of court, it has specific and detailed obligations as regards reporting on the company's affairs to the supervisory council'[1].

The supervisory board has a number of important powers. It appoints the management board; it receives regular reports from management on the state of the enterprise; it may inspect the company's books and ask the management specific questions about the company's affairs; and it can reserve to itself a right of veto over certain classes of transactions. But in other respects its ability to intervene in the affairs of the company is restricted. It cannot, in the words of the EEC Commission, 'be charged with management functions'[1]; it cannot dismiss a member of the management board before the end of his term of office except for good cause; it cannot issue positive directions to management; and even where it has reserved to itself the power to approve or veto certain transactions, it can be overruled if the management can obtain the agreement of 75 per cent of shareholders voting at a shareholders' meeting.

5. In our view a study of the West German system shows how difficult it would be to introduce something similar into the United Kingdom. For one thing, unless the two-tier board system was applied to all companies, irrespective of board level representation—a prospect which most proponents of the two-tier board do not envisage—company law would contain two separate structures for companies. Some companies would continue under the present system based on the single board of directors with their present legal duties and responsibilities; other companies with employee representatives on their boards would be subject to a new system where there were two boards, with strictly defined and

[1]EEC Commission, *op cit*, page 65.

separate functions, and two sets of directors with different duties and responsibilities. The system which applied to a particular company would be dependent neither on that company's individual needs nor on whether its board thought the system was suitable; but instead it would rest on the tests of whether a company had a certain number of employees (see Chapter 11), whether sufficient recognised trade unions in the company had requested representation on the board and the outcome of the ballot (see Chapter 10). This seems to us to be a formidable prospect both for companies and especially for those who have to deal with them, who would wish to ascertain the company law system under which a company was operating before doing business with its senior executives or board of directors. To some extent it is, of course, inevitable that employee representation on boards will introduce into law differences between companies, in that some will have employees on their board and some will not. But a statutory two-tier system would take this to extremes by creating two different and separate company law systems.

6. Furthermore, the formalism of a two-tier board system cuts right across the flexible tradition of company law within which companies in the United Kingdom have operated hitherto. It may be argued that the introduction of the two-tier board into this country does not necessarily involve the formalistic approach of the West Germans. But this is only true to a point. It seems to us that by definition the two-tier system requires careful and detailed treatment in the law. Its aim is to draw a fine dividing line between the overall responsibility of the board for strategic policy and supervision of management and the job of management to make decisions within the guidelines set by the board. This aim cannot be properly fulfilled in a statutory system unless the respective functions and membership of the board and management are dealt with in detail in the law.

7. We believe that the introduction into the United Kingdom of a two-tier board on the West German model would impose on companies a measure of inflexibility which would be detrimental to their efficient management. It is important to understand that the West German system of two-tier boards was developed during the last century, in response to demands that the shareholders should supervise more closely the work of management and long before employee representation was introduced. West German companies have therefore grown and developed in this century within the legal framework of a two-tier board system, and when employee representation was introduced, the supervisory board was the obvious place for it. In contrast as we have seen, United Kingdom law has largely left it to companies to define for themselves the role of their boards in relation to management. This has enabled them to draw up their own rules about where the job of the board ends and the job of management begins. It has meant that the distinction between the functions of supervision and management has remained fluid, responsive to the changing circumstances within the enterprise. It has also meant that no two companies have developed exactly the same method of operation or organisation. In our view, therefore, an attempt to impose the rigidity of the statutory two-tier system on British companies at the present stage in their development could be damaging to their efficiency and could restrict their ability in the future to alter their structures at top level to meet new demands on their business. If such a statutory system were introduced, companies would be required to adopt a form of board structure

and to maintain a separation of functions at top level which might bear no resemblance to the way in which they had developed their organisation over a period of years. One of two consequences could ensue. Either companies would conform to the new system with considerable disruption to their management structure, or alternatively and more likely in our view, the system would be inoperable.

8. An interesting example of the possible effects, if a two-tier system is introduced into the modern industrial state, is provided by France. Since 1966 French companies have had the option of adopting, if they wish, a formal two-tier structure with a supervisory council and management committee, the functions of each being defined in the law. According to the EEC Green Paper only a small proportion of companies have adopted this structure, and many of those who originally adopted it have now reverted to the old classical system. The EEC Commission attributed this to the tensions that existed between the supervisory board and the management committee, tensions which have been exacerbated by the fact that the management committee is largely controlled by the general assembly of shareholders:

'The reason for these developments appears to be that friction and conflict have occurred in a significant proportion of dualist companies as a result of the supervisory councils having difficulty in confining themselves to control, and trespassing on management territory. It has often been difficult to resolve these conflicts because only the general assembly of shareholders has the power to remove the management committee which deprives the supervisory council of an important means of coercion'[1].

This provides one demonstration of what can happen when there is an attempt to impose a formal separation of functions at board level upon companies where before there were informal and flexible arrangements, and shows how difficult it is to devise a law which defines realistically the distinction between the job of the board and that of management. It should be added that these difficulties in French companies arose independently of any employee representation. They could become more acute if employee representatives sat on the supervisory board. As Eric Batstone concludes, 'the evidence suggests, therefore, that the distinction between a supervisory and a management board is a difficult one to maintain in practice since the effective fulfilment of either role demands close involvement in the other'[2].

9. It seems to us that one of the major problems with the statutory two-tier system is that in its zeal to leave management free to manage, it sometimes severely limits the ability of the supervisory or top board to have an influence on company policy and to retain overall control of the company's affairs. This problem is exacerbated in countries which until recently have had a more flexible unitary board system, so that the result of limiting the powers of the supervisory board is either tension and conflict between the two tiers of control as in France, or, and potentially more serious in the context of employee representation, the development of an ineffective supervisory board. In West Germany the role of the supervisory board developed alongside the growth of the complex modern company and, as we have said, before employee representatives sat on it. During our visit we were told that it had the power to intervene

---

[1] EEC Commission, *op cit*, page 73.
[2] Batstone and Davies, *op cit*, page 22.

effectively in major questions of policy and had given employees the opportunity to influence decisions about the company's future. But we also heard of the tendency in some companies for the supervisory board, on all but the really major issues, to become a reactive and passive body, meeting three or four times a year to hear reports from management.

10. We fear that such a tendency would be increased if a two-tier board structure, with a supervisory board on the West German model, was introduced into the United Kingdom; especially if the sole reason for introducing it was to restrict the ability of employee representatives to influence the management of the company's affairs. We recognise that whatever system is devised, management will play the central role in the formulation and implementation of policy, and that boards will be very largely reliant on the advice they receive from senior executives. But we hope that employees through their representation on the board will have the opportunity to join in setting the framework of policy within which management operate and to influence decisions on major questions concerning investment, rationalisation, expansion and the like. We are not convinced that they will have this opportunity if their right to representation is on a board which is limited in the extent to which it can intervene in company policy or supervise the activities of management. The effect of the introduction of a statutory two-tier system in this country could be to enshrine in the law the dominance of management to the detriment of the interests of both employees and shareholders.

A modification to the two-tier system

11. It has been argued that the two-tier system could be modified for introduction into the United Kingdom: to ensure effective participation in decision-making it would be possible to create a top board, less restricted in its membership and functions, with more responsibility for control of the company's affairs. Denmark has recently adopted a two-tier system on these lines. The Danish Companies Act of 1973 requires that companies above a certain size must have, apart from the shareholders' meeting, a board of directors, upon which employees are represented, and a management of one or more members appointed by the board. The statute also defines the respective functions of management and the board, providing that 'the management shall be in charge of the current management of the company', and 'the board of directors shall supervise the management of the company's affairs and shall secure a warrantable organisation of the company's activities'[1]. Both the functions and the personnel of the two bodies may overlap. Management may sit on the board as shareholder representatives, but they may not be in a majority. In the crucial area of setting fundamental corporate policy, the law is specific that the board and the management are to share responsibility. The EEC Commission's description of the Danish system emphasises how much the functions of the board and management overlap:

'The board of directors is responsible for the proper management of the company and takes part in the management together with members of the management board. The members of the board of management take care of current management according to the guidelines and instructions laid down

---

[1]Quoted in Batstone and Davies *op cit*, page 55.

75

by the board of directors. Transactions which, in relation to the general circumstances of the company, are of an unusual class or importance cannot be effected by the management unless the board of directors has issued a special authorisation, except in cases where the decision of the board of directors cannot be awaited without causing essential inconvenience to the company's activities'[1].

12. This meets many of our objections to a two-tier board system on West German lines. The board on which employees are to be represented has the opportunity to be much more involved in the control of the company's affairs and in the formulation of strategic policy. It is less restricted than the West German supervisory board in the extent to which it may intervene in the affairs of management, and it may have senior executives as members of it. Furthermore, by leaving such an overlap between the functions and personnel of the board and management, it allows companies much more flexibility to define the role of those different bodies and their relationship to each other.

13. It seems to us however that the Danish system is only two-tier in a very restricted sense. It is true that in the law there is an attempt to distinguish between the different functions of the board and of senior management. But the allowance that those functions may overlap in such areas as the formulation of corporate policy, and that senior executives may be members of the board, is an admission that the distinction is difficult to define in law and even more difficult to maintain in practice. In our view it provides further confirmation of the problems in linking employee representation with the introduction of a two-tier board structure in a country where until recently companies have developed within a more flexible unitary board system. In Denmark the need has been recognised to ensure both that boards on which employees are represented are powerful enough to have a significant influence on corporate decisions, and that there is continuing flexibility in the organisation of companies at top level. But in trying to accommodate this within a statutory two-tier system, they have shown how difficult it is to reconcile effective participation and continuing flexibility with a strict and legally defined distinction between the functions of the board and the functions of senior management. This strengthens our view that in this country we should try to build on the existing unitary board system. What we propose below has many similarities with the Danish system in that it attempts to ensure effective employee representation at board level without imposing an unnecessarily rigid board structure. It differs, however, in one important respect. It does not try to define what we believe to be, and what in our view the Danish experience has shown to be, a largely illusory line between the role and functions of the board and senior management.

14. To sum up, we are opposed to the introduction into the United Kingdom of a statutory two-tier board system. We do not believe that such a system would be conducive either to effective participation in decision-making or to the continuing efficiency of British companies. In our view it is a mistake to suppose

[1]EEC Commission *op cit*, page 56.

that there is some easy distinction to be drawn between the functions of a board of directors and those of senior executives. We fear that attempts to define such a distinction in United Kingdom law could have one of two main consequences: either it would, in its desire to preserve the freedom of management, so delimit the powers of the board on which employees are represented that employee participation in decision-making would be very restricted; or it would impose strains and tensions on decision-making at top level, by requiring the adoption of an alien and rigid board structure and creating, as in some companies in France, a perpetual conflict between the supervisory and management boards over their respective functions.

Our proposals for a modified unitary board

15. We believe therefore that our twin aims of effective employee participation and efficient management can best be met in this country by introducing employee representatives on to present company boards. The role and function of those boards, however, will need clearer definition in the law, if we are to ensure that they carry the ultimate responsibility for decisions in important areas of strategic policy. As we have said in our discussions of two-tier board structures, it is of the greatest importance that employees should be represented on a board with a real opportunity to influence decision-making. A board would not have such influence if final decisions on major questions were taken outside the board by management, or if they were taken at board level but could always be over-ruled by the shareholders' meeting.

16. We propose that company law should specify certain areas, where the right to take a final decision would rest with the board of directors. The board could not delegate authority for decisions in these areas to senior management. The shareholders' meeting would however, retain a right to approve or reject the board's proposals in certain specified circumstances. We list below the seven areas in which we think responsibility should be reserved to the board. For the rest of the report we shall refer to these areas as the 'attributed functions of the board'.

17. We intend that our proposals concerning these functions should apply to boards of directors on which employees are represented. We commented above, however, that we did not wish to encourage the development of two systems of company law. It is for serious consideration therefore whether our proposals should apply to all companies irrespective of board level representation or only to those with employee representatives on their board. We discuss in Chapter 11 the application of these proposals to groups of companies.

18. The list of attributed functions is in two parts. The first part is concerned with the relationship between on the one hand the board and senior management and on the other the board and shareholders. These are the functions, which cannot be delegated to management, and in respect of which the board will have the exclusive right to submit a resolution for consideration at the shareholders' meeting:

(a) winding-up of the company;
(b) changes in the memorandum and articles of association;

(c) recommendations to shareholders on the payment of dividends;

(d) changes in the capital structure of a company (eg as regards the relationship between the board and the shareholders, a reduction or increase in the authorised share capital; as regards the relationship between the board and senior management, the issue of securities on a take-over or merger);

(e) disposal of a substantial part of the undertaking.

The second part of the list is concerned solely with the relationship between the board and senior management. These functions place the *responsibility* for decisions with the board of directors:

(f) the allocation or disposition of resources to the extent not covered in (c) to (e) above (although, of course, here the board may delegate to management);

(g) the appointment, removal, control and remuneration of management, whether members of the board or not, in their capacity as executives or employees.

19. We would not propose any alteration to the present position as regards the company's dealings with third parties: inasmuch as any transaction entered into by a managing director, for example, on behalf of a company without requisite board authority, would normally bind the company *vis-à-vis* third parties under company law as it is now, especially in the light of the amendments made in the European Communities Act 1972. The remedy and sanction would, of course, be the liability to dismissal of those who exceeded their powers.

20. We must consider how these modifications to the functions of existing boards in the United Kingdom will affect their relationship first with the senior management and second with the shareholders.

The board and senior management

21. In many respects the relationship between the board and senior management will be largely unaffected by the legal changes which we are proposing. The main change relates to the attributed functions of the board. Where company law specifies that on a certain matter ultimate responsibility lies with the board, management will not be able to take action unilaterally. This does not mean that either at the request of the board itself or on their own initiative, management will not be able to carry out the detailed work on the consideration of options and the formulation of policy in these areas. But they will be required to refer the matter to the board for a final decision. This will not, in our view, represent a major change for most companies, in that at present such important matters as changes in the capital structure or in the memorandum and articles of association of a company are almost invariably referred to the board before a decision is reached. Its importance in the context of employee representation however is that it provides an ultimate safeguard for employee representatives against the extreme case in which senior executives might try to introduce a major new policy without consulting the board of directors.

22. Apart from this, the relationship between the board and senior managers will be unaffected and will continue to develop within each company as circumstances demand. The board, as it does now in most large companies, will continue to appoint senior executives and hold them accountable for their performance, although that board will now, of course, often include employee representatives. Senior executives will continue to sit as representatives of the shareholders on the company board, if the shareholders decide to appoint them, and any executive without a seat will be able to attend the board meeting whenever the board so requests.

23. Most important of all, the board will retain full powers, within the limits of its attributed functions, to delegate authority, as it does now, to subcommittees of the board and to senior management. As we saw in the previous chapter, the delegation of considerable authority for both the formulation and implementation of policy to senior executives and their subordinates is essential to the efficient operation of companies, particularly large and complex ones. We do not believe that employee representatives will be less capable than anyone else of recognising the need for such delegation. Indeed, what we propose may encourage greater precision about the respective functions of the board and management than there is at present in many companies. Employee representatives may feel the need for clearer guidelines within the company about what matters should be discussed at board level, not just so that management may be clearer about the limits of their discretion, but also so that it is clear to employees and management alike whether a particular matter should be raised first at the board or lower down the company's structure in collective bargaining. Furthermore, the existence of functions attributed in law to the board may be a safeguard to the employee representatives against an over-delegation of authority to management.

24. This is not to say that there will not be changes in the present structure of decision-making at top level as a result of employee representation on the board. There may be some matters, for example on employment policies which as a result of employee representation will be more often discussed by the board and equally other matters which are, by agreement, less frequently referred to the board. In some companies employee representatives in time may well want the board to review the organisational structure and the way authority is delegated and exercised. But with all the changes that are made, senior management will continue to be relied upon for detailed advice on the formulation of corporate policy and for the implementation of board decisions, and at the top level will act, as now, as an informal or formal management committee. Because of their involvement in the detailed business of the company they will continue to exercise enormous influence over all aspects of its affairs from the board downwards.

25. It will be seen that we are not proposing that the law should try to define the job of management or to distinguish it from that of the board. We explained in the previous section on supervisory boards why we have taken this view. Under our proposals the onus is on the board to decide for itself where the line between the job of the board and senior management should be drawn. We expect that boards will continue to impose financial limits,

and to revise them from time to time, on the authority of senior management —without reference to the board—to commit the company to expenditure on current or capital account, to borrow money and to enter into contracts. There may also be limits on the number of employees that management may recruit or make redundant without reference to the board. On such questions as organisational changes, alterations in purchasing policy, investigation of new markets or initiation of research work, it is more difficult to devise guidelines in quantitative terms for defining which matters are of sufficient importance to be considered by the board. But in any well-run enterprise such guidelines do exist. It may be that the introduction of employee representation on boards will tend to make such guidelines more formal than they are at present, or to modify them in other ways; such developments may well be beneficial to the running of the enterprise. In our view the dividing line between the board and senior management will be more flexible and realistic if it can be defined in each company to suit particular circumstances, and if it can be varied whenever it seems appropriate to do so.

The board and the shareholders

26. It is important to describe in some detail how and why the relationship between the board and the shareholders will be affected by our proposals. One of the weaknesses, it seems to us, in continental countries which have adapted their company law to permit employee representation is that they have introduced employee representation on boards without also considering how the powers of the shareholders are affected: and the result of this has sometimes been a reduction in the effectiveness of employees' involvement at board level. We are proposing considerable changes in the legal rights of shareholders, though it will be argued below that in practice the changes may not be as great as they seem. They are necessary because, if our proposals are adopted, the new concept of a partnership between capital and labour in the control of companies will supersede the idea that a company and its shareholders (ie its 'owners' or 'members') are one and the same thing. The purpose of changing the powers of shareholders is to ensure that the board which has employee representatives on it cannot, in matters which are important to both employees and shareholders, be unilaterally overruled by shareholders. The power of individual shareholders to sell their shares remains, of course, unaffected and constitutes the normal recourse to shareholders who dislike the way a company is being run.

27. Our proposal in paragraph 18 for attributing to the board a number of functions affects the present powers of shareholders in five important areas: changing the company's constitution (ie its memorandum and articles of association), winding-up, changes in the company's capital structure, the fixing of dividends, and the disposal of a substantial part of the undertaking. These are all matters of central importance to the interests of shareholders as investors in the company: they concern the objectives and organisation of the enterprise and the long term value of the shareholders' holding in it. At present, as a general rule, in all these matters the shareholders not only retain ultimate control by approving or rejecting proposals put to them by the board but also the power of initiative by requisitioning an extraordinary general meeting

pursuant to section 132 of the Companies Act 1948. These are also issues, however, which closely affect the interests of employees and which are directly related to their future employment and pay prospects. It would be undesirable in our view to put employee representatives on a board which could not have a decisive influence on these matters, or which could find its policy changed by the passing of a resolution at the shareholders' meeting, which was not supported by the board.

28. We have suggested an approach therefore which distributes the power to take decisions in these areas between the board and the shareholders' meeting. The exclusive right to convene a meeting for the purpose of considering resolutions in these areas should belong to the board, but the shareholders' meeting should retain the right to decide whether to pass the resolutions or not. Thus, in the case of voluntary winding-up the present power of shareholders holding 10 per cent or more of the voting capital, under section 132 of the Companies Act 1948, to convene a general meeting for the purposes of considering a resolution to wind-up the company would be removed. Again, in fixing dividends the shareholders' power would lie in the right to reject a proposal put to it by the board, not to fix the dividend itself. The approval of the shareholders, where it is given, would however have to command the same majority as is required under the existing law (eg three-quarters majority of those voting in the case of a special resolution concerning a change in the company's constitution or to put the company into liquidation). A proposal to dispose of a substantial part of the undertaking does not in law (and in the absence of a specific restriction in the company's constitution), require the approval of the company in general meeting although, as the Jenkins Committee Report notes[1], it is standard practice among well-conducted companies to obtain the consent of the shareholders to such a disposal. We therefore consider that no change is necessary in law or practice.

29. In practice these changes will not be as great as they may seem. The law amended on the lines outlined above will more closely reflect current practice in large companies. We noted in Chapter 7 that the shareholders' meeting was most commonly a reactive and passive body, rarely acting of its own accord without or against the advice of the board of directors. There are few cases of shareholders initiating action in such important areas as a change in the company's constitution; and even if a resolution is duly proposed at an annual general meeting, it is even rarer for it to be carried against the advice of the board. On the payment of dividends it is most unusual for a shareholders' meeting to have the power to increase the amount of dividend proposed by the board. Most companies include in their articles of association a provision similar to Regulation 114 of Table A that 'the company in general meeting may declare dividends, but no dividend shall exceed the amount recommended by the directors'. Essentially therefore our proposals will have the effect of bringing the law into line with reality, rather than reducing any real power or valuable rights that shareholders possess. At the same time they will ensure that in the unusual case the shareholders cannot propose a change of policy in these areas without the approval of the board.

[1]Jenkins Committee *op cit*, paragraph 117.

30. Some may object to these proposals nevertheless that they take away some fundamental right of the owners to control the business in which they have invested their capital. In this respect it is worth noting that in many of the most important State corporation law codes in the United States, the shareholders do not enjoy the sole right to decide certain fundamental issues of corporate structure or policy. There are numerous examples where the law gives the board of directors the exclusive right to initiate proposals for approval or veto at the shareholders' meeting, or alternatively requires the approval of both the shareholders' meeting and the board, before a proposal is agreed. In a number of important States (eg Delaware, Illinois and New Jersey) the certificate of incorporation (roughly the equivalent of the United Kingdom memorandum of association plus a little more) can only be amended on the initiative of the board and in California the board has to approve the amendment either before or after shareholder approval has been obtained. Thus, in effect, the shareholders have only a power of veto. On voluntary dissolution many State codes give the right to initiate proposals for winding-up to the board of directors, again leaving the shareholders with power of veto (eg Delaware, Illinois, New Jersey Pennsylvania, though in each, proposals for a dissolution can be initiated by the shareholders, if they are unanimous in giving their consent or in the case of New Jersey, by consent of a lesser number if the certificate of incorporation so authorises). Thus in many parts of the USA complete shareholders' control over, for example, winding-up and the basic constitution is not always regarded as a necessary concomitant of the shareholders' 'ownership' of the business.

31. In Chapter 7 we discussed a number of other areas where the shareholders at present retain the ultimate control. We think that the right of shareholders to ratify or validate an act done, for example, by one or more directors who exceeds the powers delegated to them, or which needs approval by the company (eg payment of compensation for loss of office) should be modified. These are important powers and it seems to us illogical that once employee representatives are on the board they should remain solely with the shareholders' meeting. We therefore propose that in this case approval by both the board and the shareholders' meeting should be required. In other respects we see no need to make changes in the shareholders' legal rights. In particular, we think that the power to impose borrowing limits on the board, to appoint auditors and to require a Department of Trade investigation of a company's affairs, all of which are important means by which the shareholders can check on the activities of the board, should remain vested in the shareholders.

32. There is one other way in which the shareholders' power is reduced, and it is the most obvious. Employee representation on boards means that the shareholders will no longer be able to control all appointments to the board. We are not proposing any change in the method by which shareholders will in future appoint a proportion of the directors or by which casual vacancies within that proportion will be filled: we envisage that in general such appointments will continue to be made from the senior management of the company. Nor are we suggesting that the powers to dismiss the shareholders' appointees should be altered. But it is fundamental to our proposals that a proportion of the board (we discuss what proportion below) should be selected by the employees.

33. In the great majority of cases shareholders at present appoint the directors. As company law stands it is however possible for the articles of association to provide that the shareholders may appoint some or all directors subject to the consent of another person or, indeed, that some other person (for example a major creditor) may appoint one or more of the directors. But such arrangements can be made only by special provision in the articles of association which are, and will remain, subject to the ultimate control of the shareholders' meeting. We therefore include such exceptional cases in the general category of directors appointed by the shareholders; the new law need not exclude such a possibility; and when in Chapter 9 we speak of 'shareholder representatives' we include among that category directors appointed pursuant to articles of this kind. Similarly, a company's articles may require a share qualification for directors; this possibility can remain unchanged for directors appointed by or with the consent of the shareholders; but no such requirement should be permitted in the case of directors selected by employees.

34. In framing our proposals we have tried to strike a balance between those who believe that the board should be the supreme organ of the company with the power to overrule the shareholders' meeting in all important matters, and those who champion the rights of the company's owners to retain control over the purposes for which their investment is used. We have recognised the need to adjust the relationship between the board and the shareholders in order to ensure that employee representatives on the board have a real say in decision-making on fundamental questions like winding-up and changes in the company's constitution. We have acknowledged that it would be illogical and frustrating to the true objective of industrial democracy to put employees on the board and then allow the shareholders the power to retain control of all major decisions.

Legal duties and liabilities of directors

35. We now turn to the question of how directors' duties should change as a result of employee representation on boards. Two basic principles have guided us in making our recommendations.

36. First, we think it is important that there should be a clear statement of the basic duties of directors in statute law. We realise that this will not clarify all the complexities and ambiguities in the case law and that specific points will continue to be tested in the courts. But we believe that there must be one place where a director, and particularly the new employee representative, can see a statement of the basic duties he owes to the company as a result of his membership of the board. We would not want, however, the complex job of codification to hold up progress on the introduction of board level representation.

37. Second, we are agreed in principle that all directors should have the same legal duties and liabilities. We believe that to create two standards of directors owing different or separate duties would not be conducive to the development of cooperation between employee and shareholder representatives on the board, nor ultimately to the efficient management of the company. Nor, judging

by the unanimity of the many company managements who gave evidence to us on this point, would it strengthen their confidence in the effects on companies of board level representation. However we do recognise the TUC's concern that the employee representatives should not be put under impossible obligations which could cut them off from their constituents, or force them to pay sole regard to the interests of shareholders. We therefore propose that there should be some changes in the law regarding directors' duties to ensure that the employee representatives are able to carry out their normal and reasonable functions as representatives of the workforce.

38. The most important change, and it is a change which should be made whether employee representatives are put on the board or not, should be in the duty of directors to act in the best interests of the company, which, as we said in Chapter 7, has been defined in the courts as meaning the interests of shareholders, present and future. We recommend that all directors should continue to be required to act in the best interests of the company, but that in doing so they should take into account the interests of the company's employees as well as its shareholders. A number of formulations have been proposed to amend the law in this way—in the Companies Bill 1973, in the Industrial Democracy Bill 1975, and most recently in a Conservative amendment to the Companies Bill 1976. The formulation in the Companies Bill 1973 was:

'The matters to which the directors of a company are entitled to have regard in exercising their powers shall include the interests of the company's employees generally as well as the interests of its members' (ie the shareholders)[1].

The Industrial Democracy Bill's provision (repeated in the proposed amendment to the Companies Bill 1976) was slightly different:

'The matters to which the directors . . . of a company shall have regard in exercising their powers shall include the interests of the company's workers generally as well as the interests of its shareholders'[2].

We prefer the second formula because it places a clear obligation on directors, (ie directors 'shall have regard') whereas the 1973 Bill merely entitles, but does not require, directors to take into account the interests of employees. We think it important that the members of a parent or holding company board should also be able to look beyond the interests of the company, to those of its subsidiaries. We recommend therefore that directors of a company should be entitled to take into account the interests of the employees and shareholders, present and future, of subsidiaries and sub-subsidiaries of that company. It is for consideration whether the directors of a subsidiary company should be able to have regard to the interests of the shareholders and employees of the holding company and of its other subsidiaries.

39. It has been said that such a formulation puts the director in an impossible position, because the interests of employees are essentially opposed to the interests of shareholders, present and future, and in a crisis one interest must be paramount. It has also been objected that no change in the law is necessary, since shareholders and employees have the same interest in the continuing

---

[1] Companies Bill 1973, Clause 53.
[2] Industrial Democracy Bill 1975, Clause 1.

effectiveness and profitability of the enterprise, and one set of interests therefore includes the other. Generally speaking, we see the directors' duty to act in the best interests of the company as one of balancing a number of interests, and we agree that there is a large measure of coincidence between the interests of shareholders and employees. But at times there is bound to be conflict; instances are likely to include arguments about the priority to be given to the maintenance of employment levels or about whether investment should be in the United Kingdom or overseas. There will be cases where the representatives of employees or shareholders argue for the predominance of their own interests. But no one will be in breach of his duty for arguing a specific case at board level. At present some boards already include nominee directors, appointed by a specific shareholder interest, who nonetheless have the same legal duty to balance the interests of all shareholders. In some ways they occupy a similar position to the future representatives of shareholders and employees. The directors' job will indeed be the same as it is now: to weigh up the differing and conflicting interests in the company in order to reach decisions which they genuinely believe to be in the company's overall best interest.

40. It would be unreasonable and unrealistic not to expect the employee representatives, the representatives of the workforce, to argue strongly at board level for the interests of their constituents. Indeed one of the objectives of putting them on the board in the first place is to make sure that the employees' voice is heard at the very highest level of the company. But we are not proposing any change in the law which at present prevents the mandating of a director to vote in a particular way. This is discussed in Chapter 10. We are quite clear that an employee representative would be in breach of his duty if he voted in a particular way solely because of the instructions of his trade union. He must be a representative, free to express his opinions and to reach his own conclusions about which policies will work for the greater good of the company, not a delegate, told how to vote by his constituents.

41. In Chapter 7 we considered some specific aspects of the directors' fiduciary duty. We believe that these should be largely unaffected by employee representation on the board. There seems no reason to exempt any director from the duties concerning *secret profit* or any law which is likely to be enacted regulating *insider trading*. No director should be able to use information received in the boardroom for personal profits. We have already touched on the position concerning *outside interests* ie the duty of a director not to deprive himself of his independent discretion to consider the interests of the company, and we have concluded that while we are opposed to mandating we think it possible for an employee representative to represent his constituents' views at board level at the same time as acting in the best interests of the company. We consider the special problem of *confidential information* below. Other aspects of the fiduciary duties of directors need not be amended.

42. Another aspect of directors' duties—the duty of care and skill—poses no special problem. We pointed out in Chapter 7 that these duties were not particularly onerous and that there is scarcely any modern case of a director being held liable for negligence. The director's legal liability is measured by the standard of what is reasonable for his knowledge and his experience, and

at the very least the director is required to act as a reasonable man would. This seems to present no special difficulties for employee representatives on the board.

43. In Chapter 7 we also singled out two other important aspects of the director's duty concerning *misfeasance* and *fraudulent trading*. We explained that a director could be liable in misfeasance proceedings for actual loss suffered by the company if he had misapplied, retained or become accountable for any property of the company, or been guilty of 'misfeasance or breach of trust'. We consider that all directors should continue to be subject to such liabilities.

44. On fraudulent trading the present law is far from clear. Directors are liable in both civil and criminal proceedings if they decide to carry on business when they know that there is no reasonable prospect of the company's creditors being paid. But it has been suggested that the offence of fraud means 'real dishonesty involving, according to current notions of fair trading among commercial men, real moral blame'. Courts also have discretion to excuse a director, wholly or partly, from his liabilities if he acted 'honestly and reasonably' and ought 'fairly to be excused'. It is clear that when a company is in a precarious position there may be genuine difference of opinion on the board about whether it is safe to carry on the business or whether to do so would amount to defrauding the company's creditors. Although we do not wish to over-emphasise the chances of such differences, the employee representatives might be more strongly motivated than the shareholder representatives to seek all possible ways of continuing the business, since redundancies will be an immediate and inevitable consequence of cessation, whereas financial loss to shareholders may or may not ensue. But the judgment that all directors have to make in such a case concerns the interests and prospects of *creditors*, a matter separate and apart from any conflict of interest between employees and shareholders. We think it right therefore that in the matter of fraudulent trading as in all other respects the liabilities of all directors should be the same. But it is important that the law should make it absolutely clear that neither civil nor criminal breach of duty will be committed in respect of fraudulent trading unless the director has been *dishonest* in the sense of incurring real moral blame, or *reckless* in his judgment of the prospects of creditors when making his decision to continue trading or to vote at a board meeting for such a continuation.

Reporting back

45. We consider it very important that board members should keep in touch with and report back to those who have appointed them to the board (ie to the shareholders and the employees). We would distinguish however three different aspects of the reporting function: the report of the board as a whole to both employees and shareholders; the report of shareholder representatives to the general meeting of shareholders; and the report of employee representatives to the employees through trade union machinery.

46. At present the Companies Acts 1948 and 1967 require the board of directors to present to the annual general meeting of shareholders a directors'

report and audited accounts. We propose that this duty should continue to apply to boards of directors, when employees are represented on them. But we would add that this report from the whole board should be made not only to shareholders but also to employees in the company. This seems to us a small, but important, step in emphasising that the directors' prime duty is to act in the best interests of the company as a whole, and that both the shareholders and the employees have a stake in that company's future. In some companies this will not represent a material change in practice since they already circulate their directors' report and accounts to their employees. But in all companies it is likely that the contents and emphasis of those reports will change because they are to be circulated to employees as well as shareholders. By analogy we think it appropriate for documents which are available for inspection to shareholders to be made available to employees also.

47. Where it is the practice at present for the report and accounts to be put formally to the shareholders' meeting for adoption, we think this should continue. It is very uncommon for such meetings to reject them at present and we would not expect the practice to change. It is for consideration whether it would be possible or desirable to introduce parallel rights for employees in general to comment on, or in some cases approve, the report and accounts in the same way, but it is not an essential innovation at this stage. We welcome the Department of Trade's recent consultative document on company reports[1]. In considering what changes in law or practice should be recommended, the Department should, we believe, have it in mind that, if our proposals are implemented, many company reports will be joint reports by the board of directors to both shareholders and employees.

48. The annual general meeting of the shareholders will continue to be the occasion when the shareholders have the opportunity to hear a report from and question their representatives on the board. Whether the whole board, rather than just the shareholder representatives, should attend the general meeting is something which we believe is best left for companies themselves to settle. We would certainly not wish to prevent employee representatives attending such a meeting and answering questions along with other members of the board, and we hope in many cases that they will do so. Equally, we recognise that on occasions the shareholders and their representatives may want to meet without other members of the board present.

49. Nothing we have proposed should prevent the employee representatives reporting back to their constituents. Indeed, we wish to emphasise the importance of reporting back. It is essential to the success of board level representation that employee representatives should be in close touch with their constituents. They must make it their regular job to report on what the board is doing or proposing to do and why. They must be able to take soundings before a matter comes up to the board so that they can accurately reflect the views and feelings of the employees to their fellow directors. If they are prevented from doing so, then they will become isolated from those they represent and may even be regarded with suspicion as the agents of management. Many submissions of evidence that we received dealt with the potential or actual

---

[1]Department of Trade, *Aims and Scope of Company Reports* (Draft consultative document circulated to interested organisations, June 1976).

difficulties of employee representatives who become too closely identified with management and lose the confidence of those they represent. We do not share the view that such a development is inevitable, but we recognise it as a real danger. It is the board's as much as the employees' loss when it happens, since the major advantage to the board of employee representation lies in the greater acceptability its decisions will have if agreed to by employee representatives and in the regular two-way flow of views and opinions to and from the employees. An employee representative cut off from his constituents is able neither to reflect the views of the employees, nor to provide a channel of communication to the workforce, nor to ensure that board decisions are acceptable to the employees.

50. We think it essential, therefore, that employee representatives and the recognised trade unions within each company should develop a system of reporting back by which the representatives on the board can keep in touch with those they represent. We do not propose however that there should be a special legal duty on employee representatives to report back. It is better, we believe, for flexible arrangements to be devised to suit the particular circumstances of the company and the nature of the information which is to be reported. We discuss in detail how the reporting back might take place and what it might involve in Chapter 10.

Confidential information

51. The discussion of reporting back inevitably raises the question of whether there should be any legal limits on the right of employee representatives to disclose information to their constituents. Much anxiety has been caused in industry over this question by the comment in the TUC's 1974 report that 'worker representatives should not be unnecessarily hampered and restricted in reporting back . . . by narrow requirements of confidentiality'[1]. Behind that comment there lies a valid and understandable concern that companies may use the excuse of confidentiality to stop any meaningful communication from the employee representative to the trade unions or employees. Since then, however, the provisions in the Employment Protection Act 1975 and Industry Act 1975 have put a legal obligation on companies to disclose information to trade unions. The ACAS Draft Code of Practice on Disclosure of Information demonstrates how widely the requirements of the Employment Protection Act are to be interpreted[2]. Some companies, actively encouraged by the CBI, have already concluded comprehensive and wide-ranging information agreements. We detect a growing willingness in industry to be more open with its employees about its activities and we hope that representation on the board will lead companies even further in this direction. The benefits in increasing confidence and understanding between trade unions and employees on the one side and management on the other, to be gained through more extensive and better provision of information, are not disputed by responsible and forward-looking people in industry. Yet in practice the label of confidentiality is still used too frequently. When employee representatives sit on the board, we hope and believe that they will encourage a policy of 'open government'

---

[1]TUC *op cit*, page 37.
[2]Advisory, Conciliation and Arbitration Service. *Draft Code of Practice: Disclosure of Information to Trade Unions for Collective Bargaining*, paragraph 2.3 *et al.*

in the enterprise, and we trust that management will respond by adopting the view that no information should be concealed from employees, from trade unions or indeed from the public, unless there are good and specific reasons for doing so.

52. Companies clearly do have information which must remain confidential to the members of the board, to senior executives and in some cases to the small number of people who must have access to the information to carry out the detailed work on the proposal or project. It is not possible to generalise, however, about what is and is not commercially confidential, and rules of confidentiality can only be applied to particular circumstances. The ACAS Draft Code listed some of the matters which, though relevant to collective bargaining, might in some circumstances cause injury to the company if disclosed. These seem to us similar to many of the issues on which information would normally need to be restricted to members of the board. They are:

'Cost information on individual products, research and development plans and projects, detailed analysis of proposed investment, marketing or pricing policies, and price quotas or the make-up of tender prices'[1].

In addition to these matters some information will occasionally be discussed at board level which, if disclosed prematurely, could cause speculation in the company's shares on the stock market. Such price-sensitive information, ranging from declaration of results to discussion of proposed take-overs, will generally have to be regarded as confidential until an appointed day for disclosure.

53. There may be information other than the two kinds mentioned above, which a board has good reason to keep confidential. But we do not think that any serious problem in this regard arises merely from the presence of employee representatives on boards. Individual employee representatives are no more likely than existing directors deliberately to leak confidential information to competitors or price-sensitive information to speculators. Employee representatives may through inexperience be unsure about what is confidential, but any such problems should be solved by the chairman paying special attention to his existing duty to give guidance to his fellow directors on what part of the discussions in the boardroom are confidential.

54. Employers' fears have focussed on the duty of the employee representative to report to his constituents leading to the danger of disseminating confidential information to too many people, so that information reaches competitors or the stock market more by default than out of malice. For a number of reasons we believe that these fears will be shown in practice to have been unjustified. In the first place we think that it will usually be possible for the employee representative on the board to make an effective report to his constituents without disclosing confidential information. He will often be able to report on discussions at board level without giving sensitive figures. Second, there is no reason to think that the employee representatives will want to take any step which could damage the company's prosperity, in which employees as well as shareholders have a long-term interest. They will see therefore the

---

[1]Advisory, Conciliation and Arbitration Service *op cit*, paragraph 4.4.

importance of restricting confidential information to a very few people. Third, we think it is a mistake to assume that those who sit on boards will have no experience of handling confidential information. Many employees in the course of their daily work come into contact with information about, for example, new products and plans, the disclosure of which might damage the company. In other cases full-time trade union officials and lay union representatives are increasingly given confidential information during negotiations with companies or with government which they are quite used to keeping secret.

55. Several of these points were put to us by the TUC representatives during their oral evidence. When asked by us about the need to maintain confidentiality they accepted without reservation that there were categories of information which must be restricted to the minimum number of people. What they feared was an attempt to define in law a boundary of confidentiality, which might become a barrier to communication. When pressed by the Committee to define the boundaries of confidentiality in the specific case of a take-over or merger, the TUC representatives said that they could not accept the need for absolute secrecy if the interests of the employees were in the balance. In such a case they would want the employee representatives to be free to consult one or two senior trade unionists in the company to test opinion, but they accepted that it would clearly not be desirable to disseminate such information more widely.

56. There is a potentially more serious problem within companies in the less easily definable area of management plans, the premature disclosure of which would cause alarm in relation to employment prospects or other matters of direct concern to the workforce, even though proposals might ultimately come to nothing. There is a fine dividing line between creating unnecessary alarm by early disclosure and using confidentiality to prevent effective participation in decision-making. We believe that employee representatives will be rightly concerned to prevent the preparation of such plans without the knowledge of the whole board, but it will then only be possible to judge in each individual case whether wider disclosure is desirable or possible.

57. We were strengthened in our view on this topic by our visits to Sweden and West Germany. In both countries we were told that though satisfactory systems of reporting back had been developed, breaches of confidentiality as a result of board level representation were extremely rare. We were particularly interested in the Swedish experience. We were told in Sweden that confidentiality had seemed a major problem when the experiment with employee representation on boards started in 1973, but that management's fears had proved largely groundless. Most companies had devised a satisfactory and workable system for deciding what was confidential before employee representatives on the board reported back to their constituents. The employee representatives and the chairman or managing director spent a short time after the board meeting discussing and agreeing what could be reported back and what was confidential: both sides appreciated the value of such a system. At one company we visited the management and the employee representative distinguished three stages of confidentiality: information which could not be released out of the boardroom; information which could be discussed with one or two senior officials; and information which could be passed on to the trade union committee and to the union members.

58. As we said in Chapter 7, the present law on confidentiality is vague: but it does make it a breach of duty to reveal confidential information, for example in respect of the company's plans and projects, to people outside the board. We believe that for the time being at any rate this provision is sufficient to ensure that employee representation at board level will add no fresh problems in relation to confidentiality that cannot be solved by agreement between management and the representatives of the workforce. Our visit to Sweden confirmed our view that the best rules of confidentiality are those which are devised within each company at board level. It is much more desirable that within certain legal limits the board should work out what is confidential in a particular circumstance, than that the law should try to prescribe what should happen in every case. We therefore make no recommendations for changes in the law on confidentiality.

CHAPTER 9

The reconstitution of the board[1]

1. In his *Company Responsibility and Participation: a New Agenda* Professor Fogarty says:

'The most contentious question in Britain as elsewhere is the proportion of employee representatives on boards. Employer and management organisations everywhere and unanimously reject parity for employees. Labour movements tend, like the TUC, to take the view that anything short of parity is cosmetics . . .'[2]

We found that the question of proportions was indeed the most difficult issue in our deliberations. We devote the major part of this chapter to a discussion of the proportion of board seats to be occupied by employee and shareholder representatives and conclude that a fundamental change in the way in which companies are run will not be achieved unless there is equal representation of employees and shareholders on company boards. Having established this principle, we go on in the second part of the chapter to propose how equal representation might be introduced into United Kingdom companies and the timetable which will be necessary to ensure a smooth transition from the existing to the new system.

Minority and parity

2. We have held extensive discussions on proportions, which have clarified the options before us. We have concluded that there are three main options other than employee representatives being in a majority:

(a) unequal representation, with the shareholder representatives retaining a majority of seats and the employee representatives taking a minority (eg two thirds shareholder representation to one third employee representation);

(b) 50:50 representation, with the board seats equally divided between employee and shareholder representatives;

(c) minority but *equal* representation of shareholders and employees, entailing a third group of directors on the board.

As we explain later in this chapter we have concluded that the third approach is the best solution.

3. Both the countries we visited have experience of unequal representation on boards, where shareholders retain a majority of seats and employees are in a minority. In Sweden, the trade unions have the right to request two employee representatives and two non-voting alternates on company boards, or one representative and one alternate if the total size of the board if five or less. In the Federal Republic of Germany, until 1976, companies with over 500 employees, apart from those in the coal, iron and steel industries, have

---

[1]Mr N S Wilson's note of dissent (see page 163) is related primarily to the recommendations contained in this Chapter.

[2]Michael P Fogarty, *Company Responsibility and Participation: a New Agenda* (PEP Vol XLI Broadsheet No 554 1975), page 90.

operated under a system where employee representatives have one third and shareholder representatives two thirds of the seats on a supervisory board. For companies with over 2,000 employees, this was extended in 1976 to give employees and shareholders equal representation on the board; but the system falls short of full parity in that the chairman with an automatic casting vote is elected by the shareholders.

4. Unequal representation can, as we found during our visits to Sweden and West Germany, be beneficial both to employees and to companies as a whole. In both countries we were told that representation on the board has given employees a valuable insight into the process of development and determination of company policy at the top level and access to management information. This has been useful to employees and their trade unions in discussions and negotiations with management at other levels of the enterprise, and to senior management in helping, as one Swedish managing director put it, to 'demystify' the board's proceedings. Some industrialists we met felt that unequal representation gave employees a considerable influence on decision-making; and that the existence of a sizeable employee presence on the board meant that management paid more attention to the interests of employees both in the exercise of their executive functions and in the formulation of policy proposals. Summing up the first three years of board level representation in Sweden, the National Swedish Industrial Board concluded that the overall gains had been modest but worthwhile:

'Although one may question whether the reform *per se* has so far meant any significant increase of the influence wielded by employees, it has undoubtedly improved their opportunities of insight. In the long run it should serve to increase their influence as well . . .'[1]

5. A study of such European experience shows, however, the difficulties employee representatives encounter in influencing policy if they can always be outvoted by the shareholder representatives. It is not simply that if shareholder representatives are in a majority they can decide the extent to which they wish to ignore, take note of, or act upon the views expressed by employee representatives. They can also devise and control the framework of policy-making: the appointment of senior management; delegation of authority to management; the procedures of the board and the arrangements for provision of information to board members.

6. In both West Germany and Sweden we found for example that where they were in a minority *vis-à-vis* the shareholder representatives, employee representatives had little influence on the appointments of senior management. The Swedish Labour Attaché who gave oral evidence to us said that there had been cases of employee representatives recording their lack of confidence in the managing director, but since they could always be outvoted by shareholder representatives, this had little effect on the managing director's ultimate appointment or dismissal. In Germany Professor Däubler has pointed out that where employee representatives have only a minority of seats, 'up to now not a single case is known where they have succeeded in getting a man of their choice

---

[1]National Swedish Industrial Board, *Board Representation of Employees in Sweden* (January 1976), page 9.

on the board of directors against the vote—be it only a part—of the "majority group".[1]

7. The National Swedish Industrial Board in its review of the three-year experience of board level representation in Sweden highlighted two ways in which minority representation restricted the ability of employees to influence decision-making[2]. First, employee representatives had little control over the composition of committees of the board, particularly the powerful drafting committees, where much of the detailed work of the board was prepared. There was some evidence that during the three years in question, use of committees of the board had increased; on 70 per cent of such committees employees were not represented. Second, employee representatives found it difficult to gain access to the information they needed to take informed decisions at board meetings. There was evidence that in some companies information was not available to board members until the day of the meeting. Professor Fogarty in his analysis of German experience with unequal representation found similar trends to those in Sweden.

'It is common to find that employee representatives are once again kept away from sources of information, that the old technique of assigning important decisions to sub-committees from which employee representatives are excluded is again in use . . .'[3]

8. In our view, therefore, whether employee representatives sit on the top tier of a two-tier board system as in Germany or on a unitary board as in Sweden, unequal representation imposes severe restrictions on the effectiveness of employee participation in decision-making. It leaves control of major decisions and of the decision-making process in the hands of the shareholder representatives and management, and therefore does not fundamentally change the way in which decisions are reached or the premises on which they are based. Our argument is not so much that where shareholders are in a majority, employee representation on boards is ineffective, but rather that it is effective only in terms of certain limited objectives. As Paul Davies has concluded in his report on European experience commissioned by this Committee:

'The picture appears to be that minority employee representation on the board may increase somewhat employees' access to information and improve management communication channels, and may somewhat encourage current trends towards the breakdown of autocratic management and a recognition of the need to take social and personnel matters into account in the setting of corporate objectives, but that such representation does not provide the opportunity to change the nature of board decision-making. The reasons for this are various but the major one would seem to be that with minority representation there is no effective transfer of power from shareholders and management towards workers, and worker representatives are thus in a relatively powerless situation dependent completely on the goodwill of management and other board members'[4].

---

[1]Quoted Batstone and Davies *op cit*, page 60.
[2]National Swedish Industrial Board *op cit*, page 26.
[3]Quoted Batstone and Davies *op cit*, page 60.
[4]Batstone and Davies *op cit*, page 59.

9. Those who propose unequal minority representation of employees in the boardroom claim that participation and influence can thereby be adequately provided for employees. We reject that view; experience suggests that such influence would be very limited. Yet the same people insist that the minority employee representatives must bear full and equal responsibility as directors, in law and in practice, for board decisions. We believe that such a structure would in fact be more divisive than one in which employee and shareholder representatives are equal; the employee directors would be far less likely to accept equal responsibility in practice for decisions which could always be controlled by the majority of shareholders' representatives; and they would be more likely to adopt a defensive posture in the face of that permanent majority. It is of course easier to adapt the existing law to accommodate an unequal minority of employee representatives; but in our view such a structure cannot lead to that full participation in decision-making on the board which full responsibility implies, nor to the consequent release of constructive energies which, we are convinced, full participation will do much to produce.

10. We believe that there must be a joint approach to decision-making in companies, based on equal representation of employees and shareholders on the board. In our view it is no longer acceptable for companies to be run on the basis that in the last resort the shareholders' view must by right always prevail. There must in the future be a new legitimacy for the exercise of the management function within a policy framework agreed jointly by the representatives of capital and labour. We believe that this new legitimacy is essential for the long-term efficiency and profitability of the private sector and for the ultimate success of the economy itself.

11. We do not think that this will be achieved unless employee representatives are fully involved in, and committed to the work of the board, and share equally with the shareholder representatives the responsibility for the board's decisions. In our view it is unreasonable to expect employee representatives to accept equal responsibility, unless, through equal representation on the board, they are able to have equal influence on the decision-making process. In West Germany this was an important argument leading to the extension of employee representation from one third to 50 per cent, which was effected in 1976. In this country it has been strongly expressed by the TUC in its supplementary evidence to the Committee:

'The TUC advocates parity trade union/shareholder representation at board level in order to avoid a situation of trade union representatives being given responsibility without a real share in decision making. It is the TUC view that it is unrealistic to expect "equal responsibility" without "equal representation". Nothing could be more damaging than having to accept responsibility if the shareholders' representatives had an entrenched majority'.[1]

12. We believe that the main benefits of representation at board level in terms of improved industrial relations and greater efficiency will result from the greater acceptability to employees and trade unions of board decisions in which employee representatives have been fully included and for which they

---

[1]TUC supplementary evidence, *op cit*, paragraph 6.

have taken equal responsibility. In our view these benefits may never be realised if employees are not equally represented on the board: first, because a minority group of employee representatives will be less willing to become involved in the formulation of policy, if at the end of the process they know they can always be overruled by the shareholder majority; second, because the credibility of employee representatives in the eyes of their constituents will be reduced, if those constituents conclude from the proportions on the board, that their representatives are powerless. This view is confirmed by the West German experience of parity and minority systems, evaluated by the Biedenkopf Commission in 1970. Comparing experience of parity representation in the coal, iron and steel industries with that of minority employee representation in other parts of German industry, the Biedenkopf Commission reported that there was more commitment and cooperation at board level, where employees were equally represented:

'the cooperation between the shareholders' and the workers' representatives at the supervisory board level is judged to be better in companies with *montan* co-determination [ie with parity] than in the Works Constitution Act spheres [ie with minority]'[1].

13. Our conclusion is therefore that there should be equal representation of employees and shareholders on company boards. As we noted in paragraph 2 there are two ways in which this could be introduced: full parity representation (ie 50:50 employee and shareholder representation) as in the German coal, iron and steel industries; or equal representation of employees and shareholders plus the appointment or co-option of a third group of directors. We prefer the second of these options. We propose that in companies where all the conditions for the introduction of employee representation are met (see Chapters 10 and 11) the boards should be reconstituted to be composed of three elements—an equal number of employee and shareholder representatives plus a third group of co-opted directors. These additional directors should:

(a) be co-opted with the agreement of a majority of each of the other two groups—the employee and the shareholder representatives;

(b) be an uneven number greater than 1;

(c) form less than one third of the total board.

14. Such a system will provide an important means by which special experience and expertise can be brought into the boardroom from inside and outside the company. Our intention is that the co-opted directors should be individuals who can make a valuable contribution to the work of the board. We do not propose therefore any restriction as to eligibility for co-option, or any stipulation that they should be independent or neutral. They must, however, be agreed upon by a majority of each of the other two parts. We see this co-opted third group of directors being composed of various elements. It may be, for example, that there will be someone in the company itself—among senior or middle management—who both sides agree could be a useful addition to the board. It has been suggested to us that the shareholder and employee representatives will in the initial stages be anxious to co-opt people with proven ability from inside the firm, rather than unknown elements from outside. We think it more likely

---

[1]Quoted Batstone and Davies *op cit*, page 60.

however that the third group will be made up of people from outside the company: of the best among those who are at present non-executive directors; of senior personnel from other companies with a particular interest in or connection with the business of the company; of people with special expertise like solicitors, bankers, accountants and so on; of local and national trade union officials who would not be eligible for election as employee representatives because they are not employees of the firm (see Chapter 10).

15. The co-option of additional directors will also enable people with a broader view of the company's affairs to take seats on the board. Under our proposals the employee representatives will almost invariably be employees of the company and we expect the majority of shareholder representatives to be senior executives, so that all or almost all the employee and shareholder seats will be filled by people from inside the company. It was put to us in Germany that this could lead to 'company egoism' with too much concentration on the internal affairs of the company and too little regard to the wider context in which companies have to operate. We think that some of the co-opted directors at least will be a safeguard against such an introspective approach, and will ensure that the wider public interest is taken into account.

16. Moreover, we have noted that increasing importance has been attributed in recent years to the appointment of non-executive directors to the boards of British companies. In the words of the Confederation of British Industry they can make:

'a valuable contribution by reason of their ability:

(a) to bring to bear an independent and entirely objective and detached approach to policy matters;

(b) to give the board the benefit of their knowledge and experience in other areas over a wide field of activities'[1].

We ascertained also that the boards of United States corporations generally include a majority of non-executive directors. In 1974 the average United States board of 13 members already had eight non-executive directors from outside the corporation, and in 1975 the figure was nine[2].

17. We recognise that the normal process of decision-making on a board is by consensus rather than by voting, but if there were any tendency towards block voting, the presence of co-opted directors would act against it. Block voting is not an inevitable consequence of equal representation on the board, since within each group of employee and shareholder representatives there will be a considerable range of opinion. Nevertheless the Biedenkopf Commission found that in the German coal, iron and steel industries there was a tendency for employee and shareholder representatives to vote and act as distinct groups. The existence of co-opted directors will not eliminate this tendency but it will, we believe, reduce it. It will mean that either group will at the very least need to gain the support of a majority of the directors co-opted by both groups before they can carry or veto a proposal.

[1]CBI, *op cit*, page 37.
[2]*Industry Week*, 3 May 1976, page 10.

18. Finally our proposals build into a system of equal representation on the board a strong and effective mechanism for avoiding deadlock by creating a board which has an odd number of members. We believe that the debate about equal representation has centred too much on the problem of deadlock. Nevertheless many of those who wrote to us opposed equal representation on the grounds that it encouraged the polarisation of views at board level and could ultimately paralyse the decision-making process. Guest Keen & Nettlefolds, for example, expressed the concern of many employers as follows:

'. . . 50 per cent employee representation (on a supervisory board) should not be considered because polarisation of interests would be likely to place undue power in the hands of one man . . . who would repeatedly be called upon to give his casting vote. Such a method of reaching key decisions would be most undesirable'[1].

19. We believe that our proposal meets these criticisms, largely because we do not see the co-opted directors primarily as a means of resolving deadlock. We are, for example, suggesting that they should never number less than three, to avoid giving one person the sole responsibility for exercising a casting vote. Equally we have said that the prime criteria for choosing them should be the expertise and experience they can bring to the board, not some intangible quality of neutrality or independence.

20. We recognise that, even with this proposal for a co-opted third group, there may be occasions when the board is evenly divided on a proposal: if, for example, a director abstains on a crucial vote, or misses a board meeting due to illness or for business reasons. We consider what should happen in such exceptional cases later in this chapter when we discuss the role of the company chairman.

21. For all the above reasons we think that the addition of such co-opted directors to two equal groups of shareholder and employee representatives will produce a mixture conducive to the efficient operation of companies. While we accept that many companies are efficiently managed by their boards, we do not take the complacent view that there is no room for improvement in this respect in British industry and we are confident that the proposed new board structure will have a considerable contribution to make to greater efficiency. We have come to call this formula for board composition $2X + Y$, where X represents the number of employee representatives and also represents the number of shareholder representatives, and Y is the number of co-opted directors. We think this exactly and conveniently expresses the form of board we are proposing, and that it is a useful piece of shorthand for our discussion in the next section of how our proposals will operate in practice.

The introduction of our proposals for a reconstituted board

22. We set out above the main principles and the arguments in favour of our proposals for a reconstituted board. We now consider step by step how it could be introduced, and what procedures will be necessary at each stage to resolve disagreement about the size of the different parts, or of the whole board.

---

[1]GKN evidence, page 14.

We begin our consideration at the point where it has been agreed that there should be employee representation on the board of a company. How that point is reached is discussed in the next chapter.

23. Once it has been agreed that there is to be employee representation on the board, we think that the onus should be on the existing board of directors and the authorised representatives of the recognised trade unions in the company to discuss the arrangements for representation. The first questions to be decided are what should be the ultimate size of the board, once it has been reconstituted to include employee representation and a third co-opted group, and how many seats should be occupied by the various elements. There will also need to be discussion on the timetable within which the various steps for the reconstitution of the board should take place. We expect that during these discussions there will also be consideration of who should be the co-opted directors and no doubt at this stage some preliminary approaches to suitable people will be made. The formal task of co-opting the directors will fall, of course, to the prospective directors—the employee and shareholder representatives—who will sit ultimately on the reconstituted board. But it would be foolish to suppose that discussions about them would be delayed until the employee and shareholder representatives had been appointed. Once the employee and shareholder representatives are selected and the third group has been co-opted, the board will be properly constituted, and will take office.

24. The discussions, as can be seen from the above, have several parts to them and may be complex. The parties may want at various points to call on an outside body to give advice and perhaps to provide conciliation: we discuss the possible role of an industrial democracy commission in Chapter 12. We think it right, however, to give recognised trade unions and existing boards the flexibility to make arrangements which best suit them. Later in this chapter we consider what should happen if, at various points in the discussions, agreement cannot be reached. But we should emphasise here that we expect solutions satisfactory to both sides to be agreed readily in the majority of cases.

25. The options open to the parties for the reconstitution of the board are very wide, but it will not always be an easy task to decide on the total size of the reconstituted board or of its various elements. It has been said to us that our proposal will tend to make boards large and unwieldy. We recognise that there will be a tendency for the parties to want the X element of the board to be large, both in order to accommodate as many members as possible of the existing board and in order to secure fair representation of the company's employees. But in most cases there will be a recognition of the need to keep the board to a manageable size, if it is to remain an effective body: and therefore, the agreed size of the 2X part of the board—the employee and shareholder representatives—will often be roughly the same size as the existing board.

26. One of the pressures tending to increase the size of the new board may be that the existing board is reluctant to see any of the present directors lose their seats, either because of the difficulty of doing this in the middle of a director's term of office, or because of the disruption it would cause to the board if it were to lose one or more experienced directors at a time of great

importance in the history of the company. To ease this difficulty we propose a solution, which would enable as many members as possible of the existing board to retain their seats until the next annual general meeting of shareholders (AGM). We recognise that in many cases a $2X + Y$ board will be agreed where the number of seats for the shareholder representatives is not large enough to accommodate all the members of the existing board. In such a case any members of the existing board not accommodated in this way should retain their seats as members of the Y element, until the next AGM, when all members of the old board will retire and some or all of them will present themselves for re-election.

27. It will be helpful if we consider a number of simple examples. In the first case we assume that the existing board has 9 members and that agreement is reached on a reconstituted board of 15 members, 6 employee and 6 shareholder representatives and 3 co-opted directors. In this case the existing board would nominate 6 of its members to sit as shareholder representatives until the next AGM. The additional 3 members would sit as the co-opted directors, again until the AGM. At the AGM all 9 directors would be obliged to retire: and the shareholders' meeting would have to appoint 6 of the 9 to represent it on the board. The 3 remaining directors would lose their seats on the board, unless appointed to the third group by agreement between the shareholder and employee representatives.

28. In the second case we assume an existing board of 8 and the same reconstituted board of 15 (where $X = 6$ and $Y = 3$). In this case, following the nomination of the 6 shareholder representatives, 2 members of the existing board would remain. They would again sit in 2 of the places allocated to the co-opted directors until the next AGM; but in addition, before the new board could take office, the employee and shareholder representatives would have to agree on one co-opted director, to bring the third group of directors up to its agreed size of 3.

29. In the third case, we assume an existing board of 10 and the same reconstituted board of 15. In this case there would be 4 additional members of the existing board to fill 3 places in the Y element. One of them would therefore have to retire immediately, a matter which would have to be settled by the existing board.

30. This solution will normally avoid the need for a sudden retirement of several members of the old board, at the point when the new board takes office. It creates a useful method of transition which allows the experience of the old board to be available for up to a year to the members of the new board, and encourages a gradual adaptation rather than an overnight change. Furthermore, the period during which members of the existing board sit as members of the third group on the new board will allow the other parts of the board the time to find and agree suitable people to be co-opted as directors. It also enables them to see whether they judge suitable for co-option any members of the existing board who will be liable to leave at the next annual general meeting. The length of the transition will vary, of course, according to the date of the next AGM; in some cases it will be very short, in other cases almost a year.

We shall be discussing later in the chapter the transitional periods which have been suggested to us, and why this is the only one we are proposing.

31. Under our proposals some members of existing boards may not have seats on the reconstituted board. This raises a particular problem as regards existing executive directors who have long-term service contracts with their companies. As it now stands company law gives to the shareholders' meeting the right not to re-elect or to dismiss any director; but if he is so removed from the board his rights under such a service contract survive. The terms of many service contracts provide that removal from office as a director constitutes a breach of contract by the company; the executive director then has the right both to rescind the contract and to claim damages for breach of contract against the company. Those damages will usually be related to the sum which he would have been paid in the unexpired period of the contract (perhaps five or ten years or even more), part of which will under the existing law be exempt from tax.

32. Our proposals allow for and indeed facilitate the continuance of existing executive directors on reconstituted company boards; and it is certainly one of our aims that the top management team in a company should be kept together. Executive directors of the old board may be selected by the shareholders to fill the shareholders' seats on the reconstituted board; they may sit as co-opted directors, though we think that would happen less frequently; and in the first year of the process of reconstitution they may be among the board's existing directors who, as we have explained, may continue for up to one year in the seats which will ultimately be filled by co-opted directors. The parties, in agreeing upon the size of the board, will, we are confident, do their utmost to provide for the continuity of the company's top management team upon it. Nevertheless, it is true that the application of the 2X + Y formula could sometimes involve the removal from the board of one or more executive directors who have service contracts, either at the annual general meeting following the reconstitution of the board or possibly even before. Such cases will be unusual; but they could arise and we feel obliged to deal with the problem. Suppose an existing board consists of 13 directors of whom 10 are executive directors with service contracts; if the reconstituted board were to have 6 directors in each group of shareholder and employee representatives and 3 directors in the third group, at least one of the existing executive directors is likely to be excluded from the new board. The question arises whether the company should always be liable to the legal consequences described above for the breach of contract.

33. In framing proposals to meet this problem we have twin objectives: first, equity as between executive directors and their companies; second, facilitating continuity on company boards and keeping together its top management team. We do not believe that an executive director should be deprived of any right to rescind his service contract and leave the company where he is removed from the board before the term of the contract has expired. We think also that his right to damages in that event should continue; but we propose that in certain carefully defined circumstances, that right to damages should be limited.

34. We believe that this limitation on the amount payable as damages should apply where the director has lost his status as a director but nothing more and where that loss has been caused solely or mainly by a reconstitution of the board under the industrial democracy legislation. We therefore propose that the limitation should apply if an executive director is removed from a reconstituted board and leaves the company:

(a) where the company is willing, by a decision of its reconstituted board, to continue honouring all the other conditions of his contract (eg as to his salary, pension, term of the contract, etc);

(b) where all the seats in the group of shareholder representatives are occupied by members of the old board to which he belonged; and

(c) where at the conclusion of the first annual general meeting of the company following the initial reconstitution of the board with employee representatives, a majority of the third group of directors co-opted by shareholder and employee representatives are members of that old board.

Where those conditions apply and he nonetheless leaves the company we propose that his claim to damages should be limited to an amount equivalent to his aggregate remuneration for two years.

35. We believe that in those carefully defined circumstances to permit a director to claim more than two years aggregate remuneration for breach of contract would be unreasonable. If condition (a) is fulfilled he has lost no more than his status as director; for this we acknowledge his vested right to compensation; but where conditions (b) and (c) are met we believe that to allow him higher damages than two years' salary and fees would constitute an unfair penalty upon the company. Moreover, to allow him to claim a larger sum than this might even amount to an inducement to him to rescind the contract, take his 'golden handshake' and leave the company, when he might not otherwise do so. On the other hand, we believe that condition (b) and condition (c) might bring positive advantages to the company. They ensure that, if there is a risk of an executive director claiming damages if removed from the board, the shareholders, in selecting their representatives, and the shareholder and employee representatives, in agreeing upon the third group of directors, will pay particular attention to the selection of existing directors for the reconstituted board. This will, we believe, be a proper protection for executive directors and at the same time it will help to facilitate continuity on company boards as they are reconstituted.

The legal framework

36. Our aim is to encourage the parties within each company to reach agreement on a solution which is suited to its particular circumstances; to its size; to the number of recognised trade unions; to the size of the existing board; to the structure of management at the top level and so on. We are therefore proposing that once the principle of employee representation is agreed there should be a duty on the authorised representatives of the recognised trade unions and the existing board to negotiate a solution. As we have said, in the majority of cases we expect this to be sufficient. We must, however,

consider the few difficult cases where there is deadlock at some stage in the discussions over how large the board or some part of it should be, or where one party to the negotiations is deliberately trying to obstruct progress.

37. We think that if the parties have not reached agreement at the end of six months after the ballot proposed in the next chapter there must be some way in which either party can break the deadlock if it wishes. One solution is for the parties to agree to seek conciliation from an outside body, and indeed this is open to them at any point during the discussions. We also think that the statute itself should contain provisions about board size which can be invoked by either party at the end of six months. We believe that this will be a better incentive to the two parties to reach agreement within the six month period, than the prospect of independent arbitration would be.

38. The solution provided by the law would be based on the $2X + Y$ formula, and would state what the size of the X and Y elements should be, if the law is invoked. We think that the size of the reconstituted board should be related to the number of full-time employees in the company. As we shall explain in Chapter 11, we do not recommend that our proposals should apply to companies with less than 2,000 employees, and our discussion here about the shareholder and employee representative elements is based on that assumption. We suggest that the size of each X in the fall-back solution should be as follows:

for a company or group with   2,000– 9,999 employees: 4

for a company or group with 10,000–24,999   ,,   5

for a company or group with 25,000 or more   ,,   7

We propose that the size of the co-opted group of directors, the Y element, should be related to the number of employee and shareholder representatives, who are to sit on the new board, as follows:

where the number of employee and shareholder representatives together is less than 14 (ie $X = 6$ or less): 3

where the number of employee and shareholder representatives together is 14 or more: 5.

39. This means that if the statutory fall-back provisions were invoked in a company with between 2,000 and 10,000 employees, the size of the reconstituted board would be 11: 4 employee and 4 shareholder representatives and 3 co-opted directors. Where a company has 25,000 or more employees the size of the new board where the fall-back formula is applied would be 19. It is worth noting that under our proposals, even if there is not recourse to the statutory fall-back, a reconstituted board can never have less than 11 members, when it is first set up. This is because the co-opted directors must always number at least three, and must always form less than one third of the total board: it follows from this that the number of employee and shareholder representatives together must always be at least eight.

40. In devising this formula we have allowed that the board size may increase as a result of its being reconstituted, but not we believe to the point where it becomes unwieldy. Under our proposal the size of any board which was statutorily imposed could never be more than 19 and would frequently be less.

If we refer back to our analysis of present board size in Chapter 7, we see that most of the enterprises in *The Times 1,000* now have boards numbering six to 10 directors, although about one third of the enterprises with 2,000 or more United Kingdom employees already have boards with more than 10 directors. Our proposals therefore represent some increase in the average size of the boards of large companies.

Co-option of the third group of directors

41. When the size of the board has been settled, the next step is to select the board members. We discuss in the next chapter how the employee representatives are to be selected; and we have already explained in Chapter 8, that shareholder representatives will continue to be chosen as boards of directors are at present. There remains the question of how the co-opted directors are to be chosen, and what happens in the last resort when there is disagreement.

42. It will be the task of the employee and shareholder representatives—the prospective directors—to agree who is to sit in the third part of the board. In the majority of cases we think that agreement will be reached by those representatives after their selection and before the reconstituted board is due to assume office and that the choice of co-opted directors will not hold up the reconstitution of the board. We also think our proposal that until the next annual general meeting the Y element should be composed of members of the existing board where they are available, will in many cases provide a useful transitional phase during which suitable people can be found. Nevertheless there could be cases either before the board is operative or at the end of the year when all the former members of the old board retire, when there is disagreement over who is to be co-opted. Clearly in that case some method of resolving disagreement must be found.

43. The only solution which seems to us workable, without detracting from the principle of equal shareholder and employee representation, is for an independent body to be called in to provide conciliation. We propose therefore that if at the end of one month the employee and shareholder representatives are unable to agree on one or more co-opted directors, either party should be able to refer the matter to an independent commission, the nature of which we discuss in Chapter 12, for conciliation. In the last resort the commission should be empowered to make a binding nomination of people to sit as members of the third group. Where the commission has to act in this capacity it should be given three months in which to do so. At whatever stage the need arises, the existing board should continue in office until the commission completes the composition of the new board. This is a solution which we expect will be used very rarely, if at all. But we are convinced that it is a necessary legal provision, in order to avoid the process of reconstitution—and therefore the introduction of employee representation on the board—being delayed and deferred because no agreement can be reached on who should be co-opted to the third group on the board.

44. It is only when the co-opted directors have been agreed and the employee and shareholder representatives have been selected that the new board can

assume office. Once the board is operative we are not suggesting that it should be bound by the overall size limits, agreed originally between the old board and the recognised trade unions or in the last resort imposed by law. If for example it is agreed by the shareholder and employee representatives that the size of X or Y should be altered, then such a change can be made.

45. It should be added that the co-opted directors are full members of the board once they have assumed office and take equal responsibility for the board's decisions. Their fees and tenure of office should be fixed by the employee and shareholder representatives when the appointments to the third group are made. We would expect the normal tenure of office to be three years, with one third retiring each year. We suggest that they should only be removed before the end of the agreed term if, as with their appointment, a majority of each of the shareholder and employee groups agree.

The chairman

46. The position of the company chairman will continue to be important both to the board and to the company as a whole. The role of the chairman at present may differ from company to company: sometimes, for example, he is the chief executive of the company, closely involved in the management of its affairs; sometimes he may be a non-executive chairman playing a more supervisory role. We think it appropriate that boards of companies should continue to decide for themselves what the function of the chairman is and who, in consequence, would be best suited to fill the position.

47. We think it desirable, especially during the first few years of the reconstituted board, that the group of shareholder representatives, with its experience of the company's management, should provide the chairman; and in the initial phase, in order to ensure some continuity of leadership, we would expect the present company chairman in most cases to remain in office. We would not wish to prevent the chairman being chosen from another part of the board, if the board agrees it is desirable. We certainly envisage cases where the chairman will be chosen from the co-opted directors; and in the longer term it may be that in some companies the chairman will be an employee representative. We propose therefore that on a reconstituted board the shareholder representatives should continue to provide the chairman, unless unanimously agreed otherwise by the whole board. This we believe will mean that the chairman will usually be a shareholder representative, but it will leave open the possibility of his coming from another part of the board, if the board so agrees.

48. There remains the question of whether the chairman should have the casting vote in the case of a tied vote on the board. As we commented in paragraph 18 above, we have built into our proposals for a co-opted group of directors a mechanism by which in normal circumstances deadlock can be resolved. The $2X + Y$ board is so constituted that it has an odd number of members, so that if all members of the board vote, deadlock is automatically avoided. We recognise, however, that on rare occasions due to a director being absent on business or through illness or due to abstention the board may be evenly split, and that in such a case it will be useful to have a means

of resolving a tie. We do not think it appropriate to prescribe a legal formula to deal with this rare case, and propose that it should be left to the reconstituted board, when it takes office, to decide how this kind of deadlock is to be resolved. We expect that the board will often decide to give the chairman the casting vote, either by using the provision to that effect already in the company's articles of association, or by proposing to the shareholders' meeting the insertion of such a provision into the articles. But we propose that, where a board decides not to give a casting vote to the chairman, it should be empowered to override any provision in the company's existing articles which confers a casting vote on the chairman.

49. There are a number of ways in which a tie can be broken, other than through the casting vote of the chairman. In Germany, for example, the practice in the coal, iron and steel industries, if a member of one side of the board is absent, is for a member of the other side to abstain if a vote is taken. In Sweden the use of alternates, who attend the board even when the full employee representative is present, is established in the law. But again we would emphasise that under our proposals such devices will be needed only rarely. We hope that when board members have worked together for a short time, they will have sufficient confidence in each other for it not to matter whether a member is absent.

The overall timescale

50. The nature of the changes we are considering have led to a number of suggestions in the written evidence for some kind of period of grace or transitional phase, before board level representation is fully operative. We distinguish three distinct strands of thought in such submissions: first, that it is too soon to introduce board level representation, and that a considerable period is needed for experiment and the further development of participation below board level; second, that minority employee representation should be introduced as a preliminary step to equal representation of employees and shareholders; third, that there is a need for a short period to enable companies and trade unions to prepare for the changes and to ensure a smooth changeover from the old to the new system.

51. We strongly disagree with those who take the first of these approaches. We have argued in earlier chapters of the report why we think the time is right for the introduction of employee representation on boards, and we have dealt specifically with the arguments of those who believe that the structure of participation below the board is insufficiently developed to ensure successful participation at board level. It is unnecessary to reopen that discussion here.

52. We also disagree with those who believe that minority, and unequal, employee representation is in some way a necessary preparation for equal representation of employees and shareholders. We discussed earlier in this chapter the fundamental differences between unequal and equal representation and we remain convinced that the real change in the way companies are run and in the nature of decision-making will not occur until employees have equal representation on the board. The qualitative difference between unequal and equal representation means that it is only with the latter that a real threshold is crossed.

106

53. We do however see the force of the argument that a period of time will be necessary to enable industry to prepare for board level representation and to ensure a smooth introduction of the new system into each company. There must be time, for example, for an independent commission to be established to provide advice to the parties involved in the discussions about board level representation and in the last resort to intervene where there is disagreement about who should sit in the third group as co-opted directors. We shall propose also in Chapter 12 that there should be a major training effort to help employee and shareholder representatives to carry out their task effectively on the new boards. Both these measures, which are important to the success of our proposals, will take time to organise. Furthermore, it is essential that the sequence of events leading up to the introduction of board level representation to a company should be orderly and should at each stage allow time for a solution appropriate to that company to be devised. But we do not conclude from this that there is need for a statutory transitional period; the sequence of steps required for the introduction of employee representation, which we have incorporated into our proposals in this report, in addition to the time that must inevitably elapse between the introduction of legislation and its passage into law, should allow a sufficient period for the new system to be introduced.

54. We have discussed earlier in this chapter some of the successive steps from the introduction of legislation into Parliament to the date on which the first employee representatives take their seats on the reconstituted board. The steps in (c), (d) and (e) below are discussed in Chapter 10. The full sequence will be as follows:

(a) the passage of legislation from its introduction to the date on which it receives the Royal Assent;

(b) any additional period from the Royal Assent to the appointed day on which the statute becomes effective;

(c) a request for board level representation from one or more recognised trade unions;

(d) a ballot of all employees to see if there is the required majority in favour of representation on the board;

(e) constitution of a joint representation committee;

(f) agreement on the size of the reconstituted board;

(g) selection of employee and shareholder representatives;

(h) co-option of additional directors;

(i) new board assumes office.

55. It is impossible to say how long each of these steps may take. We cannot for example predict the length of time that will be required under (a) to introduce and pass legislation through Parliament. Nor can we be sure what period will be necessary under (b) between the Royal Assent and the date on which the statute comes into effect, though we do not envisage that it will be a long period. As regards (c)–(i), the speed with which employee representation on the board can be introduced into a company will depend on individual circumstances, and on the extent of the preliminary steps which have been taken by

companies and trade unions during the passage of legislation to prepare for the changes ahead. It is unlikely, however, even where preparations begin, before legislation comes into effect and good progress is made in discussions, that the period from the request of a recognised trade union for representation on the board to the reconstituted board taking office will be less than six months, and it might well be a year. The period could be longer than this in the difficult cases, where the existing board and the recognised trade unions cannot agree and there is recourse to the commission.

56. We also proposed earlier in this chapter that where they exist, members of the old board of directors, who are not included among the shareholder representatives, should occupy the seats in the Y part of the board until the next annual general meeting of shareholders. This we regard as a further important provision, which will help to bring about a smooth transition from the existing board of directors to the new board. It will mean that in many companies there will be a gradual reconstitution of the board and not one moment when a majority of it is completely new. It also means that experience and expertise of the existing board members will be available to the new board and to its new members for up to one year after it has taken office.

57. Even if our proposals were implemented immediately and quickly brought into effect, we think that on average it will be between two and three years from the legislation taking effect to the date on which the new board is fully reconstituted. In our view this will be a sufficient period to ensure an orderly transition from the present to the new system. Any additional period written into the law would, we believe, be merely an excuse for delaying the introduction of employee representation on company boards.

CHAPTER 10

Employee representation and the role of trade unions

1. This chapter deals with the mechanics of the system of employee representation on the board which we are proposing: how the system should be set in operation, how the employee representatives should be selected, who should be eligible to become an employee representative, how long their term of office should be, what procedures there should be for their removal from office and how they are to keep in touch with their constituents. In each case we have considered what role trade unions should play and it is to this subject which we turn first.

The role of trade unions

2. Many of those submitting evidence suggested to us that employee representation on the board should be based, not on trade union machinery, but on works councils or consultative committees which are separate from collective bargaining and which represent all employees, whether union members or not. Such councils and committees, it has often been argued, are an essential preliminary to representation on the board, encouraging participation below board level and providing the machinery through which employee representatives are appointed and can report back.

3. We are surprised that so many people in this country have placed so much emphasis on works councils and similar consultative committees. For, as a senior official of the International Labour Organisation has pointed out,

'A rapid survey of the role played by works councils around the world shows that there is often disenchantment with their functioning. There is a broad consensus in many countries that works councils have not lived up to the expectations that were placed in them when they were first initiated. Many examples could be given from various parts of the world to show that the works council is not, perhaps, an ideal means of handling employer-employee relations at enterprise level. One of the reasons for this seems to be the lack of real decision-making powers possessed by most councils. Experience has shown that a purely advisory arrangement under which workers are given information and may express an opinion, but have no influence on whether this opinion is taken into account or not is not likely to create much enthusiasm or even interest'[1].

At least one major association of employers in the United Kingdom has taken this point. The Coventry and District Engineering Employers' Association has concluded on the basis of a survey which it undertook on the European experience of worker participation that:

'The procedures, systems and institutions which have been established in most European countries for providing joint consultation or decision-making have been, until recently, largely alternatives to collective bargaining or varying forms of it. This is particularly true of works councils or committees which are a common feature of the European scene apart from

[1] J Schregle, *Workers' Participation in Decisions Within Undertakings*, International Labour Review, CXIII (January–February 1976), page 8.

109

Ireland and Great Britain. This factor has been overlooked in the debate on worker participation and industrial democracy which has tended to assume rather more for the works council system than the facts justify. It is doubtful whether employees in companies with obligatory works councils have had any more sense of involvement than their British counterparts and the survey suggests that works councils have rarely inhibited managements' freedom to decide and act accordingly. This view is substantiated by the growing shop steward movement in Europe, increasing resistance to national or district bargaining in favour of plant bargaining and the pressure for increased industrial democracy'[1].

Indeed, as the Coventry and District Engineering Employers' Association implies, works councils have generally tended to decline in importance and, in spite of recent attempts in some European countries to strengthen them, they are increasingly being overshadowed by the growth of shop steward organisation and workplace bargaining. Germany may be considered an exception to this generalisation because there works councils have extensive statutory powers; but it would be singularly inappropriate to introduce German-style works councils into the United Kingdom because their functions are generally performed here by shop stewards' organisations[2] in workplace bargaining.

4. In general the growth of shop steward and equivalent trade union organisation and workplace bargaining has proceeded much further in the United Kingdom than in Europe. The number of shop stewards and the incidence of workplace bargaining in the United Kingdom have increased dramatically over the past twenty years and have resulted in a decline in consultative committees. Research undertaken ten years ago for the Donovan Commission concluded that consultative committees:

'cannot survive the development of effective shopfloor organisation. Either they must change their character and become essentially negotiating committees carrying out functions which are indistinguishable from the processes of shopfloor bargaining, or they are boycotted by shop stewards and, as the influence of the latter grows, fall into disuse'[3].

The growth of workplace bargaining and the decline of joint consultation has, of course, taken place unevenly across the private sector, and it is still possible to point to companies with consultative committees which are the sole form of representation within the plant or which exist independently alongside the negotiating machinery. But, even where the form of the old consultative system remains, for the great majority of large companies the employee representatives are always shop stewards or equivalent representatives and the consultative machinery is closely integrated with the negotiating machinery.

5. Given the rapid and continuing development at the workplace of a representative structure based on trade union machinery, any attempt to bypass

<hr/>

[1]Ed A P Berry, *Worker Participation—The European Experience* (Coventry and District Engineering Employers' Association 1974), page 119.

[2]The phrase 'shop steward' is used generically throughout the report to refer to trade union lay representatives at the place of work.

[3]*Royal Commission on Trade Unions and Employers' Associations, 1965–68 Report*, Cmnd 3623 (HMSO 1968), page 54.

this structure would be seen as an attack on trade unions and collective bargaining and would be fiercely resisted. The dangers of proceeding with industrial relations legislation without trade union support have been amply demonstrated and we think it is impractical to contemplate a system of representation on the board which does not have the support of the trade union movement.

6. Even if it were practical in the United Kingdom to attempt to erect an alternative structure to trade unionism on which board level representation could be based, it would be undesirable. For the policy of successive governments over the course of the twentieth century, and particularly in the last ten years, has been to encourage and strengthen trade unionism and the collective bargaining which it makes possible. We have no wish to deviate from this trend. For we agree with the Donovan Commission that over a wide range of issues 'collective bargaining is the most effective means of giving workers the right to representation in decisions affecting their working lives, a right which is or should be the prerogative of every worker in a democratic society'[1]. To put it another way, since trade unions are necessary to ensure that employees have an effective voice in decision-making both within the company and within the wider society, we wish to ensure that board level representation is designed in such a way that it does not undermine the unions' representative capacity.

7. There are also other reasons why employee representatives on the board should be based on a single channel of representation through trade union machinery. Such machinery would provide the expertise and independent strength necessary to support employee representatives and to enable them to play an effective role in decision-making on the board. It would also provide an established and trusted channel of communication to and from the shop floor through which employee representatives could keep in touch with their constituents. Perhaps most important, integrating employee representatives into a wider system of representation based on trade union machinery would be the most effective way of ensuring that board level representation did not conflict with collective bargaining but that the two processes operated in a mutually supportive way.

8. What we propose in this chapter, therefore, is a system of employee representation on the board which is based on trade union machinery. In practice, we think that the trade union machinery which most employees will wish to use is that which is internal to their company, the shop steward organisation and its equivalent rather than that which is external to it, the branch, the district committee, and the national executive. We see considerable value in shop stewards being the key figures in a system of board level representation. They are almost invariably elected by trade union members at the workplace and because their constituencies are small (generally between fifty and sixty employees) they are kept in close touch with those they represent; indeed, the extent to which members are involved in the election of shop stewards and equivalent representatives and in the activities of those representatives on behalf of their constituents is probably greater than in most other bodies which are organised on democratic lines. Moreover, as the Donovan

---

[1]Donovan Commission, *op cit*, page 54.

Commission has pointed out, and the workplace industrial relations surveys of 1972 and 1973[1] have confirmed, shop stewards are 'rarely agitators pushing workers towards unconstitutional action'[1]. Rather they are generally 'supporters of order exercising a restaining influence on their members in conditions which promote disorder . . . more of a lubricant than an irritant'[2]. We think that companies in this country will find it useful to have such people on their boards.

9. It follows from our support of the principle of a single channel of employee representation through trade union machinery that our proposals in this chapter do not provide any special rights for employees who are not members of a trade union. As we demonstrated in Chapter 2 the proportion of non-unionists is generally small in the large companies in the private sector to which our proposals apply and most of these are white-collar employees, the group amongst whom unionisation is increasing most rapidly. Nevertheless, we have carefully considered the arguments put to us about the position of non-unionised employees in general; the position of particular groups of non-unionised employees; and a different but related problem, the position of employees who are represented by staff associations and professional associations which are not affiliated to the TUC.

10. Although our proposals do not make any special provisions for non-unionised employees, we do not wish to create a system whereby a trade union representing a minority can force the majority, whether unionised or not, to accept board level representation against its will. Hence we have built into our proposals a ballot in which all employees, will have the right to show whether they wish to be represented on the board of their company through trade union machinery. If the ballot is favourable, we do not see how or why we should make special provision for those who have chosen not to join a trade union and who are thus unable to speak with a collective voice. We believe that if employees wish to be represented on the board, they must be prepared to organise at lower levels to make representation on the board effective. In taking this view, we are not introducing a new principle into industrial relations. When unions engage in collective bargaining, they generally determine the terms and conditions of employment for everyone employed in the grades for which they are recognised, not just for those who happen to be union members. Employers would find it highly disruptive if this principle were not followed in collective bargaining. And we think they would find it highly disruptive if the same principle were not followed in employee representation on the board.

11. Some people have suggested to us that managers and other professional groups play a particularly important role in the running of companies and often occupy a unique position between the board and other employees—at one point representing the company in discussions with employees and at another being employees themselves—and they have argued that a special seat on the board should be reserved for these groups. Provided that professional and managerial employees are organised collectively, as increasingly many

[1]Stanley Parker, *Workplace Industrial Relations, 1973*. An enquiry carried out on behalf of the Department of Employment (HMSO 1975), page 98.
[2]Donovan Commission, *op cit*, pages 28–29.

of them are, we can see no reason why they should not be represented on the board amongst the employee representatives. But we do not think that a special seat should be reserved for them on the board by law. It would be unfortunate for legislation on industrial democracy to give the impression that certain employees had a special and presumably higher status in the eyes of the law than other employees. In any case, we find it difficult to accept that any group of employees should be able to demand a seat on the board by right unless they constitute a significant proportion of the company's total employment. The Federal Republic of Germany's Codetermination Act of 1976 illustrates the problem which arises if board seats are reserved for small groups. This Act gives the right to at least one of the employees' seats to the senior executives of the company. The provision was included at the insistence of the minority partner in the West German coalition government. As has been pointed out by its opponents, the result has been to give a group of employees constituting on average five per cent of total employment in West German companies, the right to 16 per cent of employee representation on company boards.

12. Nothing in our proposals prevents a staff association, a professional association, or any other employee organisation which is not affiliated to the TUC from being represented on a company's board. To play a role in such representation an employee organisation has only to satisfy two conditions: it must be 'independent' of the company but 'recognised' by it. The Employment Protection Act 1975 provides procedures by which trade unions may claim recognition and establish their independence[1]. If an employee organisation cannot meet these requirements, then we do not think it should be granted any rights in a law on industrial democracy.

Triggering the system

13. Regardless of what role trade unions play in a system of employee representation on the board, the system itself must first be set in motion. We have considered three main ways in which the system can be introduced: by making it mandatory, by requests from recognised trade unions, and by ballots of all employees.

14. West Germany provides the best known example of a mandatory system. There, regardless of whether trade unions, works councils or employees are interested in being represented, companies of a certain size and type must put employee representatives on their supervisory boards. In the various statutes there is no trigger mechanism as such; the law simply requires board level representation on an appointed day. In contrast, the Swedish system is optional: board representation can be requested by one or more recognised trade unions which represent over 50 per cent of the company's employees. The relevant section of the 1973 Act stipulates that:

'decisions on the establishment of employee representation shall be taken by a local trade union which is bound by a collective agreement in relation to the enterprise and represents more than half of the enterprise's employees, or similarly bound trade unions which taken together are of that extent'[2].

---

[1]Employment Protection Act 1975: for recognition see sections 11–16; for independence see sections 7–8.
[2]Act relating to Board representation of employees in joint stock companies and co-operative associations. Adopted by Swedish Parliament December 1972, Section 7. For English version see National Swedish Industrial Board, *op cit*, page 42.

The third method may be linked with the previous two and incorporates a secret ballot. Denmark provides an example of how it may work. Danish law requires that before representation on the board becomes mandatory on companies there should be a secret ballot of all employees in the company to see if a majority of them wish to be represented on the board. The right to request a ballot rests with the company's consultation committee or with one or more unions representing over 10 per cent of the workforce, or with 10 per cent of the workforce itself.

15. We think that the first of these methods is undesirable because it forces board representation on employees whether they want it or not. To operate a system of board representation for the benefit of employees who are not interested in it is a recipe for ensuring that it will become moribund. The second method, a request from one or more recognised trade unions representing more than half of a company's employees, seems a more viable proposition: it ensures that board level representation is not introduced against the wishes of the company's major trade unions, without whose support it could not be a success. This method does not directly assess the wishes of the employees themselves, however, and many individuals and organisations have suggested to us that employees, as distinct from the unions to which they may belong, are often indifferent, if not hostile, to the notion that they should be represented on company boards.

16. We believe that the most effective way of meeting this argument is to put it to the test by asking all the employees in a company what they think. More specifically, before a company would be required to accept employee representatives on its board, a secret ballot would be held. Unless otherwise agreed by all the parties concerned, the ballot would be held at the company's expense and in company time and on company property, thereby giving employees every chance to vote should they wish to do so. All full-time employees would be eligible to vote, including those on short time or laid off, but not part-time employees. In industries with very high labour turnover, unions and employers might wish to stipulate that employees should also have a minimum period of service with the company before being eligible to vote. We think it important, however, that as few people as possible are disfranchised, and that if a minimum period of service were stipulated, it should be quite short, say six months.

17. The question of what majority should be required in such a ballot proved to be a difficult one. We consider that in a matter of such impotrance to a company's employees, it is reasonable to require not only that a majority of the eligible employees who vote should be in favour of the proposals but also that such employees should constitute a sizeable proportion of the electorate. It would be possible, and not altogether unusual, to require a minimum turnout as a precondition of the effectiveness of the ballot but this could result in an abstention being as significant and, in certain circumstances, even more significant, than a vote against. In other words, abstention would be ambivalent: it could equally indicate apathy or boycott. To overcome this difficulty, we propose that, in addition to the requirement for a simple majority to vote in favour of the proposals, such majority should represent at least

114

one third of the eligible employees. It may be objected that this further requirement erects an additional hurdle for employees to overcome before employee
representation becomes effective. We do not deny this but consider that the
provision for the ballot to be held in company time on company property should
produce a high turnout. It may be objected that the appropriate proportion
should be one half, rather than one third, of the workforce. We believe that
because of illness and the geographical dispersal of employees in many large
enterprises it is wrong to assume that for any practical purposes, the effective
electorate is more than about 80 per cent of all eligible employees. On this
basis, we believe that the affirmative vote of one-third strikes the right balance
between these competing objections. Thus, if the *turnout* was only one third
of the electorate, every vote cast would need to be in favour. For a 40 per cent
turnout a majority of 5:1 would be required, (ie, $33\frac{1}{3}$ per cent of the electors
voting 'yes' to $6\frac{2}{3}$ per cent voting 'no'). Even for a 50 per cent turnout at least
a 2:1 majority (ie $33\frac{1}{3}$ per cent of the electors voting 'yes' and $16\frac{2}{3}$ voting 'no')
would be required.

18. Unless otherwise agreed by all the parties concerned, the question on
the ballot would simply ask for a decision on the principle of employee representation through trade union machinery. In other words, it would generally
not ask employees to express a view on the details of employee representation:
on, for example, the number of employee representatives who should sit on
the board, the union or group of employees from which each of them should
be drawn, or who they should be. We think that a suitable question would be:
'do you want employee representation on the company board through the
trade unions recognised by your employer?'. This question would have to be
adapted in the case of a group ballot so that the unions concerned might be
any of those recognised in the group of companies. One reason for not presenting
the details of the plan at this stage is that one or more of the recognised unions
in the company might wish to oppose the principle of employee representation,
but, if the vote went against them, they might wish to reassess their position
and be represented on the board. Another reason is that it would be difficult
to mobilise the conciliation machinery discussed below in paragraph 22 in the
absence of a decision by the employees that they actually wished to be represented on the board. We think that the Industrial Democracy Commission which
we discuss in Chapter 12 should provide a standard ballot form and explanatory
literature on the basic principles of board representation which should be
circulated to all employees with or in advance of the ballot.

19. The right to request a ballot would rest with the independent unions
recognised by the company. But difficulties might arise in requesting a ballot
in a company with several unions if one of these, a small union recognised on
behalf of only a few employees, requested a ballot in the face of opposition
from other recognised trade unions which represented a much larger proportion
of the employees. This situation would probably not arise often in practice as
in highly unionised companies the joint shop stewards committees or their
equivalents would generally take the decision to request a ballot and a single
union would be unlikely to decide to 'go it alone'. Disagreements and disputes
could arise, however, particularly if there were no joint union committee which
brought together the various trade unions in the company.

20. Hence we think that a union or a group of unions should have the right to demand a ballot only if it is recognised on behalf of grades which constitute at least 20 per cent of a company's employees. Such a provision would prevent a union representing a small proportion of workers from requesting a ballot at a time when it was unlikely to be successful, thereby preventing another ballot being held for a further two years. It would also offer some safeguard to the employer that he would not be involved unnecessarily in the expense of holding a ballot. Most important, where there were several unions it would encourage them to come together before the ballot was held to discuss the details of how employee representatives would be placed on the board, a subject to which we return later in this chapter. Although the figure of 20 per cent is to some extent arbitrary, it is probably high enough to ensure that the above objectives are achieved, but not so high as to make the requesting of a ballot, especially in large multi-plant companies, unduly difficult.

21. We think that employees are unlikely to want to discontinue a system of board representation once it is in operation. But such a possibility must be allowed for. Hence we suggest that once five years have elapsed since a favourable ballot was last held, any union or group of unions which is recognised on behalf of grades which constitute at least 20 per cent of a company's employees should have the right to request a ballot of all the company's employees to determine whether they wish to continue to exercise their statutory right to board representation. If a majority which constitutes one third or more of all eligible employees voted against the continuance of board representation, such representation would cease. This ballot would be administered in the same way as the ballot which triggered the system.

22. Any ballot on the question of employee representation on boards would be jointly administered by the company and by those of its recognised unions which wished to be involved. If there were a dispute over the request for, or administration of the ballot, any party to the dispute could refer it to the Industrial Democracy Commission, the independent agency which we propose in Chapter 12, whose decision on these matters would be final and binding.

23. The balloting process which we have recommended would give unions which were opposed to employee representation on boards an opportunity to campaign against it. It would also give all employees, whether unionised or not, the right to be involved in the decision. Where most of them were opposed to employee representation through trade union machinery, they could prevent it being introduced. We believe then that the secret ballot will be an important democratic check. We hope also that it will have the effect of involving everyone in the company in the debate about employee representation on the board. For the ballot to be a success the trade unions will have to explain to employees what is involved in board representation and employees will have to be sufficiently interested to turn out to vote. We noted in Chapter 5 the widespread belief that most employees do not want to be represented on the board and that trade unions are not democratic enough to speak on behalf of their members. The ballot we propose will allow both of these propositions to be tested.

Implementing the decision

24. Once a ballot has gone in favour of placing employee representatives on the board of a company, there are many different ways in which they could be selected. Our written evidence makes numerous suggestions, and experience in other European countries provides a variety of practical examples. The basic question is how far the law should specify the method of selection and how far it should leave the trade unions free to devise a system they think suitable. A contrast is provided by comparing West Germany with Sweden.

25. In Germany the method of selection is carefully defined by law and varies according to the size of company. The Codetermination Act 1976, for example, stipulates that an electoral panel, which is itself elected by a secret ballot of all the employees in the company, shall make the appointments to the employees' seats on the board. The employees' seats are distributed by law between trade union represenatives from outside the company and employee representatives from inside, and at least one employee representative must come from each of the major groupings in the company; the blue-collar workers, the white-collar employees, and the senior managers. In Sweden the local trade unions recognised by the company control the selection procedure. The law states the basic principles as follows:

'If more than four-fifths of the employees under collective agreement belong to the same local union this union shall elect both of the employee members. Otherwise the two local unions having the highest number of such employees shall appoint one member each'[1].

The law goes on to say, however, that this arrangement may be varied by agreement between the unions involved.

26. There is no need for a selection procedure defined by law to be as complex as that which exists in Germany, but the German example does demonstrate what must be done if a statutory procedure is to be applied to all large companies. It inevitably becomes necessary to go into detail in order to define constituencies which reflect the different interests in the company, to construct a system of nomination, and to stipulate how a ballot shall be carried out and what proportion of votes shall constitute an election. We are not attracted by the prospect of trying to do this for the United Kingdom. We doubt if we could devise a system which was flexible enough to suit all companies, and the written evidence presented to us suggests that neither companies nor trade unions would welcome being put in a statutory straitjacket.

27. We believe that the United Kingdom would be better advised to follow the Swedish example and put on the trade unions in each company the onus of devising a satisfactory method of selecting employee representatives. We have already recorded our support for the principle of representation through the single channel of recognised trade unionism, arguing that it is essential to build on the existing representative structure to ensure compatibility with trade union responsibilities for collective bargaining. But the Swedish method of selecting employee representatives, which fairly strictly ties the right of a trade union to appoint an employee representative to the relative size of its

---

[1]Section 9. (See National Swedish Industrial Board, *op cit*, page 43.)

membership in the company, could not simply be transferred to the United Kingdom. For in Sweden there are rarely more than two or three major trade unions in a company, and it is fairly easy therefore to share the two employee seats between the white-collar and blue-collar unions. In contrast, companies in the United Kingdom often recognise many unions, and we think unions would find it more difficult to agree on the number and method of selecting employee representatives, if the law required that representation should be strictly tied to the proportion of each union's membership in the company.

28. We therefore suggest that the law should close none of the options. It should merely lay on the recognised trade unions in the company the responsibility to devise whatever method of selection seems most appropriate. They could agree, for example, that there should be a strict division of seats according to the relative strength of each trade union in the company and leave each union to decide how it would fill its seats. Alternatively, they might decide that the employee representatives should be chosen by and from the joint shop steward committee or its equivalent in the company. Or, they might decide to allocate the seats to constituencies in the firm—to blue- and white-collar workers, to management, to subsidiaries of the parent, or to different plants—and then hold elections by secret ballot to choose a representative for each constituency. Or, they might hold a secret ballot of all employees in the company, presumably restricting the right of nomination to recognised trade unions.

29. The process of devising a satisfactory system of employee representation on the board will require that the various trade unions recognised by the company come together to discuss the problems involved and to agree ways of resolving them. Ideally, before requesting a ballot the recognised unions in a company would have discussed among themselves at least some of the details of how employee representatives would be placed on the board; and they would be encouraged to do so by the requirement that they must be recognised on behalf of grades which constitute at least 20 per cent of the company's employees before they have the right to request a ballot. They would also be encouraged to enter into such discussions if they wished to participate with the company in administering the ballot. In any case, once a ballot went in favour of board representation, shop stewards and other lay representatives of the various trade unions in the company would have to come together in a formal committee. For ease of reference, let us refer to this committee by the generic title of the Joint Representation Committee (JRC). In general, this committee would need to provide the continuing support for board representation and its interface with collective bargaining, a subject to which we return below. Initially, however, its two most important functions would be to negotiate with the existing board on the size and structure of the new board, and to decide how the employee representatives on the board would be selected. All the independent unions recognised by the company would be eligible to become members of the JRC and, if any such union could demonstrate to the Industrial Democracy Commission discussed in Chapter 12 that it was being excluded from membership, then the committee would be deemed to be improperly constituted, and the board would not be required to meet with it or to accept employee representatives. Such a

provision would ensure that all the recognised unions would have an opportunity to express their views on the form which employee representation on the board should take.

30. The JRC will not have an easy job. It will need to balance the conflicting claims of trade unions for seats, and to ensure that minority interests are reflected on the board even if they are not directly represented. There will be inter-union disputes, and on occasions these may be acute. But by placing on trade unions the responsibility for devising a satisfactory method of selecting employee representatives, we believe that a compromise agreed by all the parties concerned will ultimately be reached. Indeed, as we argue below, it is not the least of the advantages of our proposal that it should encourage closer working by trade unions, not only on the question of industrial democracy but on other matters as well.

31. But even with the best will in the world all the members of the JRC may not always be able to agree amongst themselves. Even if they can, the committee may not be able to agree with the existing board. Hence there must be a procedure for resolving disputes. We have already discussed in the previous chapter how disputes over the size and structure of the new board will ultimately be resolved by a statutory fall-back formula, and there is no need to repeat the details of this formula here. Suffice it to say that if the members of the JRC could not agree amongst themselves on the desirable size of the new board, then they would have to propose the appropriate figures given by the statutory formula. If the existing board preferred another figure, it would no doubt try to convince the members of the JRC of the desirability of its views. But, if the committee and the existing board could not agree, then the figure given by the statutory formula would ultimately prevail.

32. Inter-union disputes over the selection of employee representatives cannot be settled by a statutory formula; they require individual consideration. Hence if the JRC cannot unanimously agree on how the employees' seats on the board should be allocated and filled—either immediately following a favourable ballot or on any subsequent occasion when an employee representative position becomes vacant—then the dispute would have to be resolved by one or more of the unions referring it to the Industrial Democracy Commission. If all the unions involved were affiliated to the TUC, the Industrial Democracy Commission would follow the usual procedure for inter-union disputes and call upon the TUC to conciliate. In the unlikely event that such conciliation proved unsuccessful, or if one or more of the unions were not affiliated to the TUC and did not want it to conciliate, then the Commission would investigate the matter itself and make a recommendation.

33. Regardless of how the employee representatives are chosen or who they may be, and regardless of whether they are chosen with or without the help of the Industrial Democracy Commission, there must be a 'legal event' which would constitute the moment of their appointment to the board. Such an event could be arranged if the names of the duly selected employee representatives were listed on a certificate of appointment, a standard form drawn up by the Industrial Democracy Commission, and handed to the company secretary. At this moment the employee representatives listed on the certificate

of appointment would become 'prospective directors' and, as explained in the previous chapter, they would meet with the shareholders' prospective directors to agree the number and names of the 'co-opted directors'. Once the co-opted directors were determined, the employee representatives (and the shareholder representatives) would at a specified date assume office and the new board would then replace the existing board.

34. To be valid the certificate of appointment should contain the names of those selected and their period of tenure, and would need to be signed by the accredited representatives of all the unions on a properly constituted JRC, confirming that the selection had been done by a proper procedure. If a certificate were not so signed, then it would not be valid and pending consideration of its validity by the Industrial Democracy Commission the existing board would continue in office. In other words, the result for the unions of failure to agree would be that they would remain unrepresented on the board. Similarly, if a vacancy occurred for an employee representative after the board had been reconstituted, and if all the unions on a properly constituted JRC or, in the case of disagreement among these unions, all those specified by the Industrial Democracy Commission under the procedures described above, were not prepared to sign a certificate of appointment, then the vacancy would remain unfilled. In other words, the result for the unions of failure to agree in this case would be that they would have fewer members on the board than the shareholders.

35. The procedures described above would offer some protection to minority interests without allowing these interests to frustrate the majority's wish to have employee representatives on the board. If, for example, a union representing a minority interest could not get the other unions in the company to agree to allocate it one of the employee seats on the board, it would be able to refer the matter to the Industrial Democracy Commission. If the Commission upheld the union's claim, then the other unions would not be able to obtain representation on the board unless they allowed it to fill one of the employee seats. But if the claim of the union representing the minority interest was not upheld by the Commission, then it would not be required to sign the certificate of appointment, and hence it could not prevent the other unions from appointing employee representatives on the board. And in the unlikely event that one of the unions specified by the Industrial Democracy Commission was acting in bad faith and was refusing to sign the certificate simply in order to ensure that no employee representatives were placed on the board, the Commission would no doubt be requested to re-specify the list of unions so that the name of this union was omitted.

Qualifications of employee representatives

36. Although some European countries have gone into great detail about who should be eligible to sit on the board as an employee representative, specifying, for example, age and service qualifications, we think that in a system based on representation through trade union machinery the spelling out of these qualifications can best be left to the trade unions themselves. In general, therefore, we cannot see that anything would be gained by writing into the law rigid categories of eligibility which might exclude able and suitable representatives whom the trade unions wanted to appoint.

120

37. We have, however, given special attention to one aspect of eligibility: whether employee representatives should be chosen from the employees of the company, or whether a union should be able if it wishes to appoint a trade union official from outside the company. It was said to us in West Germany that the ideal was a mixture of the two. Experience there seemed to show that the outside trade union official was more able to take an overall view of the company's affairs than the representative from inside the firm who tended to concentrate on parochial matters of immediate relevance to his constituents. But strong arguments have been put to us in this country in favour of restricting eligibility to the employees of the company. From industrialists the argument has been that only employees of the company will have sufficient commitment to it to be effective and reliable directors. From some trade unions the argument has been that only employees will have the necessary direct involvement in the company's affairs.

38. We have already said above that we expect the method of selecting employee representatives to be built on trade union machinery. We expect this machinery generally to result in the selection of company employees, and more often than not of shop stewards. The members of the Joint Representation Committee will probably in most instances act as an electoral college and select employee representatives from among the community of shop stewards or equivalent representatives in the company. This seems to us desirable, as we think that the cause of effective representation will be furthered if employee representatives are chosen from among those on the company pay-roll who have already demonstrated that they can command the support and confidence of the workforce. If they cease to be employees of the company after they are appointed to the board, they should be allowed to remain there, if they wish, until their term of office expires or they are recalled by their constituents (see paragraphs 40–42).

39. Although we think the employee representatives on the board should generally be chosen from among the employees of the company, we would not want to exclude altogether the possibility that a full-time official from outside the company might be chosen to represent employees on the board. Such representation might be desirable and necessary where, for example, labour turnover is very high, employment is thinly spread over numerous establishments, or employees spend much of their time out of the country. In such isolated cases, we think it should be possible for the Secretary of State for Employment, in consultation with the Industrial Democracy Commission, to issue an order which would enable a full-time union official to act as an employee representative on the board of a company.

Term of office, pay and facilities of employee representatives

40. We believe that employee representatives should be appointed to the board for a reasonable period and that they should be eligible for reappointment. Clearly, employee representatives will be more effective when they have received training and when they have experience of how the board operates. For this reason alone, it would be undesirable for them to be continually changing. It is the normal practice at the moment to appoint directors for three years, with one third of them retiring each year. We think that this

practice is desirable. Hence we suggest that the term of office of all directors, including those representing employees, should be three years and their appointment should be renewable. In the first instance, however, some directors will have to be appointed for a period of less than three years to enable their terms of office to be staggered in such a way that one third of them retire each year.

41. We think that there must be machinery by which in exceptional circumstances an employee representative can be removed before the end of his term of office, parallel to the shareholders' right to remove a director by ordinary resolution. It would be impossible for an employee representative to make an effective contribution to the board if he did not have the support and confidence of his constituents, and hence we cannot agree with those who have suggested to us that there should be no right of removal. If the accredited representatives of *all* the unions which had signed the certificate of appointment demanded the dismissal of any person named on that certificate, then we think that person should cease to be a director. Clearly, the person accredited by a union to sign the certificate of appointment on its behalf should not be someone who is named on that certificate.

42. The power of removal from office should be used exceptionally, however, and in normal circumstances the employee representative should be allowed to serve his full term of office. We have already made it clear in Chapter 8 that the employee director is to be a representative and not a delegate. The power of removal should not be regarded as a method by which the trade unions can in effect mandate their representatives. The proper place for an expression of confidence or lack of it must normally be at the end of the representative's term of office, when it is decided whether he should be reappointed or not.

43. We have received conflicting views on the question of whether employee representatives should receive a fee for serving on the board. Some people have suggested to us that employee representatives should receive a director's fee since serving on the board will involve extra work and responsibility. Others have argued that if employee representatives are to retain the confidence of their constituents and to continue to be representative of them, they should not receive a fee.

44. We agree with the latter school of thought. To pay employee representatives a fee for serving on the board, on a scale something like that of present non-executive directors, would undoubtedly cause them to be regarded with suspicion by their fellow employees. It would thereby undermine the effectiveness of employee representation on the board. It would also be inequitable. Shop stewards carry extra work and responsibility in the companies in which they work, and they do not receive a fee in addition to their wages. And executive directors often do not receive a fee for serving on the board: their service agreements normally provide that they should receive only the salary which they are paid as an employee of the company. Hence we think that the law should stipulate that any director who is an employee of the company, whether he be a representative of the shareholders or of the employees, should not be entitled to a director's fee in addition to salary.

Other directors—the co-opted directors and any non-executive directors which the shareholders might appoint—would be entitled to fees, and the size of these would be determined by the board.

45. Although employee representatives should not receive a special fee, they should obviously not suffer financial loss as a result of performing directoral duties. Their expenses must be covered and they must be reimbursed for any loss of earnings. Indeed, if they are required to attend to board business outside normal working hours, then, as is often the case with shop stewards who attend meetings called by the company outside normal hours, they should receive the overtime rate of pay laid down for the job they usually perform. This would also apply to members of the JRC.

46. If employee representatives are to be effective representatives and effective directors, they will require a range of rights beyond those directly associated with attending the board. In addition to receiving board papers, employee representatives will need to maintain contact with their constituents, to keep in close touch with the JRC and to discuss issues informally with other directors, senior managers, and perhaps outside experts. Accordingly, they will need, with due notice to their immediate supervisors, to be able to take time off as of right. They will also require access to an office and a telephone, secretarial assistance of a confidential nature, and perhaps other facilities.

47. The principle of granting time-off with pay and other facilities to employees engaged in trade union and public activities is already widely accepted in industry; indeed, it is laid down in the Employment Protection Act 1975[1], and the Advisory, Conciliation and Arbitration Service has recently published a draft code of practice on the subject[2]. We think that the Industrial Democracy Commission which we discuss in Chapter 12, should issue a similar code of practice dealing with the facilities which should be given to employee representatives on boards of companies and members of the JRC.

Reporting back

48. We emphasised in Chapter 8 the importance of employee representatives keeping in touch with their constituents; if they do not, they will be of little use to the board or to those they represent, for they will not provide the necessary communication link between the two. Here we briefly discuss what reporting back may involve.

49. Reporting back to the membership is generally a central feature of trade union organisation, and hence the law does not need to require that a system of reporting back should be created. It need only emphasise the desirability of this practice and leave it to the recognised unions to work out how employee representatives can best be included in the existing union communication network within the company. Indeed, one of the reasons we have opted for a single channel of representation through trade union machinery is that it provides an excellent means by which employee representatives can keep in touch with their constituents.

---

[1] Employment Protection Act 1975, Sections 57–62.
[2] Advisory, Conciliation and Arbitration Service, Draft Code of Practice, *Time-off for trade union duties and activities* (HMSO 1976).

50. An obvious starting point for any system of reporting back would be the Joint Reresentation Committee. It would provide a continuing reference point for employee representatives, and they would be expected to report regularly to it. The members on the JRC would then have the task of making reports to other parts of the trade union structure—the branches of individual unions, joint shop steward committees, or other joint union committees—which in turn would have the job of disseminating information more widely to the union membership and to employees as a whole. The employee representatives themselves might occasionally make reports to these lower-level parts of the trade union structure and on occasions to groups of employees, so that the hierarchical system does not cut them off from those on the shop floor.

51. This is only one way in which a system of reporting back might be developed. There are numerous other options open to the unions. If they wished, they could create a special structure to deal with reports from employee representatives on the board, or, where a company has a works council system which formally involves trade unions, they might decide to use it as one of the channels of communication. The form of the reporting back machinery will no doubt vary from one company to another. But whatever form the machinery takes, it must enable employee representatives to keep in touch with those they represent.

Employee representation and collective bargaining

52. We noted in Chapter 6 that the view has been expressed that there is a fundamental and irreconcilable incompatibility between board level representation and collective bargaining. The clearest statement of this view came from the Electrical, Electronic, Telecommunication and Plumbing Union (EEPTU), which argued that the job of trade unions is through collective bargaining 'to consider, contest, and oppose, if necessary, the exercise of managerial prerogatives'. 'It is not the responsibility of work people to manage the enterprise'; indeed, 'it is essential that trade unions retain their independence'[1].

53. We agree with the EEPTU that trade unions must retain their independence. But we do not see why this independence need be compromised by representation on the board. If, as we propose in Chapter 9, the employee representatives on the board are equal in number to the shareholder representatives, and if the former are backed by the strength of the trade unions in the company, they will carry both weight and influence on the board. Indeed, they will be able where necessary to oppose a policy not only on the board but also in collective bargaining.

54. More generally, we see no necessary contradiction between board level representation and collective bargaining. Rather, we believe that they are similar and complementary processes. Both contain elements of co-operation and conflict, harmony and discord. Both by their very natures involve the mutual dependence of union and management. Perhaps most important, both have the same basic objective: to enable employees to participate in decision-making in the enterprise in which they work. And hence both involve participation in 'management', not in the sense of participating in the executive tasks

---

[1]EEPTU evidence, paragraph 24 *et seq.*

which must be performed to implement major company policies, but in the sense of participating in the formulation of these strategic policies. As the TUC has pointed out in its report on industrial democracy, 'the extension of joint control or joint regulation in any form, including collective bargaining, is a *de facto* sharing of the management prerogative'[1]. In short, board level representation does not raise any new issues of principle for trade unions which already engage in collective bargaining. It simply creates an additional means by which they may influence the managerial process, particularly those aspects of this process which collective bargaining is inadequate to handle by itself.

55. Some people have suggested to us that one way of avoiding any confusion and conflict between board level representation and collective bargaining would be to require employee representatives to relinquish all other union offices, such as being a shop steward, once they are on the board. We think this is an unrealistic and unhelpful proposal which, by reducing the co-ordination of trade union policy in collective bargaining and at board level, might produce the very confusion and conflict which it was attempting to avoid. The only example we know of employee representatives at board level being required to relinquish office was in the British Steel Corporation when the original board representation scheme was introduced in 1968. It had the effect of alienating employee representatives from the unions and the union membership, and when the scheme was revised, the requirement that employee representatives on the board should not be union office-holders was dropped.

56. It has also been suggested to us that confusion and conflict between board level representation and collective bargaining could be avoided in practice if employee representatives were prohibited from taking part in those board discussions and decisions which concern strikes, lock-outs and collective agreements. Such a provision is contained in the Swedish legislation on board representation. But we discussed the effects of this provision when we visited Sweden, and we found that the provision had rarely operated. In practice, we were told, boards did not often become involved in matters of this sort and when they did it was most unusual for the employee representatives to be excluded. When collective bargaining matters were important enough to be brought to the board, then it was found valuable to have the employee representatives involved in the discussion. We think that a similar practice would develop in the United Kingdom, and hence we can see no reason why the law should try to prevent employee representatives from considering an area of the board's work on which they are particularly well qualified to comment. Nor should the absence of such a provision give them an unfair advantage in collective bargaining. For employee representatives are most unlikely to demand that senior management reveal their bargaining position and strategy and, if they did make such a demand, they would almost certainly not be supported by the shareholder representatives and the co-opted directors.

57. We have considered whether any specific recommendations and legal provisions need to be made about the role of the reconstituted board when there is an actual or potential industrial dispute. There are three possible

[1]TUC, *op cit*, page 37.

alternatives. The first is for all matters in negotiation to be considered by the board without any limitation on any member's right to participate and vote. The second is for those on both sides directly interested in the dispute to be disqualified from voting. A third answer would be to recognise that the 2X + Y formula does enable the shareholder representatives along with the co-opted directors to insist that the management negotiating position is not the subject of detailed and practical consideration by the board. We believe that this approach is the practical one and that it would be very divisive on the reconstituted unitary board for the law to determine circumstances in which members on one side or the other would be precluded from participating and voting on these matters. Where such a matter does come to the board, however, an employee representative who finds that an instruction to take industrial action amounts in effect to a mandate on him to vote on the matter in a particular way should, on normal principles of company law, be obliged to declare this to the board and abstain from voting on it.

58. There is a provision in the Companies Act 1948, however, which requires directors to disclose their interests in contracts made by their companies, and many companies' articles of association preclude directors from voting on matters in which they have a personal interest. If this provision were left unchanged, it might be interpreted to preclude employee representatives from taking part in board decisions concerned with collective bargaining and industrial relations. Hence we propose that the law should state that employee representatives should not fall within these provisions simply because their contracts of employment give them an interest in the matters discussed or the decisions taken by their board.

59. As we have repeatedly argued throughout this chapter, the best way of ensuring that board level representation and collective bargaining do not in practice become confused and conflict is to insist that both processes be firmly based on the single channel of trade unionism. Indeed, our belief in the validity of this argument is the main reason we have not been attracted to the proposal that employee representation on the board should be based on a substructure of works and company councils which is divorced from trade union machinery. Although the advocates of this proposal have suggested that this new structure would not interfere with collective bargaining, we do not see how such interference could be avoided in practice. The decisions made by any such structure must inevitably have implications for collective bargaining. If this structure were not based on trade union machinery, the potential for conflict would be much greater and the objective of ensuring greater trade union commitment to the implementation of the board's policies would be much more difficult to achieve.

60. In contrast, the structure we have proposed to support board level representation—the Joint Representation Committee and its supporting structure of shop steward and equivalent committees—would not only be compatible with collective bargaining, it would also be a catalyst which would stimulate the changes needed in the machinery of trade unionism if it is to cope successfully with the new issues which are likely to be raised by representation on the board. In particular, it would fill any gap which might exist

in trade union machinery at company level and encourage closer working between trade unions on a wide range of issues. By so doing, it would not only ensure employee representation on the board and collective bargaining did not conflict, it would also create a new and positive relationship between them which would be of immense benefit to British industry.

CHAPTER 11

Application: size of companies, groups and multinationals

1. We discuss in this chapter how widely our proposals should be applied to companies, to company groups and to multinational enterprises. This raises a number of important problems, particularly with regard to the relationship between a parent company and its subsidiaries and sub-subsidiaries, which must be solved if employee representation on the board is to be a success. A failure to deal with them properly could open up such loopholes and exemptions in the law that the principle of board level representation itself might be endangered.

Size of companies

2. Our proposals in Chapter 8 concerning the duties of directors are intended to have universal application to all companies in the United Kingdom; they represent positive improvements in company law which are desirable in themselves. We have left open for consideration the question whether our proposals concerning the functions of the board and the role of the shareholders' meeting should apply only to those companies in which board level representation of employees has been introduced, or to all United Kingdom companies. Moreover, we believe that the right to employee representation on company boards should apply only to enterprises with a large number of employees. It is in large enterprises that the problems discussed in earlier chapters—the alienation of the workforce, the remoteness of decision-making, the lack of communication between management and employees—are liable to be most severe and that board level representation can make the most impact. It is here also that a high proportion of employees are members of trade unions, which we see providing the representative structure on which effective board representation can be built.

3. Where should the dividing line be drawn? We decided early in our deliberations that the most appropriate criterion of size was the number of employees in the enterprise. This is in line with most European practice. The West German system now has two main dividing lines. The 1976 law applies to companies with over 2,000 employees, whereas the Works Constitution Act of 1952 applied to companies with over 500 employees, and still applies to companies with between 500 and 2,000 employees. The Swedes applied their 1973 law to companies with over 100 employees, and after three years' experience have decided to reduce this to 25 employees. In the Netherlands the law is more complex and relates to companies with a certain level of capital and with over 100 employees or which are subject to the legal obligation to have an enterprise council. In Austria there is no limit at all: the law applies to all joint stock companies.

4. To some extent any dividing line is artificial and may in a very few cases encourage companies to restrict their size or in the case of groups to reorganise their structure in order (wholly or partially) to avoid being subject to the law. Since we have decided, however, to apply our proposals to large companies, it is inevitable that a line should be drawn. We therefore recommend that our

proposals for employee representation on company boards should apply to all enterprises with 2,000 or more employees in the United Kingdom. The provisions should apply to the ultimate holding company of a group which *in toto* employs 2,000 or more people in the United Kingdom, as well as to any individual company which employs 2,000 or more people in the United Kingdom, whether or not it is part of a group.

5. From our statistical survey in Chapter 2 we estimate that some 738 enterprises employing in all 6 or 7 million people in the United Kingdom, (one third of total employment in the private sector), would be affected by these proposals. If subsequently the limit were to be lowered to enterprises with 1,000 or more employees in the United Kingdom, another 500 or so enterprises employing perhaps three quarters of a million people in the United Kingdom, would be brought within its scope.

6. We believe that at this stage the enterprises to be brought within the scope of our proposals should be those employing 2,000 or more people in the United Kingdom. Thus, the size threshold might remain fixed for a period of three to four years by which time a thorough review of the operation of the legislation should have been made. But, assuming that an independent review of the operation of the legislation had then become available, it might be possible for the Government to lower the threshold to enterprises employing 1,000 or more people in the United Kingdom, by means of a statutory instrument rather than a new Act of Parliament. The statutory instrument should, in our view, be an Order laid before Parliament in draft, requiring an affirmative resolution by both Houses before it could be signed by the Secretary of State and become effective.

Possible exemptions

7. It has been suggested to us in evidence that certain types of companies, or companies operating in certain sectors of the economy, should be exempted from the provisions of any new legislation on employee representation on company boards. The exemptions allowed for in other European countries are described by Eric Batstone[1].

8. Apart from multinational companies, which are dealt with later in this chapter, particular sectors for which exemptions have been suggested, usually through the bodies representing their collective interests, are: banking; insurance; shipping; construction; hotels and catering; broadcasting and the press. The following reasons seem to lie behind these suggestions:

(a) the application to such companies of legislation additional to the Companies Acts (eg the Merchant Shipping Acts, the Insurance Companies Act 1974, the Industrial Assurance Act 1923, the Independent Broadcasting Authority Act 1973, etc);

(b) the geographical spread and fragmentation of their activities (eg public houses, building sites);

(c) high labour turnover;

---

[1]Batstone and Davies, *op cit*, page 15.

(d) employment of part-time workers, seasonal workers or a high proportion of foreign nationals;

(e) special considerations of confidentiality (eg credit ratings of a bank's customers).

9. It will be for those who prepare legislation to consider in detail the case for any such exemptions. The problems of high labour turnover, the employment of part-timers and seasonal workers, etc are largely dealt with by the procedures which we propose for testing the desire of any workforce to be represented on the board (see Chapter 10). Our views about the availability to employee representatives of confidential information are set out in some detail in Chapter 8, and they apply as much to banks as to any other companies. We found on our visit to Sweden that Swedish banks had encountered no difficulties in regard to confidentiality from the presence of employee representatives on their boards. Generally speaking we are opposed to exemption for particular groups or classes of companies or particular sectors of industrial or commercial activity, and in our view the necessity for consequential amendments to other statutes should not stand in the way of the application of our proposals to particular sectors of the economy.

Groups of companies

10. The application of our proposals to groups of companies is one of the most important parts of our report. In this section we are concerned exclusively with the application of board level representation to groups of companies all of which are incorporated under United Kingdom law; but much of what we say will be pertinent to our discussion of multinational groups in the next section. Virtually every enterprise identified in Chapter 2 as employing 2,000 or more people is also part of a wider group. Large industry in the United Kingdom is organised in pyramids of holding and subsidiary companies. In some instances the ultimate holding company in the group itself employs less than 2,000, but one or more of its subsidiaries or sub-subsidiaries may employ 2,000 or more, and of course in the enterprises under discussion the *group as a whole* satisfies this criterion. The 738 *enterprises* employing 2,000 or more people in the United Kingdom will therefore translate into a larger number of separate *companies* employing 2,000 or more. No precise figure can be given, but the number is likely to be of the order of 1,800.

11. We mentioned the diversity of group boards and decision-making structures in Chapter 7. It is often difficult to define the relationship between the group holding board and its subsidiary boards and to identify the level at which decisions are taken. But each subsidiary company is a separate legal person and its directors fall under the duties laid upon directors by the law. In Chapter 8 we proposed changes in the law about directors' duties. Directors should be obliged to consider the interests of their company's shareholders and employees. Further, directors of a holding company should be enabled to consider the interests of shareholders in and employees of a subsidiary company; and it is for serious consideration whether directors of a subsidiary should be enabled to consider the interests of employees of and shareholders in the holding company, and indeed, in all companies in the group.

130

12. In some instances, a subsidiary board may in practice be closely controlled in respect of its decision-making powers. Some group holding companies regard their subsidiaries—in particular, their wholly-owned subsidiaries—as instruments to carry out group policy. In this type of group the subsidiaries resemble in function the divisions of an enterprise constructed as one large company, although in law of course the board of directors of a subsidiary company is essentially different from any such 'divisional board' in that the subsidiary company is a separate legal entity. At the other end of the spectrum there are conglomerate groups in which the holding company acts rather as an investment holding company, taking decisions about the financial affairs of the group but exercising much less control in other respects over the management of the subsidiary companies. Across this spectrum diversity is increased by the varying patterns of subsidiaries which are wholly-owned and those which are not. Where the group is more closely controlled from the top, the parent company is able to integrate a subsidiary's management into the group managerial hierarchy, and senior managers of the subsidiary may even be accountable to the management or board of the parent. Executives may sit on several boards within the group; a director of the parent holding company may sit on one or more subsidiary boards; the chairman or managing director of a subsidiary may sit on the parent company's board. In this type of group although there is a number of separate legal units, the management personnel and policies of the group can be effectively co-ordinated from the top. A group may include elements of different kinds, some subsidiaries being allowed greater independence of action, others being more tightly controlled by the holding company.

13. This diversity of group structure makes it difficult to devise provisions which achieve effective representation of employees at every point in the group where major decisions are taken. Nevertheless we regard such representation as essential to our proposals. But we also recognise that proposals on groups must be consistent with the operation of a group as an economic unit; for it is no part of our task to prevent or hinder the continued operation of business in the private sector on a group basis. Our aim in what follows is to reconcile the principle of effective employee representation with the continued operation of efficient groups of companies.

14. The feature currently common to all holding companies in the different varieties of groups is the power to control the composition of the board of directors of the subsidiary. Such control is normally available to the holding company by reason of its ownership of more than 50 per cent of the voting share capital in the subsidiary. This is reflected in the legal definition of holding and subsidiary company in Section 154(1) of the Companies Act 1948:

'For the purpose of this Act, a company shall . . . be deemed to be a subsidiary of another if, but only if,—

(a) that other either—
   (i) is a member of it and controls the composition of its board of directors; or
   (ii) holds more than half in nominal value of its equity share capital; or
(b) the first mentioned company is a subsidiary of any company which is that other's subsidiary'.

15. We shall return later to the adequacy of that definition in the context of our proposals for employee representation on boards. For the present our discussion is based upon that current legal definition; and in particular, we adopt the usage of Section 154(1) in that our references to 'subsidiaries' must normally be taken to include 'sub-subsidiaries'. Moreover our discussion of the 'holding company' usually refers to the ultimate holding company. Section 5(1) of the Companies Act 1967 provides (with certain exceptions which will need to be re-examined) that in the case of a subsidiary company:

'there shall be stated in, or in a note on, or statement annexed to, the company's accounts laid before its general meeting the name of the body corporate regarded by the directors as being the company's ultimate holding company and, if known to them, the country in which it is incorporated'.

16. The right to employee representation on the board should apply to groups of companies as well as to individual companies. In most groups the strategic decisions about policy affecting the group and the individual companies within it are taken at the level of the holding company; board level representation would be incomplete if it applied only to large operating subsidiaries and not to the board at the apex of the pyramid of decision-making. Representation only at subsidiary level would be rightly regarded by employees as unsatisfactory. It is true that practice in other European countries has varied; but generally there is provision for representation of the group's employees at holding company level. In Sweden one of the recognised failings of the 1973 law was that it did not provide for representation on both holding and subsidiary company boards so that employees were often excluded from the board on which many of the major decisions were taken. We learned that some companies had set up small holding companies with less than 100 employees so that they escaped from the legal requirements under the law about board level representation. These defects were remedied in the 1976 statute.

17. In the Netherlands, if there is representation on the group board then the subsidiaries are exempt. We recognise that one reason for this is to ensure that the parent company can control the subsidiaries and to this question we return below. While there may be special reasons for this solution in the context of the Dutch scheme for employee participation in the selection of members of supervisory boards, we do not think that subsidiaries should be exempt from our different proposals on board level representation. Wholesale exemption for subsidiaries would impose drastic limitations on the employees' ability to influence major decisions; and, while representation at the level of the group holding company board is essential for influence over strategic policy decisions, representation at the subsidiary level is also of importance if employees are to know that they can bring that influence to bear at the level of the company which is their immediate employer.

18. We therefore believe that our proposals should apply *both* to the board of the holding company in a group where the aggregate workforce employed in the United Kingdom by all companies in the group is 2,000 or more, *and* also to any subsidiary company in the group which by itself employs 2,000 or more full-time employees in the United Kingdom. The right of recognised unions to demand a ballot, discussed in Chapter 10, should apply independently to

each such subsidiary as well as to the holding company in the group. There would, however, be no right to representation on the board of a subsidiary which employs fewer than 2,000 employees in the United Kingdom; and in the remainder of this section references to 'a large subsidiary' should be understood to refer to a subsidiary company of which the number of United Kingdom employees is 2,000 or more.

19. It would be inconvenient always to require a separate ballot among the workforce of each large subsidiary as well as the group ballot. On the other hand, even where a large majority of employees in the group voted affirmatively, the employees of any one large subsidiary might vote negatively or fail to produce the required majority. We recommend therefore that in a group ballot the unions recognised on behalf of grades which constitute 20 per cent of the employees of a large subsidiary company should have the right to ask for a separate count of the votes cast by employees of that subsidiary company. Those votes should then both be included in the group total and be used as a test of employees' opinion equivalent to a separate ballot in that subsidiary.

20. In the case of the group holding company the appointment of the employee representatives to its board would be effected by the recognised trade nnions in the group as a whole in accordance with the proposals set out in Chapter 10. It has been said that this would present difficulty in, for example, the case of a conglomerate group where a large number of unions may be involved drawn from different industries. We recognise this problem, but we believe that our proposals are quite practicable in that situation. The machinery outlined in Chapter 10 for the settlement of disagreements between recognised trade unions could be adapted to the diverse structures of groups; and in particular we are confident that the Trades Union Congress would play an important role in this process. Moreover, trade union co-operation is continuously developing for the purposes of collective bargaining and consultation; and we foresee that our proposals on groups will provide a further incentive to the development of such inter-union co-operation in a group of companies.

21.[1] Representation on the board of the group holding company should, as for any other company, be on the basis of the proportions proposed in Chapter 9: equal numbers of shareholder and employee representatives and a smaller group of agreed co-opted directors. This would provide a framework within which a co-ordinated group policy for board level representation in subsidiaries of the group and, indeed, for participation at all other levels than the boards throughout the group, could be devised. The diversity of group structures makes it essential that the law should be flexible enough to suit the organisation of each economic enterprise. The aim should be for management and unions and the co-opted directors to decide how and where decisions are taken in the group and in consequence at what level employee representation is appropriate. We are confident that in practice many managements and unions will wish to get together as soon as possible after legislation is enacted, in many cases before it is passed, to devise or improve the policy for overall participation in the groups as a whole. Where participative structures already exist below board level, as in most large companies they do, discussions of them on the group holding

---

[1]Mr N S Wilson's Note of Dissent relates in part to the proposals contained in paragraphs 21 to 32 of this chapter.

company board can only lead to improvements; where there is a gap to be filled, the new constitution of the group holding company board will, we believe, act as a catalyst for the speedy formulation and implementation of better procedures throughout the group.

22. The reconstituted board of a holding company should regard as one of its priorities the review of machinery for employee participation in the group as a whole. Employee representation might be secured by agreement on the board of a subsidiary which itself employed less than 2,000 employees. Account could be taken both of the industrial relations substructure and of the position of a subsidiary in the group, eg whether it was wholly or partly owned, in devising such a group policy. We believe that there would be a role here for advice from or, eventually, a Code of Practice drawn up by the proposed Industrial Democracy Commission described in Chapter 12. The Commission could be of use both to management and unions in setting out the factors which in the light of experience generally should be considered in devising a policy on participation to suit the needs of the group's management and employees.

23. We now turn to the problem of *legal* control by the holding company of a subsidiary company. There are two main respects in which that control by a holding company would be affected by our proposals compared with the existing situation. First, employee representation on the reconstituted board of a large subsidiary on the lines proposed in Chapter 9 would take away the holding company's power of complete control over the appointment of all directors to the board of that subsidiary. The holding company, exercising its votes as shareholder by decision of its own board, would be able to appoint only the shareholder representatives. The rest of the large subsidiary's board would be made up of those appointed by the subsidiary's employees through trade union machinery and a smaller number of directors co-opted by agreement between the shareholder and employee representatives. This represents a transfer of power from the holding company to the subsidiary which might prevent the operation of group policy and threaten the continued existence of a group of companies as a viable economic unit. Second, the changes in company law which we think necessary to prevent a board being overruled by a shareholders' meeting on certain fundamental issues would restrict the right of the holding company to control the subsidiary. In Chapter 8 we proposed that certainly in companies with a reconstituted board, and possibly even in all companies, the power of the shareholders to initiate resolutions concerned with five areas (winding-up; amendments to memorandum or articles; changes in capital structure; dividends; and disposal of substantial assets) should be removed, leaving the board with a power of initiative in relation to such matters. If this were applied to groups, the dominant shareholder or (where it is wholly-owned) effectively the sole shareholder in the subsidiary—ie the holding company— would be deprived of its right as a shareholder to secure changes in a subsidiary's constitution or structure by way of resolution at the shareholders' meeting. It would be dependent upon the initiative of the subsidiary board.

24. Thus, of the proposed changes in company law, the two which create problems in regard to the economic viability of groups are the new composition of the reconstituted board and the restriction of the rights of shareholders. A variation in our recommendations in regard to the composition of the board of large subsidiaries provides, we believe, an answer to both problems.

25. We are convinced that the proportions of the elected shareholder representatives and of the employee representatives should, in the absence of agreement to the contrary, remain equal on the board of a large subsidiary in a group. Furthermore, we believe that the most satisfactory result on the board of such a subsidiary, as for any other large company in which a ballot has produced an affirmative vote, will be for the smaller third group of directors to be co-opted to the board by agreement between those two groups of representatives, one of which represents the holding or parent company. Even on the board of a large subsidiary, whether wholly or partly owned, such co-opted members would have an important role to play; in a large operating subsidiary, for example, which retained some independence in its activities from the holding company, such co-opted members might well bring to bear on the company's problems special knowledge and experience of great value, whilst at the same time being able to take account of the economic policies of the group as a whole. But we recognise that if the law went no further than this, then, even though the holding company could now command the composition of the shareholder representatives, it would be left without effective *legal* control over the policies of the subsidiary. In law, whatever happens in practice, the board of the large subsidiary company would be able, as reconstituted, to block the implementation of group policies, either for a long period or in some cases for ever, to the possible detriment of employees and shareholders in the group as a whole and of the community at large. In particular, technological changes and investment planning in the group could be obstructed by a subsidiary board since, even if the holding company's shareholder representatives on that board approved of them, the rest of the board might oppose them.

26. In consequence we consider that special provision must be made by the law to avert such a situation on the board of a large subsidiary and that the best way to do this is through the co-opted third group of directors. We repeat that we would wish to see those directors co-opted by agreement between the employee representatives and the holding company's shareholder representatives wherever possible; and the law should provide for this to be the primary and preferred method of their appointment. Where, however, agreement on the co-option of some or all of those directors is impossible to achieve within a given period between the other two groups of representatives on the board, we propose that, in the interests of group viability, the holding company should in the last resort have the power to appoint them. This power should extend also to the removal of existing directors, however appointed, and the appointment of new ones in their place.

27. Such appointments would of course be made by the board of the holding company and the representatives of the employees in the *group* would sit on the group holding company board where it had been reconstituted following an affirmative ballot of the workforce in the group. What appears, therefore, at first sight to be a severe modification in regard to subsidiary boards of our proposals concerning proportions of directors would not, we think, in practice lead to such a major difference. First, any sensible management and responsible directors representing the holding company, as dominant shareholder, would, we are sure, normally wish to secure agreement with the employee representatives of the subsidiary on the directors to be co-opted on to the board of the subsidiary company. The pressures to reach genuine agreement with the employee

representatives would be real. It is true, of course, that the knowledge that the holding company could in the last resort appoint the third group of directors to their subsidiary board would not be absent from the minds of the employee representatives when considering the nominations made by the shareholder representatives appointed by that holding company. That leads to a second consideration already mentioned, namely the composition of the board of the holding company itself. Decisions about appointment of the holding company's shareholder representatives on the board of the large subsidiary will be taken by the board of the holding company. Where the group workforce has balloted in favour the board of the group holding company will enjoy effective employee representation along the lines proposed in Chapter 9, so that it will speak not with the voice of the holding company's shareholders or management but with the voice of its reconstituted board as a whole.

28. A complication arises in the case of sub-subsidiaries. We take a sub-subsidiary company which employs 2,000 or more employees and which is part of a pyramid group of companies. The company which holds the majority of its equity shares is a subsidiary of the group holding company, and for convenience we refer to that company as the 'intermediate' company. If an affirmative ballot leads to the reconstitution of the board of the sub-subsidiary, the shareholder representatives on its board will be appointed by the inter-mediate company. But, if agreement between employee and shareholder representatives on the sub-subsidiary board proves impossible, which company is to have the residual power to appoint the third group of directors to that board: the group holding company or the intermediate company? We recom-mend that the ultimate group holding company which controls group policy should have that power.

29. We appreciate that the shareholder in the sub-subsidiary will not be the group holding company but the intermediate company. Nonetheless the group holding company can ultimately control the composition of the board of the intermediate company (either by controlling the appointment of all directors, as is currently the case, or, where the board of the intermediate company is reconstituted, by exercising if necessary its residual power of appointment of the third group of directors as proposed above). Even where the intermediate company is allowed considerable independence in running its affairs, in the last resort real power in the group will vest in the group holding company. We believe that company law should ascribe the legal power to appoint the third group of directors on the sub-subsidiary's board to the group holding com-pany's board which is where real power resides. (The name of the ultimate group holding company would appear both in the sub-subsidiary's accounts and, as we explain below, in the 'instrument of control' registered with the Registrar of Companies.) Furthermore, we are confirmed in this conclusion by the fact that, in the example we have taken, it will always be possible to hold a group ballot and reconstitute the group holding company's board with employee representatives, since by hypothesis the group workforce will be 2,000 or more whereas the intermediate company may well be a subsidiary with fewer than 2,000 employees; in that event no right to employee representation on its board can arise. The protection of the employees' interests in effective representation in the group requires that this residual power should reside in a board which itself may be reconstituted as a result of an affirmative ballot.

30. We think it is useful to draw an analogy in the case of groups between the residual power which we would give to the group holding company to appoint the third group of directors to subsidiary or sub-subsidiary boards, and the functions of the Industrial Democracy Commission described in Chapter 12 to make such appointments. The role of the Commission in groups would be restricted to the power in the last resort to appoint the third group of directors to the board of a reconstituted holding company. For boards of subsidiaries and of sub-subsidiaries the group holding company board itself would fulfil that role. We think this analogy in its role should be extended; the group holding company should be allowed to appoint only the same number of the third group of directors as the Commission would have been able to appoint under the statutory fall-back procedure described in Chapter 9. The fact, however, that the group board is to have this role strengthens our belief that the power should be vested in the board at the apex of the group pyramid on which employee representation can eventually be claimed. It has been argued that some existing boards of intermediate subsidiaries which are allowed independence in their affairs by the group holding company would be affronted at seeing the board of the group holding company appointing directors to 'their' subsidiaries (the sub-subsidiaries in the group). But even if that were so in some cases, it remains true that even if the group holding company did not have this legal power to appoint directly, it could still exercise it indirectly down the line through its control of the composition of the boards of those intermediate companies. On balance, therefore, we prefer the solution of ascribing the exceptional residual power over appointments of the third group of directors on both subsidiaries *and* sub-subsidiaries in the group directly to the board of the ultimate holding company of the United Kingdom group.

31. We have also considered whether this residual power to appoint the third group of directors on the board of a large subsidiary or large sub-subsidiary, after it has been found that agreement in their co-option cannot be reached, should be limited to group holding companies of which the board has already been reconstituted to include employee representatives of the group workforce and a co-opted third group of directors. It can be argued that such a limitation of the residual power is required in order adequately to protect the interests of the employees. But on balance we have decided that no such limitation should be introduced; the need for effective co-ordination of group policies is just as great whether or not the holding company has a reconstituted board. Moreover, where the recognised trade unions have secured representation for employees on the board of the large subsidiary or sub-subsidiary, they will in principle be able to require a group ballot and achieve representation on the group holding company board after an affirmative vote. We recognise that in some groups—especially conglomerates—it may be more difficult for the unions to secure a favourable vote in a ballot among the diverse workforce of the group than among the workforce of one large subsidiary. But we believe that in many groups employee representation will be secured at group level together with, or not long after, representation on subsidiaries, and the effective representation of employees on the group holding board will in practice be the better long-term answer to this problem than the exclusion by law of holding companies which have no employee representatives from the exercise of the residual power. It is, however, to be remembered that in this section we are discussing groups of

137

United Kingdom companies; and it will be for consideration below whether the same conclusion can be reached when a multinational group is under discussion, where the ultimate holding company is situated abroad.

32. If the solution outlined above were adopted in regard to the composition of the boards of subsidiaries, we believe that our other recommendations on company law need not be modified in relation to groups. The rights of the holding company as shareholder in the subsidiary (or of the intermediate company in a sub-subsidiary) would be limited by our proposals in Chapter 8 —certainly if the board of the latter company were reconstituted; possibly even if it were not. Those limitations would confine the power of initiative to call a shareholders' meeting and move resolutions on the five matters there set out (winding-up; amendments to memorandum or articles; changes in capital structure; dividends; and disposal of substantial assets) to the board of the subsidiary (or sub-subsidiary). But the composition of the relevant boards would, in the last resort, now be sufficiently within the control of the holding company to ensure that group policy was not thwarted by a failure of the subsidiary board to introduce any such resolution. In the light of this residual power to control composition we do not recommend any further modification of our earlier proposals on shareholders' powers. Indeed, in the case of a large, partly-owned subsidiary with a reconstituted board, we think it wrong that there should be a right for minority shareholders to initiate resolutions on such matters and we dislike the prospect of conferring a special right on a controlling shareholder. Accordingly, we consider that that initiative should rest with the board of its subsidiary.

33. We considered a further problem. It arises where the boards of a holding company and of a large subsidiary company have both been reconstituted on a 2X + Y basis. The board of the holding company has the power to appoint the shareholders' representatives on the subsidiary board. It might be argued that, if the law made no further provision, the board of the subsidiary might eventually come to contain a majority of directors who in practice were representatives of employees. It is said that this could occur in the following way: if the employee representatives on the holding company board secured the agreement of the majority of the co-opted directors on that board they might ensure that one or more of the persons appointed to the board of the subsidiary as representatives of the shareholder (ie the holding company) would in reality represent the employees. For example, it is said that the holding company's employee representatives might persuade the co-opted directors that the holding company should appoint one of their own number to be a 'shareholder representative' on the subsidiary board. Such a person might then vote with the employee representatives on the subsidiary board and form with them a majority to co-opt directors to the subsidiary board who were really acceptable to employees' interests only. This would produce the result that the subsidiary board contained in practice a majority of directors who were effectively representatives of employees, even though at least one of them posed as a holding company's 'shareholder representative'.

34. We regard any such sequence of events as highly unlikely; and we are confident that employee representatives on a holding company board would not normally consider acting in this way or, if they did, that the co-opted directors

on that board would not agree to their plan. Even so, we do not wish our proposals to be open to this criticism, however theoretical it may be. For it is no part of our intention to make recommendations which could possibly produce such a result.

35. In consequence, we make the following recommendation to meet this eventuality. Where a holding company board resolves upon the names of persons to be appointed as its shareholder representatives on the board of a subsidiary, such a resolution should not be valid unless it is passed with the affirmative votes of a majority of the shareholder representatives on that holding company board. Thus, if the reconstituted board of a holding company were composed as five, five and three, appointments to the board of a subsidiary company would require the votes of seven directors, of which at least three would need to be votes cast by shareholder representatives. The same solution should be applied to the board of a sub-subsidiary; in that case the appointment of shareholder representatives to the sub-subsidiary board would be validly made by the board of the intermediate subsidiary company (its dominant shareholder) only if the majority of shareholder representatives on the intermediate company's board had voted for these appointees.

36. We are reluctant to make proposals which involve inquiry inside the boardroom about how particular directors voted on a given occasion. We believe that boards will continue to operate largely by consensus and, as we have explained in a previous chapter, we anticipate that block voting will be rare. Nevertheless, on this specific question of a holding company's appointments of shareholder representatives to the boards of its subsidiaries we consider that the law should make an exceptional provision of the kind described above, in order to avoid even the possibility that the apparent balance of the $2X + Y$ formula should conceal a majority of persons representing employees.

37. The need, however, to introduce special provisions in favour of holding companies in United Kingdom groups has led us to reconsider the definition of 'holding' and 'subsidiary' company as now set out in Section 154 (1) of the Companies Act 1948. We have concluded that this definition will not be satisfactory in the new context for company law created by our proposals. This is particularly the case in regard to a take-over by acquisition of shares of a company which itself has a reconstituted board.

38. We take as an illustration of the problem an independent company of which the board has been reconstituted, with equal numbers of shareholder and employee representatives and an agreed third group of co-opted directors, and in which industrial relations and productivity have improved consequent upon the increased participation of workpeople in its affairs. A second company, contrary to the wishes and recommendations of the independent company's board, acquires a majority holding in the latter's shares. If the independent company automatically becomes a 'subsidiary' of the second company (as it would if the definition in Section 154 (1) remained unchanged) the second company would be able not only to replace the shareholder representatives on its board but also, by virtue of the proposal above for a residual power for holding companies, control the appointment of its co-opted directors. A

transaction on the stock market would thereby destroy what employees in the hitherto independent company had come to regard as effective employee representation on their company's board.

39. We are convinced that, whereas our proposals in earlier paragraphs are necessary to provide for the continuance of group enterprise, the results described in the previous paragraph should not be permitted. They could deal a severe blow to the new confidence in management enjoyed by the employees of the acquired company and lead to the destruction of the fruits of the new participative structures and a loss of morale also on the part of that company's management. Even if the second company in our example had a reconstituted board with employee representatives on it, we still consider that the purchase of the majority of the shares of the independent company is not by itself sufficient justification for such a change in the residual power over the hitherto independent company's affairs.

40. We believe, therefore, that the existing definition of 'subsidiary' company should be altered. In order to provide the necessary protection for reconstituted boards, for employees' interests as represented upon them and for management which has successfully adapted itself to what may well be a new style of management, we think that the definition of the subsidiary company should include an additional requirement, namely that the *board* of one company should have executed a document acknowledging the fact of control by another company. This document we have come to call an 'instrument of control'. Such devices are known to other legal systems; in the Federal Republic of Germany company law knows of a 'contract of control' by which one company becomes the subsidiary of another, and certain proposals of the EEC Commission relating to groups have affinities with the West German structure. The 'instrument of control' which we suggest would be a great deal simpler than the German 'contract of control', though there is some analogy between the two, and we are confident that our proposals would not clash with further developments that may come at the European level.

41. The 'subsidiary company' would in future be defined as one in which another company either (i) was a shareholder and controlled the composition of its board of directors or (ii) held more than half in nominal value of its equity share capital, *and* which, in either case, had executed and registered an instrument of acknowledgement of control by that other company. In the case of sub-subsidiaries the instrument would name the ultimate group holding company as well as the intermediate, or immediate holding, company.

42. The instrument acknowledging control would be registered as a public document with the Registrar of Companies. It need be no more than a brief statement setting out the acknowledgement of control; a model instrument in that form which a company could adopt should be set out as a schedule to the new statute. But the parties should be able to add to the brief model instrument; and in particular, guarantees or undertakings made by the offeror company in the take-over should, if incorporated in the instrument, have legally binding force. The instrument would be registered under the names of both holding and

subsidiary companies. The instrument would cease to have effect when the Registrar removed it from the companies' register; this he would do if the holding company either ceased to control the composition of the subsidiary's board or ceased to hold more than half of its shares, or if both companies agreed that the instrument should be rescinded. Both companies would be under a duty to notify the Registrar of any of these events.

43. To safeguard existing groups of companies, the statute should provide that a company which is a subsidiary under the current definition in Section 154(1) at a given date (possibly the date of the new Act coming into effect) is deemed to have executed an instrument of control—in its model form unless the company registers an amended version—in respect of its existing holding company. The new definition would thus have no harmful effect on existing groups. But new take-overs would be affected. The board of a company for whose shares a bid is successfully made would have the chance to negotiate with the offeror company. Even if the latter company replaced the shareholder representatives on the offeree company's reconstituted board with its own appointees, the employee representatives and the co-opted directors would still have the opportunity to demand that certain conditions be met before the board agreed to execute the instrument which would make that company the other's subsidiary in law (for example, an undertaking as to asset-stripping, or a statement about future employment prospects). If no such instrument were negotiated, it is true that a successful offeror company might try to assert its will by ensuring that its shareholder representatives on the board did not agree to suitable replacements for the existing co-opted directors before their tenure of office ended; but in such a case the Commission could be relied upon in the last resort to reappoint them or to replace them with suitable persons. In practice we envisage such negotiations between the two boards accompanying or preceding the take-over bid; and it is most likely that an offeror company would not make a bid unconditional unless it could be sure that the offeree company's board was willing to execute an instrument of control in agreed terms. We recognise that certain adjustments of stock market practice would be required in the face of this new definition of 'subsidiary'; but we are convinced that effective employee representation on company boards will need the protection of such an instrument in the face of new share take-overs. Company take-overs cannot expect to be unaffected by these new developments.

44. Even if our recommendations on proportions of employee representatives were not followed and employees were in a clear minority on the subsidiary board as against the shareholder representatives, we are all agreed that, if the benefits of participation are not to be at risk of destruction by share transactions, the introduction of an instrument of control would still be needed. Further, we propose that the new definition should be introduced for all companies. It would, first, be inconvenient and confusing for company law to have two definitions of 'subsidiary' according to whether a company had a reconstituted board or not. Second, we see advantages in the proposal from the point of view of management; the managers in an offeree company would, we believe, welcome the opportunity for their board to be able to negotiate terms with the new corporate dominant shareholder before their company became its subsidiary and before it acquired the extended legal powers of a holding company.

The voice of the new dominant shareholder would no doubt be persuasive in such negotiations; but undertakings of importance to the workforce and to the management of the offeree company might well be incorporated into the instrument of control. It has been suggested that subsequently the holding company could, by its residual control of the new subsidiary's board, ensure that such undertakings would be rescinded by 'agreement' between the companies; but while there would no doubt be a risk that this might happen, and it would be legally possible, in practice we believe that the opposition to such rescission by the employee representatives, and perhaps by some co-opted directors, on the subsidiary's board would be a serious inhibition against such conduct.

45. The other areas of company law in which the definition of 'subsidiary' is of major importance relate to group accounts; the ownership of shares; the restriction upon financial assistance for purchase of a company's own shares; disqualification of auditors; Department of Trade inspectors; prohibition of loans to directors; the duty to disclose directors' shareholdings and, probably, in future the expected legislation on insider trading. Of these areas we believe that the new definition would create difficulties only in respect of the last two where it might be necessary to extend a director's duties to disclose shareholdings and not to trade in shares to a sphere of 'associated' companies of wider scope than the newly defined holding and subsidiary companies.

46. Finally, we are convinced that our general consideration of groups has strengthened the case for the reconstituted unitary board as against the introduction of supervisory boards and management boards into company law in the United Kingdom. On the one hand, if the holding company and each large subsidiary or sub-subsidiary had to have its own supervisory board, the formal two-tier solution would involve much greater legal complexity. Rules would have to be laid down (as in West Germany), for example, about the permissibility of cross-membership between the various boards (eg could a member of one company's management board be on another's supervisory board?); and the definition of each board's powers would be intricate. On the other hand, if a group is to have only one supervisory board at the level of the ultimate holding company, the employee representatives would operate at a level quite remote from the employees in subsidiaries and sub-subsidiaries and employee representation would become quite ineffective. Our conclusion in Chapter 8 that the modified unitary board is the right way forward for company law in the United Kingdom is particularly confirmed by the problems which arise in connection with groups of companies.

Multinationals

47. Our proposals so far have been concerned with groups of companies, all members of which are incorporated under United Kingdom law. Multinational groups, where part of the enterprise is overseas, pose additional problems. Two different types of multinational enterprise may be distinguished for our purposes: the British-based multinational where the ultimate holding company is incorporated under United Kingdom law but part of the group's operations is carried out by subsidiaries overseas; and the foreign-based multinational where one or more of its subsidiaries are incorporated under

United Kingdom law (or operations are carried on in the United Kingdom through an unincorporated branch) and the ultimate holding company is overseas. As we saw in Chapter 2, both are important to the British economy, and our proposals must therefore take careful account of the special problems which they present.

Multinationals with parent companies incorporated in the United Kingdom

48. The problem of the British-based multinational centres on the position of its overseas employees. It has been said to us that it would be unjust for representatives of a group's British employees to sit on a board which takes decisions affecting the unrepresented employees of the company's overseas subsidiaries. Some have argued that we should consider excluding from our proposals those enterprises which have a majority of employees overseas, in order to avoid the representatives of the minority imposing their will on the unrepresented majority.

49. Of the various European systems, only the Dutch system (and to some extent the Norwegian system) makes a special provision for home-based multi-nationals. The holding company is exempt from the provisions of the law if the majority of the group's employees work abroad. However, because the holding company is exempt, the Dutch subsidiaries become eligible for employee participation in the selection of the members of the supervisory board, and there are further special provisions to ensure that the holding company can control the operations of its subsidiary. No other country exempts its multinational companies in this way, and no-one we met in West Germany or Sweden suggested that there should be exemption. It was generally accepted that if the part of the group incorporated in the home country employed the requisite number of employees, then it should be subject to the national law.

50. It would clearly be unjust to exclude some employees in the United Kingdom from representation at board level just because they worked in a group which had employees overseas. If an enterprise employs as many as 2,000 people in the United Kingdom, then its operations here are considerable; and the United Kingdom employees should have the right to representation. The problem would not be solved by requiring British multinationals to have one board where all strategic decisions affecting United Kingdom employees were taken and another board responsible for overseas interests. The group must have a top board with ultimate responsibility for allocation of resources on a world-wide basis, and that board's decisions will affect all employees. Representatives of the United Kingdom employees must therefore have the right to be involved in strategic decisions affecting the whole group: in questions such as whether the group's operations should be expanded at home or overseas or how resources should be allocated amongst all subsidiaries in the group. We saw in Chapter 2 that at least 51 per cent of the enterprises in *The Times 1000* which employed 2,000 or more people in the United Kingdom also have some employees overseas; to exclude half of the largest enterprises in the country would make nonsense of our proposals. Even if the exclusion were confined (as in the Netherlands) to home-based multinational enterprises the majority of whose employees are overseas, we have identified 35 groups (there are probably

143

more) which fulfil this condition. The dividing line is, in our view, an artificial one, and we could not recommend the disfranchisement of the United Kingdom employees of this number of enterprises.

51. We recognise that it is an imperfect system that leaves unrepresented a proportion of employees in a group, particularly when they are in a majority. But in the absence of international action on this question it is an imperfection which we can do little or nothing to remedy unilaterally. It would be impractical for United Kingdom law to attempt to require the representation of employees living in another country under another legal system on the main board of a British-based enterprise. Boards of holding companies will, however, if our recommendation in Chapter 8 is accepted, be entitled to take into account the interests of employees of subsidiary companies, including overseas subsidiaries. We should expect that the reconstituted board of a British-based multinational, including representatives of the United Kingdom employees, will be more interested than at least some existing boards in the effects of policy decisions on the overseas employees of the group, in the ways in which they are collectively represented and their views canvassed, in their terms and conditions of employment and so on. Such concern may lead to the establishment (or in a few cases the strengthening) of direct links across national frontiers between trade union representatives in different units within the group. Indeed, proposals which may eventually enable this problem to be dealt with on a European basis are already under discussion within the EEC in the context of the proposed law on groups discussed in the EEC Green Paper[1]. We understand that European trade unions, through the European Trades Union Confederation have made the specific recommendation that, where trade unions concerned in the parent company of a group of companies based in the EEC have taken advantage of the opportunity of employee representation on the board, representatives of other employees in this group in other EEC countries should be entitled to share the right of representation on the holding company board. This would appear to be a logical development at European level in the longer term. In the meantime and in other parts of the world than in Europe, we believe that reconstituted boards of directors of British-based multinationals, conscious of the inherent (though inevitable) imperfection in our proposals, may regard the absence of any legal provision for representation of overseas employees as a problem for which practical solutions should be sought, rather than as an opportunity or invitation to ignore the interests of one part—often a large part—of the group's workforce.

Foreign-based multinationals

52. Where the multinational is based abroad and the British company is a subsidiary of a foreign holding company, the problem is to ensure some form of meaningful representation on the subsidiary board. It is possible, of course, providing that the subsidiary is incorporated under United Kingdom law, to require employee representation on its board if it employs 2,000 or more people. In order to ensure the application of the law to all large enterprises in this country controlled by foreign-owned companies, we must consider that

[1]EEC Commission, *op cit*, Appendix A.

such enterprises may not always be subsidiary companies. At present some foreign companies operate through branches in the United Kingdom, which are not incorporated under the Companies Acts. Though these are now few in number, more foreign companies might use this tactic if it provided a way of avoiding employee representation on the board, and if such avoidance seemed to them desirable. The simplest way of dealing with this possibility might be to require that any enterprise employing 2,000 or more people in this country be incorporated under United Kingdom company law. But there could be valid reasons for operating as an unincorporated branch, and if the employees of the branch did not wish to be represented on the board (or its equivalent body, if any), then it would appear pointless to make incorporation mandatory. A more flexible solution would be to specify that the right to request a ballot should belong to recognised and independent trade unions in any foreign-controlled enterprise, whether or not incorporated, employing 2,000 or more people in the United Kingdom, and that in the event of an affirmative decision the enterprise should be incorporated under United Kingdom law, or organised on some other mutually agreed basis that provided satisfactory representation of the employees on a body equivalent to the board of a United Kingdom subsidiary company.

53. The most difficult question concerning foreign-based multinationals is the relationship between the United Kingdom subsidiary board and the overseas parent. This relationship is not the same as that between a subsidiary company board and its United Kingdom parent, since the board of the latter would be subject to our proposals, and might therefore be reconstituted to include employee representation. The board of a foreign parent company could never be so composed under any provision of United Kingdom law. Therefore, the provisions for ultimate control of subsidiaries by the top board of the group, described earlier in this chapter, may not be appropriate for groups in which the ultimate holding company is overseas and whose board includes no employee representatives.

54. The crucial issue is the residual power of the parent to appoint the third group of directors, in the event of failure by the two other groups on the board to agree on co-option. It is important to emphasise the residual nature of this power. The boards of large subsidiaries in the United Kingdom whose workforce had balloted for representation would be reconstituted on the basis of equality between employees and shareholders, with co-option of the third group of directors. This would normally cause no serious problems, in our view, since the objectives of the two groups would be the same, namely to secure an able and balanced board that would successfully direct the company's future development, to the benefit of all. But the residual power of the ultimate holding company's board to appoint the third group would be a known fact. It would also be known, in the case of a British-based group, that the top board either already included employee representatives, on a basis of equality, or at least was capable of being reconstituted on that basis, provided trade unions in the group as a whole could co-operate with each other and mobilise the opinion of the whole workforce in support of such a move. This situation would, we believe, make the dilution of the principle of equality, inherent in the crucial residual power, generally acceptable to the employee representatives

on the subsidiary company's board. But if that power lay with a foreign parent it might appear to the British employee representatives that the formula of the three parts of the board did not really provide equality at all; that the overseas owners of the group had a clear power to appoint a majority of the board; and that attempts to co-opt an agreed third group of directors might be perfunctory on the part of the shareholder representatives. Even if this were not so, and the third group were successfully co-opted to both other groups' satisfaction, it would be generally realised that the overseas parent retained ultimate control, that group policy in relation to the British subsidiary might change over time, and that policies proposed from the overseas headquarters, even if opposed by the employee representatives and co-opted directors could always be enforced by a threat to remove and replace the co-opted directors.

55. The proper analogy to consider, therefore, may be between two British enterprises, one of which is owned by a number of predominantly British shareholders, the other by a single foreign shareholder. The arrangements for employee participation in the two types of enterprise should be the same, it might be argued, since to make any other arrangement would be to discriminate against the employees of the foreign-owned company and in favour of the foreign shareholder, who would have a greater degree of control than the shareholders of the British group. At a time when there is concern in many quarters about the power of multinationals and the need to achieve more control over their activities by the national governments of the countries where they operate, it might be wrong for new legislation on industrial democracy to discriminate by excluding them. On a board with equal representation, the sole or dominant shareholder, whether an individual or a corporation, may in any case be able to exercise more effective control than an amorphous group of shareholders, since he can formulate specific plans and present them coherently, whereas a group of shareholders must rely on its representatives to evolve policy and can develop no detailed plans of its own. The sole or dominant shareholder (in the case we are discussing, a foreign enterprise) should therefore have no grounds for complaint about sharing power with the employees in the enterprise on a basis of equality, or about leaving the ultimate power to appoint the third group of directors, in the case of deadlock, to the independent Commission.

56. Moreover, the British employees of foreign multinationals already feel at a distinct disadvantage, compared to employees of British groups, in the sense of their ability to influence overall company policy. They will be looking to the recommendations of this Committee and to subsequent legislation to provide more effective mechanisms for the expression of their interests in policy-making, on an equal basis with the representatives of capital. To provide what could be seen as one law for British-based groups, and another, more favourable to the owners, for foreign-based multinationals, might be to negate the hopes of a particularly important group of employees.

57. Against these concerns we must attempt to balance the argument that business is international, and that the correct analogy is not between two British enterprises which happen to have different kinds of shareholder, but between two groups of companies, one of which is based here and the other overseas. The relationship between the holding company and the board of the subsidiary

146

must, it is claimed, be the same for both of them, since the need for groups to function as centrally controlled economic entities is the same, wherever their headquarters may be. To grant to a subsidiary company's board an exceptional and indeed decisive degree of independence from its parent, simply because that parent is foreign, would be to discriminate against foreign capital. This would arguably involve a degree of interference with the control of subsidiary companies which we would not propose for subsidiaries of British groups. If foreign governments were to attempt to provide such independence for the subsidiaries of British-based multinationals in their countries, we should have cause to complain. Therefore, this line of argument concludes, the proposal is not only inequitable but would disturb foreign governments and foreign capital, and have a deleterious effect on inward investment, which plays an important part in the economy of the United Kingdom.

58. Finally, it may be claimed that the application of equal employee and shareholder representation in its pure form to the boards of United Kingdom subsidiaries of foreign-based groups would be seen as an attempt to impose through the medium of national law an element of control over multinationals, which by their nature can only effectively be controlled by international means. It would not act as a control, therefore, but merely as a deterrent to potential investors in the United Kingdom.

59. We have summarised the arguments for two possible solutions to this problem, because we feel that they are both strong, and to some extent convincing. We believe that a middle way should be found. In normal circumstances the $2X + Y$ formula should apply to the boards of United Kingdom subsidiaries of foreign parents and we emphasise again our belief that difficulties in reaching agreement on co-option of the third group will be rare. Where, however, no agreement can be reached about the Y directors we believe a distinction must be drawn between the immediate United Kingdom subsidiary of the foreign parent and United Kingdom sub-subsidiaries in the group. With regard to the immediate United Kingdom subsidiary (ie the top United Kingdom company in the pyramid) the procedure for a ballot and reconstitution of the board should be initially the same as in a top United Kingdom holding company. The ballot could, where the subsidiary itself employs 2,000 or more, be a ballot of its workforce; otherwise it would be a ballot of the United Kingdom group workforce that amounts to 2,000 or more. After the two equal groups of prospective directors are selected, if they cannot agree upon the third group of directors to be co-opted, either of the two groups of prospective directors may approach the Industrial Democracy Commission and if conciliation does not produce an agreed solution, the ultimate appointment of the third group of directors should be made by the Commission. But before that is done we propose that a further step should be taken. In the case of the top United Kingdom subsidiary of a foreign parent, the Commission should be obliged to ascertain the wishes of the foreign parent and to consult the Secretary of State for Industry, and should be statutorily obliged to take those views into account before reaching its decision. That decision would be legally binding and the person or persons appointed would form part of, or all the third group of directors of the top United Kingdom subsidiary company just as in the case for resolution of deadlock by the Commission in United Kingdom companies.

The difference lies simply in the obligation to consult and take into account the views of the foreign parent and the British Government.

60. This solution would mean that the board of the top United Kingdom subsidiary company of a foreign parent could, with a modified procedure, be reconstituted on the basis of a genuine $2X + Y$ formula. It therefore seems appropriate to give to the board of that top United Kingdom subsidiary the residual power to appoint the third group of directors on the reconstituted boards of large sub-subsidiaries further down the pyramid in the group. It would be inappropriate to involve the Commission and the Government in the fall-back procedure for appointing the third group of directors on all the large sub-subsidiaries; and to give the residual power to the foreign parent alone would raise all the problems and objections rehearsed above. We propose therefore, that the powers of the Commission to appoint Y directors in consultation with the foreign parent and the British Government should apply to an immediate or top United Kingdom subsidiary of a foreign parent; and that subsidiary should have the exceptional residual power to control the Y seats on the boards of large United Kingdom sub-subsidiaries below it.

61. The reason for this proposal is that we envisage the possibility of a foreign parent company claiming the same residual rights to appoint the third group of directors on the board of a subsidiary as a British holding company would possess and the further possibility that to allow it to do so might be in the national interest. But it would not necessarily be so, and to allow foreign-based multinationals to exercise that residual right in any circumstances that suited them would be an invitation to them to use the reality or the threat of that power to secure effective majority control of the board and thereby undermine the equal partnership between capital and labour which is the foundation of industrial democracy as we see it. The judgment as to where the national interest lies should rest with an independent body, and since the problem would relate to the operation of the legislation which we propose, it would be natural for the Industrial Democracy Commission to undertake this task. But the political and economic implications of particular cases might be such that the Government of the day should be involved in the decision, and it is for that reason that we stipulate consultation with the Secretary of State for Industry.

62. An examination of how the procedure would operate in practice should further clarify the reasons for the proposal. It should also show how foreign holding companies and the directors of their United Kingdom subsidiaries are likely to behave, in the light of what might happen if failure to agree at the level of the United Kingdom board led to recourse to the legal procedure. Failure to agree on the co-opted directors could occur either during the process of reconstitution of the board following an affirmative ballot, or later, when a co-opted director retired from the board and his re-election or the election of a replacement became due. The procedure of referral to the Commission would be the same, whether failure to agree was preventing the new board from becoming legally constituted in the first place, or whether the shareholder representatives were pressing for the removal of the co-opted directors in order to replace them with their own nominees and thereby achieve a majority of votes on the board.

63. Two examples may be useful. First, suppose that a foreign parent company, opposed to the concept of equal representation of shareholders and employees, decides deliberately to veto all nominations for the third group of directors, except their own, who would in effect be additional shareholder representatives. The prospective employee directors may then refer the matter to the Commission, who would ascertain the views of the parent company and of the Government (as well as the views of the prospective employee representatives) before making a binding decision. It may be supposed that the Commission would be strongly influenced by the parent company's refusal to give a real $2X + Y$ board even a chance to prove itself. The Government might believe that the damage which the foreign parent company might inflict on the economy, if the decision went against it, would not be so severe that it should be permitted to impose a majority of its nominees on the board, without at least attempting to operate within the statutory system. The Commission might then advise the parent company that the decision was likely to be unfavourable, and even at that late stage agreement on the co-opted directors might be reached; or, if the parent company remained obdurate, the Commission would be obliged to exercise its ultimate power of nominating to the board people who were genuinely independent of either side in the dispute, and willing to serve.

64. Second, suppose that a reconstituted board has been operating successfully for some time in the top United Kingdom subsidiary, and the foreign parent decides that a certain course of action (for instance, a modernisation scheme involving redundancies) is necessary, but the employee representatives and a majority of the co-opted directors oppose the scheme. The parent informs the Commission of its desire to remove and replace the co-opted directors, and explains its reasons. The Government, consulted either formally or informally, might (or might not) conclude that the majority on the board were being unreasonable in their opposition, and that the damage to the economy that would result from preventing the parent company from implementing its proposal would be severe. Accordingly, the majority on the board might be advised that the decision was likely to be unfavourable to them, and once again it might be possible to resolve the dispute without going to the extreme length of permitting the foreign holding company to remove and replace the co-opted directors. That last eventuality would, however, be the final sanction.

65. It may be argued that the involvement of Government in what are essentially business decisions is undesirable. We think that this is an unrealistic view of the interdependence of labour, capital and Government in a modern industrial state. We believe that the involvement of Government in specific disputes about the membership of boards of top United Kingdom subsidiaries of foreign-based multinationals will be rare, but we regard it as the most appropriate means of resolving the difficulties that could conceivably occur where the balance of power between the various elements involved must be extremely delicate, and where the question of national interest should be the decisive factor.

66. A question has been raised concerning the relationship of these proposals for equal employee representation on the boards of foreign controlled subsidiaries in the United Kingdom and the international obligations of the British

149

Government. In this connection we considered the OECD Declaration and Guidelines on Multinational Enterprises of 21 June 1976 to which the Government has a commitment[1], and the European Economic Community Treaty. The OECD Declaration records that member countries should accord to foreign controlled enterprises,

' . . . treatment under their laws, regulations and administrative practices consistent with international law and no less favourable than that accorded in like situations to domestic enterprises . . .'[2]

The Guidelines in the section on *Employment and Industrial Relations* state that multinational enterprises should,

' . . . within the framework of law, regulations and prevailing labour relations and employment practices, in each of the countries in which they operate, . . .

(4) observe standards of employment and industrial relations not less favourable than those observed by comparable employers in the host country'[3].

Our view is that our proposals do not involve less favourable treatment for foreign controlled enterprises and are a practical way of ensuring that they observe standards in industrial relations parallel to those that would be observed by British companies.

67. There are also obligations under the EEC Treaty not to introduce new restrictions on the right of establishment (Article 53) and to observe the right of those in other member states,

'to engage in and carry on non-wage earning activities, to set up and manage undertakings and, in particular, firms and companies . . . under the conditions laid down for its own nationals by the law of the country where such establishment is effected . . . ' (Article 52).

Our proposals involve no restriction on the right of establishment and are devised to ensure that the conditions for carrying on large undertakings are parallel for British companies and for foreign controlled companies. To enable foreign controlled enterprises to avoid effective employee representation on the boards of their British subsidiaries would indeed make the conditions unequal as between British companies and foreign controlled companies operating in the United Kingdom.

---

[1] *International Investment: Guidelines for Multinational Enterprises.* Cmnd 6525 (HMSO 1976).
[2] *ibid,* page 1.
[3] *ibid,* pages 7 and 8.

CHAPTER 12

Two consequential proposals: an Industrial Democracy Commission and the provision of training

1. In this chapter we consider some questions of great importance to the success of employee representation on boards. We discuss the need for an independent industrial democracy commission to provide advice and information on detailed matters of implementation which are inappropriate for treatment in statute, to conciliate where parties are in dispute about how board level representation should be introduced and, in the last resort, to impose a binding solution. This has been referred to in previous chapters as the Industrial Democracy Commission. Here we review the functions of such a Commission and suggest how it might be composed and what its relationship to other bodies should be. We then look at the important question of the education and training needs that will arise from the introduction of employee representation on company boards and at how these needs may be met.

2. But the first aspect of implementation on which we wish to lay emphasis is the need for the provisions and implications of the new legislation to be clearly understood by a very large number of people. The legislation will of necessity be complex, and the language of legislation is unfortunately all too often impenetrable except by experts. Although we believe that most people will accept the basic concept that enterprises in the the private sector should be jointly run by those who have a financial stake in them and those who work in them, the fact is that present law and practice are founded on entirely different principles. We mentioned in Chapter 2 that over seven million employees are liable to be affected by our proposals: with their families, they account for a substantial proportion of the population; and the indirect effects of our proposals will obviously not be confined to them. For all these reasons, we recommend that the Government and other interested parties give special and serious consideration to the problems of explaining the meaning of the legislation. We suggest that something considerably more wide-ranging than the normal means of publicising new laws will be needed.

3. Our proposals straddle the already blurred dividing line between company and industrial relations law. This is particularly important in the context of enforcement and sanctions, where quite different traditions have developed. In company law, the practice is for points of dispute—whether a director is in breach of his duty or a board has exceeded its power, for example—to be tested in the courts and, as we commented in Chapter 7, the activities of companies are regulated by the extensive and complex statute and case law. In contrast, the preference in industrial relations law, particularly in the last few years, has been to encourage the resolution of disputes without recourse to the courts, and to provide for a number of intermediate stages of advice, persuasion, conciliation and arbitration to bring the parties in dispute to agreement. This approach is based on the view that it is not conducive to good relations within an enterprise either to bring disputes between management and trade unions before the courts or to force a solution on unwilling parties by means of penal sanctions.

4. Some of our proposals—particularly those in Chapter 8 regarding the duties of directors, the functions of boards and the powers of the shareholders —fall squarely in the field of company law, and it seems to us appropriate that in these areas the traditional means of enforcement—namely the courts— should be used. In many other areas, however, we propose that within a legal framework the main parties in a company—the recognised trade unions and the existing board or, in other cases, the employee and shareholder representatives on the new board—should have considerable freedom to decide how employee representation on the board should be introduced. This extends to such matters as the selection of the employee representatives and the reconstitution of boards. We believe that where we have proposed an obligation on the parties to negotiate an agreed system, it is more appropriate that the enforcement procedures of industrial relations law should apply. The success or failure of industrial democracy depends in our view on co-operation between management and trade unions. To foster this co-operation the law must provide machinery which encourages the resolution of disputes through negotiation and agreement, and only has recourse to the courts in the last resort. We believe that the appropriate machinery is an independent Industrial Democracy Commission, which can provide advice, conciliation and ultimately decisions for those within a company whose task it is to devise an agreed system of employee representation on boards.

An Industrial Democracy Commission

5. We have referred at various points in previous chapters to the role and functions of such a Commission. It will be useful to draw together those references here in order to get a clearer picture of the considerable task the Commission might have to perform.

6. One of its main and constantly developing tasks will be the provision of information and advice on the operation of the industrial democracy legislation. It will need to build up a fund of expertise, knowledge of what has been done in practice both in Britain and abroad and understanding of the new legislation, as well as having some experience of industrial relations generally. Such advice and expertise could be invaluable to the management and trade unions of a company during their discussions on how board level representation should be introduced.

7. Another important part of the Commission's work will be the formulation of codes of practice covering certain aspects of employee representation. We identified in earlier chapters some areas where a code of practice would be more appropriate than strict legal requirements: for example, the way in which a holding company might devise a policy of participation for a group of companies; methods of selection of employee representatives; the conduct of ballots; and the provision of facilities for employee representatives and for members of Joint Representation Committees.

8. We turn now to the various points in the process of introducing employee representation on boards where we think the Commission will, under our proposals, have an important role. At the very beginning of the process we have

recommended that, in a company or group with 2,000 or more employees, the trade union or unions recognised on behalf of at least 20 per cent of those employees should be able to request a ballot to test opinion in the company or group on the question of employee representation on the board. There are two possible sources of contention here, though we would expect them to arise only rarely: first, whether a company has 2,000 employees; second, whether a union is recognised for a particular percentage of the company's employees. In the case of dispute on the first point, we believe that any party to the dispute, either union or management, should be able to seek from the Commission a ruling on whether the company or group has 2,000 or more employees. The Commission's decision on this should be final and binding.

9. The second point concerns a question of recognition. There is already a procedure under the Employment Protection Act 1975 by which a union can seek recognition from an employer. This involves, in cases where an employer refuses recognition, an appeal to the Advisory Conciliation and Arbitration Service (ACAS) and ultimately to the Central Arbitration Committee, which can make a binding award. We think it would be confusing if a dispute as to the percentage of a company's employees which a union represented were to be settled by entirely separate machinery. We propose therefore that if a dispute should arise on this matter, it should be referred to the Commission, and the Commission should seek the advice of ACAS. ACAS might then undertake the investigation of the matter and report to the Commission, which would have the power to issue a certificate as to the percentage of employees for which the union or unions concerned were recognised.

10. The next stage of our proposals is a ballot of all employees. We have already said in Chapter 10 that the Commission will have an important role in advising on the conduct, and in some cases providing independent supervision of the ballot. We suggested that the Commission should have the job of devising a standard form of ballot paper and standard accompanying literature, which the company would use unless management and trade unions agreed otherwise. On occasions the Commission may also be asked to interpret the result of a ballot, to decide, for example, whether the requisite percentage of employees voted in favour or, in the case of groups, where the ballot also concerned board level representation in a large subsidiary, to establish the percentage of employees in such a subsidiary who voted in favour.

11. Following an affirmative ballot, the Commission may be called in to provide conciliation, either between management and trade unions, or between a number of trade unions. The first point on which disagreement may arise is the size of the board. As explained in Chapter 10, the way in which deadlock on this issue would ultimately be resolved is by either party invoking the statutory fall-back procedure, which would determine the size of the board by reference to the number of employees in the company or group. But before the size of the board was finally determined in this way there would be an opportunity, if both parties requested it, for the Commission to conciliate between them. Second, the formation of the Joint Representation Committee (JRC) may cause problems. We consider it so important that the JRC should properly represent all the recognised trade unions in the enterprise that we have proposed (in Chapter 10) that there should be a specific right of appeal to the Commission by a union

which considers itself unfairly excluded from it, and that the Commission should have the power to declare the JRC improperly constituted. Clearly, there will be scope for conciliation between the parties involved before any disagreement on the composition of the JRC becomes subject to these statutory procedures.

12. We also believe it is important that the Commission should use existing expertise in providing conciliation, rather than set up its own procedures. Where there is a disagreement between unions affiliated to the TUC, the Commission should always refer the matter to the TUC for settlement under the TUC procedures for resolving disputes between affiliated unions. In other cases it should seek the help of the conciliation officers of ACAS who have established expertise in conciliating between unions and between unions and management.

13. We recognised in Chapter 10 that there must be a legal event, when the selection of the employee representatives becomes effective, and we proposed that this should be the signing of the certificate of appointment by all members of the JRC. We envisage that it will be the Commission's job to draw up a standard certificate of appointment. We have also proposed that any recognised trade union dissatisfied with the selection of employee representatives should be able to appeal to the Commission on this point. The Commission should have the power to investigate any such complaint and to make a binding decision on the validity of the appointment and, if necessary, to declare that a certificate of appointment need not be signed by the dissenting union.

14. The last possible point of disagreement is on the appointment of the co-opted directors. We propose in Chapter 9 that at the end of a stated period either party should be able to seek conciliation from the Commission and that, in the last resort, the Commission should be able to decide that specified persons should form the third group on the board. We also suggested in Chapter 11 that the Commission should have a further role in regard to multinationals. Where the representatives in the United Kingdom could not agree on the appointment of the co-opted directors on a top United Kingdom subsidiary board, or where the overseas parent requested the right to appoint the third group in order to control the subsidiary board, in the last resort we propose that the Commission should be able, after consultation with the parties concerned and the Government, to make a binding decision.

15. Finally, we believe that the Industrial Democracy Commission would be well placed to monitor and evaluate the operation of the legislation we are proposing. Breaking new ground as it does, the legislation will require review and may require modification after a period of a few years. We therefore recommend that the Commission should, from its inception, be charged with monitoring the experience of the measures in practice. The exact date or dates on which it would be appropriate for it to make recommendations on the operation of the law need not be determined in advance. A duty to report annually to Parliament on its work would be normal, and it may be best to leave to the judgment of the Commission's governing body the decision on an appropriate time to suggest any changes. We believe however that it would be right for the Commission to be charged with initiating a particularly careful and wide ranging review, three years after the new legislation comes into force.

Constituting the Commission

16. We have carefully considered whether these functions should be carried out by a new independent body, or added to the existing responsibilities of ACAS, which has an established reputation in providing advice on aspects of industrial relations and conciliation in disputes between management and trade unions. On balance we believe there should be a new independent Commission with clear terms of reference and a recognisable identity, whose sole responsibility is to ensure the smooth operation of the industrial democracy legislation. The work of the Commission will be different from that of any existing body, in that it will be equally concerned with industrial relations on the one hand and with company law and administration on the other. Its working contacts will be with trade union representatives and officials, with the top management of companies, and with bodies representing a variety of professional and other interests. It will need to establish and maintain equally close liaison with the Department of Trade and the Department of Employment, and links with other government departments and independent agencies. There will be European and international aspects to its work. It will have the power to appoint people to company boards. These functions could not, we believe, be satisfactorily discharged by ACAS, even if that body were to be reorganised and strengthened, since the aims and objectives of ACAS are related entirely to industrial relations, and its strength lies in the coherence of its various tasks. To widen the ambit of ACAS to include the new field of industrial democracy would not only fail to ensure that the important tasks described in this chapter were carried out as well as possible, but would also subject ACAS itself to damaging strains and pressures. In sum, we see a need for a new and single-minded body. This will be felt especially during the period of introduction of board level representation of employees. When the first major review proposed in the last paragraph is undertaken, the future of the Commission itself should also be reviewed.

17. The new body should not, however, duplicate functions already carried out by ACAS. We have therefore proposed that the existing expertise of ACAS should be used in two fields: where there is a dispute about whether a union is recognised for 20 per cent of a company's employees; and where the parties in dispute agree to seek independent conciliation. This we believe will avoid unnecessary and costly duplication of staff and resources.

18. It will be valuable to involve both sides of industry in the work of the Commission, and we suggest that the governing council should be a tripartite body with representatives of employers and trade unions and others with relevant experience. Since matters of company law and of industrial relations are closely involved, the appointment of the body, and especially of its chairman, should be made either by the Secretary of State for Trade in consultation with the Secretary of State for Employment, or *vice versa*. We do not think that there should be a large permanent staff, and indeed we would emphasise the need to avoid the creation of a further bureaucracy. It is difficult at this stage to estimate the staffing and budgeting that will be required. Two factors are important however. First, the Commission will not have its own conciliation service and will call on ACAS for help. Second, apart from its advisory role, its main activity will be in the resolution of disputes and difficulties; but in the great majority of cases we expect employee representation on boards to be introduced by agreement, without recourse to the Commission.

155

Training needs

19. If our proposals are implemented, many people will become directors of major British companies for the first time. Most will bring to the board valuable experience as employees of the company, and as lay trade union representatives (such as shop stewards) used to participating in decision-making through collective bargaining. Nonetheless, few of these new directors will have senior managerial or executive experience and for almost all of them the work of the board will be new and unfamiliar. At the same time, many executive and non-executive directors will find themselves working with a new group of colleagues and dealing with issues of company policy on a new basis. Much of this inexperience and unfamiliarity will only be overcome by actual participation in the work of reconstituted boards. But to facilitate the process, we believe that a substantial training programme will be essential, to equip both employee and shareholder representatives to co-operate effectively at board level in the formulation of policy and the supervision of management. If insufficient attention is given to the establishment of a training programme, then the success of board level representation itself will, in our view, be endangered.

20. We must consider first the size of the training effort that will be required. If legislation applies to the 738 or so enterprises with 2,000 or more employees in the United Kingdom, we estimate that the number of company boards within its scope, including both group holding companies and large subsidiaries, may be in the region of 1,800 (see Chapter 2). Not all will be affected immediately by board level representation, however, since the appointment of employee representatives will only take place where employees through their trade unions request and vote for it, and the process will take longer in some companies than in others. It is also difficult to estimate the average number of directors there will be on the reconstituted boards. The divergence in the size of company boards which we noted in Chapter 7 seems likely to continue after the introduction of employee representation, though it has to be admitted that the overall tendency may be for the size of boards to increase. It is unlikely that in the majority of large companies there will be less than five employee representatives and five shareholder representatives on the board. If we assume for argument's sake that the average number is seven or eight, and that during the first three years of the new law's operation the process is set in motion and boards are reconstituted in between one-half and three-quarters of the 1,800 eligible companies, then there will be an initial training need for between 6,000 and 11,000 employee representatives and a substantial training need for shareholder representatives. After the first few years the numbers requiring training will depend on the rate of change in the membership of reconstituted boards and on the number of companies affected for the first time. Assuming some turnover of representatives, and taking into consideration the need to develop more advanced follow-up courses for longer-serving representatives, the permanent training need, although below the initial figure, is still likely to be considerable. Moreover, training will not end at board representatives. Our recommendations have implications for other levels of union organisation, particularly with reference to the pivotal role of the Joint Representation Committee at enterprise level. All union representatives on this body, whether elected to sit on the board or not, will have new and wider functions as a result of our recommendations, which must be catered for in training programmes.

21. We expect that the large majority of shareholder representatives on boards of directors will continue as now to be senior executives of the company. Some of them may have little experience of negotiation or consultation with representatives of employees, because their functions or main experience lie in such fields as marketing or research, where working contacts are generally with management colleagues or with people outside the firm, rather than with large sections of the workforce. For such executive directors the fact of working at board level with the employee representatives will in itself be educational. But it may be found that comparative ignorance of labour matters constitutes an obstacle or disadvantage that might be overcome by some formal training in this field. The same may be true of some co-opted directors, who, as we have said, will usually have special expertise to contribute to the board, but may not have experience of working with trade union representatives. It will be up to individual companies to decide how and where such training may best be provided and we would expect that schools and institutions of management and business education will want to adapt their existing courses to meet such needs.

22. The provision of formal training for employee representatives who find themselves members of company boards for the first time will require substantial expansion of facilities. There may in some quarters be misunderstanding about the purpose of such training. Its purpose, as we see it, is to equip the employee representatives with the necessary ability to take part in the more technical aspects of the board's work. For this, some acquaintance is needed with the presentation of financial information, basic economics, management information and control systems, some aspects of company law and so on. The aim is not to turn employee representatives into experts in any of these areas, but to provide them with sufficient understanding to grasp and question proposals put to them by professional management. While the acquisition of technical skills will be an important element in any training for employee representatives, this should not however be the sole preoccupation. As this report has consistently stressed, employees will be on the board as representatives of the workforce elected through trade union machinery and not as traditional directors. One aim of training courses for employee representatives will be to explore the nature of their role, function and responsibilities in relation to the company and the workforce as a whole. The relationship of employee representatives on the board to other forms of joint regulation below board level and the role and function of the JRC will, for example, be an important area of concern. In the long run we believe that the value of the contribution which employee representatives will make on the board will depend less on their mastery of the tools used in the professional practice of management than on their personal qualities of judgment and leadership and their ability to interpret and represent the views of their constituents.

23. The amount of training, in terms of time, which new employee representatives may need is a matter on which we have formed no hard and fast views. If, however, the training is to be worthwhile, we believe it is necessary to think in terms of a residential training course or courses, lasting between two and six weeks in all. The duration and structure of courses will undoubtedly vary with differing circumstances. We were very impressed by the extent of the training programmes devised in Sweden by the blue collar and white collar

trade union confederations for new employee representatives. Each new representative is given three or four weeks residential training at one of the trade union colleges during the first two years of board membership. The training is divided into units of about one week, provided for employee representatives at six-monthly intervals. This enables basic training to be given quickly to a large number of representatives, and means that the later units can be devoted partly to some of the practical problems the representatives have encountered during their first year on the board.

24. Facilities already exist which can form a basis for the expanded training effort. The TUC already has an important role in developing and providing courses for shop stewards, lay union representatives and trade union officials at the TUC Training College, and individual trade unions are also rapidly expanding their educational facilities. In the public sector there are some 150 educational bodies, including colleges of further education, districts of the Workers Education Association, polytechnics and extra-mural departments of universities, providing TUC approved courses for union representatives. These have over 100 full-time tutors on trade union studies and in 1975 provided about 1,150 such courses for 16,500 students. There are also many institutions both inside and outside the public sector including some of the bodies cited above, concerned with management education. The Department of Education and Science in its written evidence has drawn our attention in particular to the 11 Regional Management Centres established since 1971 which act as focal points for management education in their regions. The existence of these considerable facilities helps to put into perspective the additional provision needed as a result of employee representation on boards, which we have estimated at between 6,000 and 11,000 people in the first few years.

25. This brings us to the question of who should have responsibility for the content of courses. The TUC has argued to us that it is impossible to separate the training needs of employee representatives who become board members from those of elected lay trade union representatives and full-time trade union officials, and therefore that any new training should be regarded as an extension of the TUC approved courses already provided at the TUC college, at individual trade union colleges and at other educational institutions; the central organisation and supervision of the new training courses should therefore be in the hands of the trade union movement. The contrary view has been put to us however by some academics and representatives of industry, that the training should be regarded as more than an extension of existing trade union education services. The role for which employee representatives are to be trained is different from their traditional function of collective bargaining, involving as it does co-operation with the representatives of shareholders in the control of companies. Therefore, it is argued, both sides of industry must be involved in the provision of new training; the job of supervising course content and allocating resources should be in the hands of a joint industry body such as perhaps the new Industrial Democracy Commission.

26. We think that the best approach is to build on present practice, whereby a variety of institutions with relevant expertise co-operate in developing and providing courses in the fields of trade union studies and management education. Much of the content of training programmes for employee representatives will

be directly related to the courses already provided for union representatives and officials. The TUC and individual unions should therefore continue to work together with the education service in devising suitable courses. In addition, since matters of company law and administration, financial control, etc, will be important constituents of the training, those responsible for arranging it may wish to call on the resources now available in institutes or schools of management and business education, especially in the public sector.

27. Apart from the question of who is to conduct this programme, there is also the question of who should pay for it. We think that the same principles should apply here as in the previous paragraph; and the present practice, which includes a Treasury grant to trade unions administered through the TUC, should be continued. A considerable amount of money will be needed, if an adequate training effort on the scale we envisage is to be mounted. It is difficult to estimate exactly how much. If it is assumed that the initial training for over 6,000 people would consist of residential courses of about four weeks, at a cost of about £400 per person, then the total cost over the first three years, in addition to what is already spent on trade union education, could be more than £3 million. This relates only to employee representatives on boards of directors and makes no allowance for the training needs of members of Joint Representation Committees. Nor does it take into account any capital outlay on extra facilities or the cost to industry of paid time off for representatives to attend the courses. It may be contrasted with current public expenditure on management education in the United Kingdom, which in the further education sector alone (ie excluding independent management institutions and universities) is expected to be in the region of £60 million during the same period of three years.

28. In view of the amount of money needed initially to meet the new training requirement, we think it unrealistic to expect either the trade union movement or industry itself to bear the whole of the additional cost. Both will have essential parts to play in identifying the representatives' training needs and in providing facilities and expertise to help with the training. But we think it right that the Government itself should directly bear a large part of the cost of the initial training. Training is a necessary part of a scheme to which the Government, if it accepts our recommendations, will have committed itself. The justification for such a course of action would be, of course, that the Government shares our view of the benefits to the nation as a whole that may come from the extension of industrial democracy in the form of employee representation at board level. It is appropriate that an incidental and (by comparison with other forms of public expenditure) moderate cost should be paid out of public funds.

Conclusion

1. Our terms of reference required us to consider the way in which an extension of industrial democracy by means of representation on boards of directors could best be achieved. As a result, a large part of our report has been taken up with questions of organisation, administration, company law and other matters requiring detailed examination. We have not, however, interpreted our terms of reference narrowly and in the earlier chapters we have discussed some of the wider issues raised in the current debate about industrial democracy and in the evidence presented to us. It is to these larger issues that we wish to return in conclusion.

2. During our inquiry we found a widespread conviction, which we share, that the problem of Britain as an industrialised nation is not a lack of native capacity in its working population so much as a failure to draw out their energies and skill to anything like their full potential. It is our belief that the way to release those energies, to provide greater satisfaction in the workplace and to assist in raising the level of productivity and efficiency in British industry—and with it the living standards of the nation—is not by recrimination or exhortation but by putting the relationship between capital and labour on to a new basis which will involve not just management but the whole workforce in sharing responsibility for the success and profitability of the enterprise. Such a change in the industrial outlook and atmosphere will only come about, however, as a result of giving the representatives of the employees a real, and not a sham or token, share in making the strategic decisions about the future of an enterprise which in the past have been reserved to management and the representatives of the shareholders.

3. We do not seek to minimise the fundamental nature of the changes which this will entail, if they are to be successful, particularly in the traditional attitudes of many on both sides of industry. Nor do we claim that such changes will act as a panacea in eliminating conflict from industrial relations. What we do believe is that, if such requirements as we have proposed are carried through, they will release energies and abilities at present frustrated or not used and thereby create a framework which will allow conflicts of interest to be resolved with greater mutual advantage. And we are encouraged in this belief by the success in improving industrial relations which neighbouring countries in Europe, with differing economic and social systems, have had in following this path of development.

4. In fact, the debate about industrial democracy is much less about the desirability of moving in the direction of greater participation (which many would accept as inevitable), than about the pace of change and the need to extend such participation to the board. We fully accept the argument about the necessity for participation at levels below the board. Indeed, our proposals for employee representation on the board entail a joint trade union representation committee at company level, which we describe in Chapter 10; the importance of this aspect of our recommendations should not be underestimated. Nonetheless, we believe that the crucial test which alone will carry conviction and create a willingness to share responsibility is an acknowledgement of the right of

representatives of the employees, if they ask for it, to share in the strategic decisions taken by the board. Participation at other levels may prepare the way, as we believe it already has in many British companies, but we are convinced that only when this test has been faced and passed will the way be opened to develop a new relationship and a new confidence between employees and management.

5. For the reasons we have set out in Chapter 8, we believe it is membership of a reconstituted unitary board, rather than a supervisory board, which will provide for effective participation in decision-making, will foster the efficiency of British companies and, despite the changes involved, will be more compatible with our company law and administration. Moreover, most large enterprises form part of groups of companies, and effective participation in groups can, as we have proposed in Chapter 11, be achieved by reconstituted unitary boards at different levels but will certainly not be provided by a supervisory board with effective powers only at group level.

6. We have deliberately avoided recommending a system which on the appointed day should have universal and immediate application. We believe that all employees should be involved in a ballot and that if a sufficient majority is obtained, then the process of reconstituting the board should take place. This is a half-way house between enabling legislation and universally mandatory legislation.

7. Although we would limit the role of legislation, we are clear that the law will have to be altered, as it has had to be in all other countries which have introduced employee representation at board level. Once this has been done, then we are confident that—as in the other countries which have made the change—management as much as the trade unions will see the need to make a success of the new relationship. Furthermore, they will soon recognise the benefits to be derived from the new arrangements by companies, by management and shareholders, by unions and employees and thus by the nation as a whole.

8. Sooner or later, we believe, this is a decision which will have to be taken, whatever government is in power. Postponing it will not make it easier, may well make it more difficult, to take. We believe that the change in attitude of the TUC and their willingness to accept a share of responsibility for the increased efficiency and prosperity of British companies offer an opportunity to create a new basis for relations in industry which should not be allowed to pass. We should certainly consider what may be the consequence for the future of British industry of a failure to seize this opportunity, of doing nothing or (more characteristically perhaps) of doing too little too late. For if we look beyond our immediate problems it appears to us certain that the criterion of efficiency in the world of tomorrow, even more than in that of today, will be the capacity of industry to adapt to an increasing rate of economic and social change. We are convinced that this in turn will depend upon the extent to which the measures of adaptation that are necessary are recognised and adopted with the assent of a workforce whose representatives are involved equally and from the beginning in the processes of decision-making.

9. Several submissions have drawn our attention to the parallels between political and industrial democracy. They have argued that, just as in the nineteenth century the shifts in economic power to the middle and working classes made it essential to harness that power to the benefit of society, by extending the suffrage, now is the time to provide scope for the growing power and unused capacities of organised labour, by giving them representation on the boards of large enterprises.

10. The fears expressed in the nineteenth century in face of proposals to give more people the right to vote did not stop short of the subversion of the constitution and the dissolution of society. Once the franchise was extended, however, the fears were forgotten and the Reform Acts were seen as essential to the country's stability and prosperity. We believe that over 100 years later an extension of industrial democracy can produce comparable benefits and that our descendants will look back with as much surprise to the controversy which surrounded it as we do to that which surrounded the extension of the political suffrage in the nineteenth century.

BULLOCK, *Chairman*

G S BAIN

CLIVE JENKINS

JACK JONES

DAVID LEA

K W WEDDERBURN

NICHOLAS WILSON[1]

ROBIN HOPE *Secretary*

DAVID NORMINGTON *Assistant Secretary*

13 Bloomsbury Square
London WC1

14 December 1976

---

[1]Signed subject to the following note of dissent.

Note of dissent by Mr N S Wilson

1. As the report indicates, it was not possible for me to agree with the majority on the composition of the reconstituted board of directors and the treatment of groups of companies. Although both matters are important they nevertheless do not affect the essential conclusions concerning the introduction of employee representation on unitary boards and the methods by which this should be achieved.

2. The most important point of departure from the majority occurs at a critical point in the argument of the report—namely in relation to the composition and structure of the board. I would wish to see a different solution to the problem of the proportion of employee representatives which I believe would be less divisive and complex and yet more realistic and practical. It would, moreover, eliminate many of the problems (notably those in relation to groups of companies) which the majority's recommendations on board composition create.

3. The question of proportions is crucial, and I believe that the majority, in determining the proportion or number of employee directors, have worked from an erroneous premise, namely, that the number of employee representatives should precisely equal the number who are (theoretically at any rate) appointed by the shareholders. The justification for employee representatives is to give employees a voice at the board room table so that they can (in the words of the TUC's pamphlet *Industrial Democracy*) 'participate in and influence decisions'[1]. It follows that the number of employee representatives for a given company ought to depend on the size, structure, homogeneity (or otherwise) and other characteristics of the body of employees who are to be represented. Put negatively, it should not depend on the size or composition of the management element of the board. Equality of representation is said to be justified by the requirement that employee representatives should have equality of responsibility with other directors. But this is to confuse two quite distinct issues: representation is concerned with numbers and proportions whereas responsibility is not capable of quantification. What is meant by 'equality of responsibility' is that *each* member of the board has identical duties and, since all directors would, if the majority's proposals are adopted, be obliged to have regard to the interests of employees, there is neither inconsistency nor contradiction in proposing minority representation whilst expecting all directors to have identical responsibilities. If equality of responsibility is used in any other sense, it must of necessity assume a degree of coherence within groups of directors and a polarisation of their attitudes which is at variance with the consensual method by which, as the majority acknowledge, board decisions are generally reached.

4. It is true that the German *montan* industries have experienced equality of representation but in West Germany employee representation is on the supervisory board, whereas the majority of the Committee (including myself) believe that, in introducing employee representation, it is right to adapt our own unitary board system rather than to attempt to introduce the German two-tier board

---

[1]TUC, *op cit*, page 37.

structure. But it does not follow that equality of representation of employees and shareholders can be introduced on to unitary boards, modified as suggested in the main report, with the same success that attended its introduction in companies in the *montan* industries in Germany. The supervisory board has limited and clearly defined functions; management is not represented on the board and its meetings are formal and infrequent. In other words, management is, by and large, left to manage the enterprise. By contrast, if employee representatives were to be appointed to a unitary board which was precisely composed of three groups, the decision-making processes would inevitably be adversely affected and management would constantly be involved in compromise, canvassing and negotiation with the other elements of the board, to the detriment of their proper entrepreneurial function. Indeed, the very composition of the board would institutionalise and accentuate the conflict between employees' and shareholders' interests and would work against the essential cohesiveness and unity of purpose which is the hallmark of every successful board.

5. To avoid the risk of polarisation and to deal with what is described as the exceptional case of deadlock, the majority therefore propose to introduce a third group of directors. Hence the formula which has come to be known as $2X + Y$. I do not accept that the formula is necessary: its adoption will tend to create larger boards (which are thus liable to be less effective) and it presupposes a causal or logical connection (which in my view does not exist) between the size of the management and employee elements of the board.

6. However, even if equality of representation were desirable, there are three reasons which compel me inescapably to the conclusion that the addition of a third group of directors is not the optimum solution of the problem. In the first place, the $2X + Y$ formula imposes on a body which, it is generally accepted, needs as much flexibility in its composition and operation as possible, a structure which is at once too rigid and too mathematically precise to be practical. To ensure the maximum efficiency of a board it is essential, in my view, that it should not be constrained by algebraic considerations. It is unreasonable to require that there should always be equal representation of employees and shareholders and that the third group of directors should be an uneven number. To do so means that the co-option (for example) of an additional management director or indeed the retirement or dismissal of any director—be he employee, management or 'third group' director—could necessitate the retirement or appointment of at least one other director for no better reason than to eliminate an imbalance. There is scarcely a worse reason for making a board appointment or for requiring a retirement. Secondly, the formula will, I fear, inevitably involve a process, conscious or unconscious, of 'horse-trading' in the selection of the third group of directors, the overall effect of which will be a tendency towards polarisation—the very thing which their introduction was designed to avoid. Thirdly, the fact that it is necessary to provide for the possibility of shareholder and employee representatives being unable to reach agreement on the identity of the third group of directors highlights the artificiality of the formula and the fragility of the solution. A board which is unable to reach agreement on its own composition will scarcely be united by an imposed solution involving the appointment of further directors by a third party.

164

7. To summarise, therefore, I find it impossible to believe that the 2X + Y formula is a meaningful advance on the outright parity representation system which (as the Economist Intelligence Unit remarked) 'makes no provision for resolving any particular difference between the two sides except by means of some haphazard form of arbitration or compromise'.[1]

8. For these reasons, it is my view that the *number* of employee representatives should be determined by reference to the number of the employees to be represented in the manner envisaged in paragraph 38 of Chapter 9, without any limitation being imposed on the composition of the remainder of the board. In other words, the shareholders should be able to appoint a majority of the members of the board. The advantages of such a scheme are as follows:

(i) the presence of employee representatives would add the required new dimension to board discussions, but the fact that they were in a minority would greatly reduce the risk of polarisation of attitudes and would hopefully lead to a less divisive working of the board;

(ii) since it has been decided that employee representatives should be selected through trade union machinery (which inevitably cannot be representative of non-organised employees) and since, furthermore, it is virtually impossible to accord rights of representation to overseas employees (and most of the companies to which the legislation will apply have a sizeable number of overseas employees—Table 2 to Chapter 2 indicates that overseas employees represent in aggregate almost one quarter of the total number of employees of enterprises in *The Times 1,000*), I believe that minority representation of United Kingdom employees would constitute a more equitable allocation of boardroom influence and give rise to less concern (justified or otherwise) on the part of the unrepresented employees both at home and abroad;

(iii) the scheme would involve much less alteration to the size and composition of boards of existing companies to which the new legislation would apply—a practical advantage which should not be underestimated if the disruptive effect on the operations of the companies affected is to be minimised;

(iv) in particular, the scheme would not involve the introduction of the third group of directors. Quite apart from the difficulty of finding an adequate number of people of sufficient ability to fulfil this role for all the companies to which the new legislation would apply, it would in all but the most exceptional cases dispense with the obligation to introduce on to the board new directors who have no existing connection with the company or its activities; and

(v) virtually all the problems which arise in relation to groups fall away: the holding company would have the right to appoint a majority of the board of every subsidiary by virtue of its shareholding, in the same way that the shareholders of the holding company would have the right to appoint a majority of the board of that company.

---

[1]Harry Shutt (editor), *Worker Participation in West Germany, Sweden, Yugoslavia and the United Kingdom*, QER Special No 20 (The Economist Intelligence Ltd, 1975).

9. Even assuming the implementation of the proposals recommended by the majority in relation to holding companies, the only justification for applying the $2X + Y$ formula to subsidiaries appears to be the quest for uniformity. I can see no economic or social justification for the inclusion of Y directors on the board of large subsidiaries. Accordingly, even if the formula applies to ultimate United Kingdom holding companies, I believe the simpler solution of the holding company having the unqualified right to appoint a majority of the board of its subsidiaries should still be adopted.

10. There is one final but essential point to be made. 'Industrial Democracy' is a phrase which at the time of the Committee's appointment was known to few and understood by fewer still. Since that time it has been thrust into the forefront of public debate more swiftly than any other concept of comparable importance in recent years. As a result, the Committee's recommendations, if they were to become 'legislative opinion', would be far in advance of public opinion at large. This fact has overwhelming significance: recent history in the field of industrial relations illustrates more vividly than words the importance of social legislation keeping pace with public opinion. The lesson to be drawn is that there are limits to the rate at which legislation can successfully achieve 'social engineering' in advance of social evolution. Despite the justification for employee representation—which I regard as beyond challenge—one cannot ignore the genuine hostility to the concept on the part of a large section of middle and upper management and the relative apathy on the part of many other employees. Such a setting is scarcely an ideal one for the introduction of radical legislation in an area of such importance. Inevitably any proposed legislation involves a calculus of and balance between the group interests whose conflicts the legislation attempts to adjust, but in my judgment in the short, and even medium term, that balance is more likely to be found by introducing employee representation on the basis suggested above than that proposed by the majority. Participation and influence in policy and decision-making can be readily and effectively achieved by such a method without the necessity of regulating the composition of boards of companies to which the legislation will apply in such a rigid and potentially divisive manner.

NICHOLAS WILSON

14 December 1976

Minority Report

by Mr N P Biggs, Sir Jack Callard and Mr Barrie Heath

Contents

I. The Committee's remit

1. The Committee's remit required it 'to consider *how* such an extension' (representation on Boards of Directors) 'can best be achieved'; it did not require the Committee to consider *whether* 'a radical extension of industrial democracy' should be achieved by the representation of employees on Boards of Directors. The proposals in this Minority Report therefore represent, in our considered view, the best ways of fulfilling what we regard as a far from satisfactory or even wise remit.

II. The case for a Minority Report

2. The issues which the Committee have debated during the year go to the heart of the management of those key industrial resources on which the country's prosperity depends and are therefore of great—and incalculable—importance. If the right solutions can be found, the benefits to the nation, to industry and to individuals will be enormous; a misjudgment could lead to disaster.

3. Although we were able to reach full agreement with our colleagues on the Committee on a number of the relevant issues, there are some solutions favoured in the Majority Report which, we know from experience, are not likely to be in the interests either of the people who work in industry or of the nation. The issues which divide us are not details of mechanism; they are fundamental, and it is for this reason that we have produced a Minority Report. In doing so, we record our regret that we were unable to benefit during the preparation of the report from the help and advice of Mr John Methven who, prior to his resignation from the Committee, gave us much wise counsel.

4. We present this Minority Report in the confidence that our views will have the support of large sections of the industrial community. We believe that those who work in industry are not ready for the radical changes which the Majority Report aims to achieve. In the Trade Union movement itself there is abundant evidence of conflicting thinking on this subject. In the debate at the 1974 TUC Congress and subsequently, a number of the major unions with extensive membership in the Private Sector have sought to introduce flexibility into the policy of the TUC and they have argued that the approach of the TUC General Council has been dominated by the views of the unions which preponderate in the Public Service to which its recommendations for the appointment of 'worker directors' in the Private Sector would not apply. The efforts of the dissenting unions to bring about a change of policy have led to confused debate but no resolution of the differences. These differences appear to have been ignored by our colleagues who have signed the Majority Report.

5. Furthermore, large numbers of employers are strongly—and, they believe, justifiably—opposed to precipitate action; and 'middle' management, a particularly hard pressed element of immense significance in our society, regard with dismay developments from which they might be excluded and which in their view would be likely to affect adversely the speed and quality of decision-making in their companies.

6. We were unable to satisfy ourselves that sufficient notice has been taken of the evidence[1] and advice of those who work in industry—employers and employees alike—whose views and experience are most relevant and most valid. It would be exceedingly unwise for the nation to disregard their practical realism and accept the theories of those who see this debate as a means of changing the structure of society in this country and who would seek to bring the Boards of the Private Sector under Trade Union control.

---

[1]Comments on an analysis of the written submissions to the Committee are included as Appendix A to the Minority Report.

7. We were asked, in our remit, to take particular account of the TUC report on industrial democracy, and we do indeed recognise the powerful advocacy of the TUC, the Labour Party and the Fabian Society as pointing one clear way for the Committee to go. We are, however, not convinced by the evidence that these voices, powerful though they are, carry wide based support in the country as a whole. The Committee has received contrary opinion not only from the great majority of employers, but from some strong and powerful Trades Unions and the National Consumer Council as well.

8. In these circumstances, we would have preferred a broader remit and a different outcome. Some of the debates to which we have listened seemed to us to have been describing situations which do not correspond with our experience of industrial life in the United Kingdom, where there is a fragmented Union movement; where large and important sections of the employee force belong to no Trades Union at all; and where there is a Trades Union movement which is wholly committed to participation through collective bargaining and deeply divided about the problems involved in sharing power in industrial enterprises within the private sector. The Majority Report takes scant account of these realities.

9. 'Industrial democracy' is a term which can all too easily be applied to a wide range of developments, some good, some, in our view, bad. The debates of the last year have only served to strengthen our view that, whereas the development of effective structures of employee participation from the grass roots level would do nothing but good for British Industry, the appointment of 'worker directors'—by which we understand people from the shop floor elected or appointed directly on to Boards of Directors as we know them now—would not be helpful. Certainly it is unwise to impose 'democracy' on those who are unwilling or unready to receive it.

10. This country needs a profitable and competitive private sector. Meeting that need must be a fundamental objective in the light of the dismal economic performance of the UK in comparison with that of its overseas competitors in terms of industrial growth, productivity, share of world trade and rate of inflation.

11. Industrial democracy can play its part in this process if it enables a more open and effective sharing of the real and practical problems of industry to take place. That cannot be achieved through a simple capitulation to strong sectional pressure. It must involve an increased accountability by management for the human, material and financial resources which the community makes available to industry and a more openly expressed concern for the rights and interests both of shareholders and of employees. The fundamental task which faces the country is that of stimulating some new upsurge of effort to improve the effectiveness of British companies in the task of generating wealth for the community.

12. Everyone who works in industry has a part to play in this task. We recognise that greater involvement in many aspects of decision-making is a rational aspiration of a work force which is better educated and better informed than ever before, and we believe that a greater degree of appropriate involvement of employees in company affairs and a greater agreement on company objectives should lead to improved relationships and help to produce a more efficient, a more competitive British industry.

171

III. Aims

13. It is necessary to be clear at the outset about the aims of any proposed new legislation. The TUC policy statement makes clear its view that the purpose of industrial democracy is to extend the power—'control' is the word used by the TUC in the report to the 1974 Congress[1]—of organised labour. Whilst the signatories to the Majority Report have not argued their case on the basis of the TUC 'control' proposition, it is clear to us that in many circles control by, and the exercise of much increased power by, the Trade Unions is regarded as a main objective.

14. We believe that any legislation that the Government wishes to introduce should—

(a) improve the effectiveness of companies in their task of generating wealth for the community as a whole;

(b) ensure that Boards of Directors are legally and demonstrably account-able for their actions to their employees as well as to their shareholders;

(c) satisfy the aspirations of employees for involvement in the formulation of decisions which closely affect their work.

---

[1] 'The whole concept of a greater degree of industrial democracy is the achievement of work people collectively of a greater control of their work situation'.

IV. Criteria

15. The criteria which would have to be met if our aims were to be fulfilled are listed below, and any subsequent proposals should be matched against them—

(a) The quality and speed of decision-making must not be impaired and improvement in industrial efficiency must seem likely.

(b) Proposals must involve representatives of all categories of employees in the planning and implementation of change.

(c) This involvement must be democratically achieved while—

- allowing flexibility to reflect the choice of those involved;
- not interfering with existing arrangements for collective bargaining;
- involving all relevant groups and parties;
- providing adequately defined and genuine roles for those involved in formal structures.

(d) The legitimate rights and aspirations of all interested parties must be recognised.

(e) It must be recognised that progress has to be made from many different states of development in many different structures.

(f) Hence there must be due regard for the evolution of the changes required, and in particular—

- development of provision of information procedures;
- changes in attitude and structure of managements, other employees, and trade unions;
- education and training, both generally and for those having specific roles;
- and, where they do not exist, the formation of what the majority report calls 'substructures' as an essential precursor and (subsequently) complementary arrangement to any form of board representation which may be adopted by a company.

(g) There must be emphasis on voluntary negotiation and evolvement of structures and procedures.

V. Proposals

(a) 'Substructures'

16. It is, we believe, common ground between ourselves and the other members of the Committee that the effectiveness of any form of Board level employee representation, where adopted, will depend to a large degree on the effectiveness of sub-board participation arrangements or 'substructures'. There is, however, between ourselves and at least some of our colleagues, a difference in approach to the justification for, and purposes of, these arrangements below Board level.

17. Our own first hand experience of companies which operate in West Germany leads us to believe that it is the German insistence on effective Works Councils separated from the union negotiating system, representing all employees and given extensive powers, which is one of the key factors in the success of the German system of employee participation. The German view (which we share) is that representation on a top board in any company would be meaningless without this under-pinning because—

- there would be no mechanism, through representation at Board level alone, for dealing with the issues which most concern employees;
- there would be no adequate communication link between employee representatives at Board level and the employee force as a whole.

18. It is perhaps worth recording at this point, in view of arguments in favour of using existing trade union machinery for this purpose, our conviction that this is in practice particularly weak on matters of communication up and down the line and that it would certainly be totally inadequate to undertake the critical task which is implied by our concept of an effective substructure for Board level participation.

19. The advantages we therefore see of participation arrangements below Board level are these—

- proof of the desire of all parties to work together co-operatively, as well as to bargain collectively where relevant;
- a base from which to elect 'top' board representatives;
- a training situation which will help to fit the successful candidates for such office;
- a way of involving a significant number of employees in day-to-day issues.

20. We believe that the substructures can be powerhouses of ideas, wisdom, and influence on a company's activities, and that they are essential complementary arrangements to any form of board representation.

21. The precise form of these arrangements cannot and should not be defined; rather they should be evolved to suit the circumstances existing in each plant and group of companies.

22. There are certain vital conditions for the effectiveness of substructures—

- all employees must take part in a ballot to approve the arrangements;
- all trade unions involved must be signatories and agree to participate;
- the structure involved must make provision for representation of all levels and every category of employee, whether belonging to a Trade Union or not;
- there must be agreement that the purpose of the arrangement is to further the success of the enterprise, and hence the well being of all involved in it, by constructive co-operation;
- no such arrangement should conflict with existing collective bargaining procedures;
- there must be a right of appeal to some form of arbitration if any party fails to co-operate, eg by withholding information or acting unilaterally in a way contrary to the general good of the company.

(b) The electoral base

23. In framing our proposals, we recognised the justifiable aspirations and power base of the Trade Unions, and also certain differences of opinion within the Trade Union movement. We considered other sections of the industrial community, particularly management, whose combined skills and experience are responsible for ensuring that the plans and day-to-day administration of industry are sensibly conceived and effectively carried out. Last, but far from least, we had a duty to the vast numbers of citizens outside industry whose standard of living so largely depends on the efficiency and economic achievement of British industry.

24. Clearly, Trade Unionists will play a major part in whatever arrangements are eventually implemented. The policies of Trade Union organisations will (and should) influence the attitudes of Trade Unionists within the enterprise as they play their parts in the internal participation structures—as happens in West Germany.

25. It is one of the great strengths of political democracy in the free world that every citizen has equal political rights and that no one has to belong to a particular party or organisation in order to exercise those rights. No citizens have to demonstrate their belief in collective representation before they can vote for a representative in Parliament. It would make a mockery of democracy as we know it to limit the rights of employees in any system of industrial democracy to those who have opted for collective representation through a Trade Union.

26. This basic and fundamental principle of democracy has obvious implications in the industrial field. It is integral to the West German system and is one of the few points on which the EEC in its recent Green Paper stands hard and fast.

27. We therefore cannot accept proposals which exclude any group of employees. Any proposals for the election of representatives either to an Employee or Company Council or to a Board level appointment must provide for the involvement—in terms of eligibility to vote and eligibility for election—of all adult employees with specified minimum lengths of service, whether or not they are members of a Trade Union. If the Trade Union membership within the organisation is strong and united, the Unions will have nothing to fear from such a procedure.

(c) Representation at board level

28. There appears to be a serious misconception of how, in our experience, Boards of Directors of UK Companies operate in practice; and we wish to add that our first hand knowledge of the operation of Boards of Directors in parts of the world other than the United Kingdom, coupled with discussions which we have had with industrial leaders in other countries, leads us to believe that we can with confidence generalise about the operation of Boards of Directors throughout the world.

29. Boards of Directors (at least of the larger Companies) are constituted in such a way as to bring to bear that range of skill and experience which is necessary for the resolution of the highly complex technical, commercial and financial problems with which an enterprise is faced. A power struggle between conflicting interests is highly inappropriate for this task; what is needed is the distillation of the combined wisdom of the Board until a consensus is reached.

30. The decision-making ability of a Board thus lies in its corporate strength and the signatories to this minority report, for all their considerable first hand experience of the working of Boards of Directors, can recollect very few occasions on which they have been involved in a policy decision arrived at through a vote by members of the Board.

(d) Role of elected representatives

31. It is, in our opinion, incompatible with the recommendation of the Majority Report that employee elected representatives should take their place on an existing Unitary Board of Directors, which is in effect the apex of a Company's management team, consisting primarily of persons with appropriate specialist and/or professional experience and training to fit them to plan and control the company's operations as executive directors.

32. Moreover, no one should be misled into believing that the comparative objectivity with which complex economic and human problems are brought into focus by the professional Boards of our large companies in the Private Sector could be maintained, let alone improved, by the injection into these Boards of representatives of powerful sectional interests, whether or not organised by the Trade Unions. We are completely opposed to the introduction into existing Boards of representatives of special interests of any kind which might provoke confrontation or extend the scope of collective bargaining into top level management decision-making. The dilution of management expertise, the confusion of objectives and the risk of a blocking vote emerging from the recommendations of the Majority Report seems to us to be a sure recipe for decline in management leadership and initiative; this is basic to our views and is not simply a question of proportions.

33. In short, to introduce employee elected representatives into existing Unitary Boards of Directors would—

- create considerable conflict of interest for the employee elected representative when the issue under discussion was one which was negotiable with the very Trade Union to which the representative himself belonged;

- place employee elected representatives in the wholly invidious position of being obliged to sit in on discussions to which they might have nothing to contribute because they were not properly equipped to contribute to this particular type of deliberation;

- cause a massive disruption in the membership—and therefore almost certainly in the effective workings—of existing Company Boards at a time when the country can least afford such disruption;

- induce further disillusionment, resentment and frustration in managers, particularly the most able, who in a number of respects are already treated inequitably and whose positive and constructive response to any employee representation proposals is essential;

- introduce a possible element of conflict and thus create a decision-making system which would certainly be slower and probably less effective than that which exists at present.

Such a course could not possibly be a right one to take.

34. The proposals on proportions of representation on Unitary Boards could also be regarded as the thin end of the wedge, a method of infiltration which could lead eventually to Trade Union/worker control of what are in effect the management boards of the Private Sector of industry. There is no evidence available in any part of the world to suggest that this form of control would be likely to be beneficial to British industry.

35. Our recommendation, subject to the creation or existence of a suitable substructure, is that if there is to be employee representation at board level it should be on *Supervisory Boards*. We recognise the existence in this country of a wish (not confined solely to questions of industrial democracy) for the introduction of some appropriate form of monitoring device to ensure that directors discharge their duties properly. A Supervisory Board is an appropriate device for such a purpose. It is here that the voice of employees can most usefully be heard. We accept the arguments in the Majority Report for confining such arrangements to companies with 2,000 or more employees[1].

36. We do not, on the other hand, accept the criticisms and rejection of the two-tier system (which entails the establishment of Supervisory Boards) and our reasons are set out in full in Appendix B to this report. We consider that insufficient consideration has been given to the working of the system in West Germany, the only European democracy in which there is any length of experience, or to how such a system might be adapted to meet the special needs of our own circumstances.

---

[1]Holding Companies employing fewer than 2,000 should not be exempt if their subsidiary companies collectively employ 2,000 or more.

37. Such arguments as have been adduced are either of a technical or formal nature—and as such open to serious challenge—or are inconsistent with the manner in which advocates of the Unitary Board system propose that it should be established. In the paragraphs which immediately follow we express our views on the constitution, duties and responsibilities of Supervisory Boards.

(e) Supervisory Boards: constitution

38. As we see it, the Supervisory Board, where established, should not involve itself with the detailed decision-making of existing Boards of Directors, not even with determining policy; but should be primarily concerned with the quality of the management of the company and its capacity to run the company profitably and competitively with due regard for the appropriate interests involved and to enable the company to continue operating in a climate of public confidence.

39. As regards constitution, it is essential to bear in mind that the governments of countries in Western Europe with practical experience of employee representatives on boards have been careful to ensure that the balance of representation is such that neither impasse nor employee representative majority situations can arise. Any proposals for the constitution of Supervisory Boards in this country must recognise that, on certain issues, there could be a direct conflict of interests between the different categories of Board membership. Therefore, a means of resolving such a conflict must be provided. To refer to external arbitration would be unwieldy, time-consuming, and might bring into a public forum issues which neither party would wish to be so discussed. It follows that the mechanism for resolution must be an internal, built-in feature of the system.

40. To these ends, we propose that a Supervisory Board, where adopted, should consist of—

One third elected by employees;

One third elected by the shareholders;

One third independent members.

Included in the one third employee elected representatives should be at least one member from the shop floor payroll, one from the salaried staff employees, and one from management.

41. The independent members should be individuals who have experience which will enable them to take a constructive interest in the affairs of the company and who have clearly and demonstrably no direct association with either of the other two parties represented on the Supervisory Board. They should be elected by an affirmative vote of at least two thirds of the employee elected representatives and of the shareholder elected representatives voting together. This proposal has the additional advantage of corresponding to current EEC thinking as represented in the Community's draft European Company Statute.

42. In the event of a continuing failure of the requisite number of candidates to achieve a two-thirds vote, the matter should be referred to a General Meeting of shareholders who should appoint the independent members.

43. The size of the Supervisory Board would, in our view, best be determined by the Chairman of the Supervisory Board and the Chairman of the Management Board jointly, but it should not be less than nine members. One of the shareholder elected representatives should be Chairman of the Supervisory Board, and should, if necessary, have a casting vote.

44. In this way, an appropriate degree of involvement in the supervision of a company's activities would be provided for employee elected representatives, with minimum alienation of existing members of management and without impairing the efficiency of existing Boards' decision-making processes.

(f) Supervisory Boards: powers, duties and responsibilities

45. If a Supervisory Board is to serve a useful purpose, it should not be a watchdog without teeth. It should exercise general supervision over the conduct of the company's affairs by the Board of Management, but should not participate directly in the management of the company, nor be empowered to initiate policies. It should be empowered to—

- approve, after appropriate consultation, appointments to the Board of Management;

- dismiss, subject to a unanimous vote of all members of the Supervisory Board, one or more of the members of the Board of Management;

- approve the remuneration of the members of the Board of Management;

- receive regular reports from the Board of Management on the progress of the company and have the right to any information on the management of the company which substantially affects its profitability or liquidity;

- have the responsibility of submitting to the shareholders such matters as are required by law or regulation of the Stock Exchange or any other body required to be approved by or reported to the shareholders, including proposals for—

  - winding up the company;
  - changing the memorandum and articles of association;
  - making changes in the capital structure of the Company;
  - exceptionally large expansions or contractions;
  - disposal of a substantial part of the undertaking;
  - approving the annual accounts;
  - payment of dividends.

46. The effect of this proposal would be to leave the existing structure, organisation, and purpose of Boards of Directors in the UK substantially unchanged, but it would introduce a new and, we believe, important element of accountability.

179

47. The accountability which Boards of Directors already have to the General Meeting of Shareholders would be strengthened and clarified by the presence of shareholder elected representatives on the Supervisory Board, and a completely new dimension of accountability would be introduced by the presence of employee elected representatives who would thus be fully involved in the major strategic issues of the Company. The presence of an independent third party is necessary, we believe, both to ensure that the interests of the community at large are taken into account and in particular to prevent deadlock and minimise sterile conflict between the other two parties.

(g) The pre-requisites for change

48. It is essential that changes of Board structure of the magnitude envisaged, either by ourselves or by our colleagues who have signed the Majority Report, should be firmly based if they are to succeed. The new 1976 law in Germany has followed a century of debate, fifty years of experiment and twenty-five years of practical experience. The new Swedish laws have evolved gradually over at least twenty-five years, since the first 'co-operation agreement' between the Swedish Employers' and Labour Organisations, providing for the establishment of Works Councils as a basic foundation on which participation should be based, was signed in 1946. Indeed, we know of no country in the world in which mandatory representation at board level has not been preceded by an extensive mandatory development of sub-board structures which have been seen as important both as structural building blocks and as means of developing in practice the willingness of the parties to work together to a single aim.

49. The pre-requisites for change in any company's board structures should therefore be—

- an Employee or Company Council, established in accordance with the terms of an agreed Code of Practice and representative of all employees in the enterprise, should have been in operation for at least three years, and it should be supported by effective sub-structures right down to the place of work;

- a ballot of all employees should have been called for either by the unanimous approach of all independent Trade Unions recognised by the Company or by a two-thirds majority of the Employee Council;

- the ballot, which should be secret, should show the support of a simple majority of all employees who had completed one year's service in favour of having a Supervisory Board (as defined above).

(h) The election of employee representatives

50. The Majority Report concludes that the process of selection of employee representatives for board seats should be left to the Trade Unions in the company in question. Apart from the unacceptable disenfranchisement of a proportion of the company's employees, this greatly underestimates the potential dangers and difficulties. Experience of inter-union rivalry, even over relatively trivial matters, leads us to have grave fears about the disruption which could result.

180

51. The Majority Report does, however, confirm the view of most submissions to the Committee in stating that employee elected representatives should be employees of the Company. We strongly agree with this conclusion. Knowledge of a Company's affairs, and identification with its objectives, as well as strong links with the body of employees, are essential and are most likely to be found in this way. However, the effective execution of the role proposed is such a demanding one that other conditions are also essential. We believe that no candidate should be eligible unless he or she has—

- been employed by the Company for a minimum of ten years;
- been a member of a sub-board council/committee for not less than three years;
- undergone adequate and appropriate training to enable him or her to participate effectively in the Supervisory Board discussions.

52. Elections must conform to proper standards of secrecy, and should be valid only if—

- not less than three candidates are proposed for each office;
- not less than 60 per cent of the electorate cast effective votes.

53. Candidates for election should be nominated in writing

either by ten employees

or by an independent Trade Union recognised for negotiating purposes by the Company.

54. Tenure of office of successful candidates should be as defined in the Companies' Articles of Association, subject to earlier termination on ceasing to be employed by the Company. Exceptionally, earlier termination could be achieved by a successful call for a new ballot by 60 per cent of the electorate, but recall would not be possible under any other circumstances.

(i) **The functions and responsibilities of employee elected representatives**

55. Proposals to enable representatives of employees to share responsibility and power on any type of board are fraught with difficulty, not only for the proper conduct of the enterprise, but also for employees and their representatives. There is evidence from opinion surveys that many employees themselves recognise this and do not want to go down this road, and this view is supported by the submissions of some of the large unions which gave evidence to us. Of course, they may be persuaded to the contrary, but we believe that this view of industrial democracy of those who would be most affected reflects a genuine conflict and difficulty which should not lightly be brushed aside.

56. It centres on the ambivalent role of the employee elected representative being obliged to share board decisions in the interests of the enterprise and, at the same time, being responsible in some way to his union membership. The original TUC Report was clear on this issue when it stated that 'the responsibility of worker representatives would be to Trade Union members employed

in the firm rather than to the annual general assembly of shareholders'. This corresponds correctly with the basic drive of the TUC document which sees industrial democracy as a means of extending the power and control of organised labour. However, the West German position is equally clear that employee elected representatives on Supervisory Boards are no different in their responsibilities from other members of the board. This should also be the position in the UK and on this point we are in agreement with the Majority Report, although the reference in the latter is, of course, to representation on Unitary Boards.

57. The aspect of confidentiality has already received much attention—and rightly so in our view—but of at least equal importance is the recognition and acceptance of the concept of the company, and the common duty of all directors to act at all times for the success of the Company. The same duty should apply equally to all members of Supervisory Boards since without such collective responsibility and commitment to the success of the organisation, the direction and management of a Company would be impossible.

58. We consider that those who have acquired experience in the substructure should have relatively little difficulty in this respect, since a proper understanding of Company issues is inherent in holding office under such arrangements.

59.   With regard to 'reporting back' to constituents, we stipulate two requirements—

- that it be executed through the fully representative substructure in order to involve all employees and with a proper regard for the need for confidentiality where this can be shown to be in the best interests of the enterprise;

- that there can be no question of employee elected representatives being 'mandated'; as also indicated in the Majority Report, they must act within the Board in accordance with all the facts and opinions available to them.

VI. Fundamental issues

60. The preceding paragraphs set out the framework within which we believe that legislation should take place if the Government is determined, in spite of the difficulties and dangers, to introduce new laws on the basis of the remit which we have been given. Fundamental to these proposals are five issues to which we attach the greatest importance and on which we believe there should be no compromise—

(a) that where a secret ballot reveals a majority of employees in favour of representation at board level, such representation should be on Supervisory, not Unitary Boards;

(b) that the employee representation should always constitute less than half of a Supervisory Board;

(c) that the employee representation should include at least one representative of all categories of employees—from the shop floor payroll, from salaried staff employees, and from management;

(d) that the issues of board level representation should not be voted upon until a complementary 'substructure' of an Employee Council had been established and operated effectively for a specified number of years;

(e) that all employees (not just members of Trade Unions) should be involved in elections both to Employee Councils and to Supervisory Board appointments.

VII. Practical problems

(a) International companies

61. There are real problems relating to companies based in the UK with substantial overseas interests. It would be inequitable and undemocratic for matters affecting the employees, Boards and the minority shareholders of subsidiary companies overseas, many of which are long standing and substantial companies in their own right in their own countries, to be decided by bodies on which the only employees represented were those of UK companies.

62. The EEC Commission has given considerable thought to this issue without reaching any conclusion. The matter must nevertheless be dealt with. Our proposal is that—

Employee elected representatives on the Supervisory Boards of Companies having expressed their views and declared their interests, should not be entitled to a vote in cases of disagreement over a major investment project outside the UK or matters which are wholly the concern of a subsidiary company overseas.

(b) Subsidiary companies

63. It is possible to argue that proposals for employee representation at board level should operate equally for the boards of subsidiary companies and for the subsidiaries of subsidiaries and so on.

64. The result would be a total structure of intolerable complexity, for instance—

- some subsidiaries would fall within the criteria by which Supervisory Boards had to be established, others would not;
- in some groups, large plants would be operated as divisions or branches, in others as legal entities—there would thus be a total lack of uniformity in industry generally;
- it would ignore altogether the practical problems of operating major groups under which many matters normally reserved for boards of independent companies (eg in relation to capital expenditure, finance, dividends, executive appointments, pensions, etc) are made at the centre of the group management structure;
- it could militate seriously and dangerously against the efficient operation of the group as a whole.

65. We believe that an employee or company council is the most appropriate means of obtaining employee involvement at the subsidiary company level, and that, for the time being at least—

companies which are subsidiary to other companies incorporated in the United Kingdom should not be subject to the proposed legislation.

66. If, however, in spite of the anomalies arising, any legislation has to be applied to large subsidiaries, then—

(a) employees should elect representatives only to the Supervisory Board of the subsidiary company and not to that of the holding company as well;

(b) the rights of the Supervisory Board of the subsidiary company should exclude any rights relating to the appointment and dismissal of their Management Board.

The latter provision is, we believe, essential if the management cohesion of a group of companies is to be maintained. The Supervisory Board of a subsidiary company would nevertheless have rights of recommendation to the Management Board of the holding company in respect of the membership of its own Management Board.

67. Subsidiaries of foreign companies should not be included in the legislation. Many of these, in the future, may be controlled by other European companies and it is probable that EEC regulations will prescribe the appropriate procedures. In no circumstances should overseas investors be put in a position where they could be outvoted by a combination of employee directors and co-opted directors. No solution could have more disastrous results than this on the establishment and/or development by overseas companies of industrial enterprises in the United Kingdom.

68. The issues set out in the preceding paragraphs on subsidiary companies are more fully explored in Appendix C.

(c) Major financial institutions—clearing banks and insurance companies

69. The major financial institutions, eg the clearing banks and the large insurance companies, must, in our view, receive separate and special consideration. This is examined in Appendix D, and our conclusion is that there is a strong case for the specific exclusion of such institutions from any provisions relating to employee representation on any form of board.

(d) The Fragmented British Trade Union Movement

70. The German DGB is made up of 16 Trade Unions. There are over 100 Trade Unions affiliated to the British TUC. Most German companies deal each with only one Trade Union. Most British companies deal with several, some with ten or more in the UK alone.

71. This is as much a problem for the Trade Union movement as a whole (and is recognised by the movement as such) as it is for management and for the nation. We have, however, been sufficiently impressed by the number of industrialists in West Germany who have expressed the view that any form of co-determination would be unworkable in a fragmented Trade Union situation to wish to record a note of caution and to suggest that the Government would be unwise to proceed with any legislation without any clear undertaking from the TUC and its constituent Unions on the way in which the problem of fragmentation will be resolved.

72. At present, we do not see how the genuine differences of union policy on the subject of industrial democracy can be resolved at the workplace in such a way as to make either our proposals, or those of the majority report, work effectively and without inter-union strife.

VIII. Legislation

73. Legislation can and has been used to influence certain aspects of industrial relations, but its recent history must indicate that there are grave dangers to good industrial relations in adopting too arbitrary a policy in terms which are inflexible and premature.

74. Our preference is therefore for a minimum of legislation providing no more than a framework within which a company might choose to work, a safeguard to ensure a necessary minimum of progress and a protection against more radical developments which might be damaging to the country's wealth-producing capacity. The provisions we feel to be desirable are—

(a) amendment of the Companies Act to confirm the rights and duties of directors (ie for members of existing Boards and, under the optional arrangements which we are proposing for larger companies, members of Management Boards) to manage the Company's affairs within the Memorandum and Articles of Association with due regard to the interests of shareholders, employees and other interested parties;

(b) a requirement for all companies within the scope of the report to conclude an internally agreed form of domestic participation arrangement below the level of the board within four years of the legislation being enacted. This should be flexible, but, to ensure effectiveness, should conform to certain criteria which should be contained in a Code of Practice. Rights of appeal to arbitration in cases of 'non-performance' should be included;

(c) necessary enabling legislation which would allow formation of a Supervisory Board as described in paragraph 38–43, subject to the pre-requisites regarding substructure, and specifying clearly the rights, duties, powers and means of election of all members of such a Board.

IX. Change, credibility and confidence

75. In the Majority Report there is considerable discussion of the need for change in the field of industrial democracy, and the reasons which make it particularly appropriate for such change to be implemented at this time. We agree in principle with much of this analysis, and particularly with the argument that greater involvement in the planning and implementing of developments in industry will enrich the lives of employees and increase industrial efficiency.

76. If industrial democracy is extended in a way which meets what we believe to be the essential criteria described in Section IV, the potential for good, for the nation and for the individual, will be great; but should the extension be 'radical' to such a degree that it increases conflict rather than encourages co-operation, it will lead not only to disappointment but to disaster. We therefore close our report by stating our conviction that the extension of industrial democracy requires application of the highest skills in devising and managing the changes involved at company level.

77. If they are to succeed, the wisdom of the steps to be taken by any company must be recognised and accepted by many different people, not only in this country—by managers and all other categories of employees, Trade Unions, Boards of Directors, shareholders and consumers—but also overseas, where we are increasingly dependent on our industrial credibility with our friends who invest in Britain, with our overseas customers and with the international bankers.

78. It cannot be stressed too strongly that there is no evidence whatsoever that the changes proposed in the Majority Report will be beneficial and the risks are enormous. If ever there was a case for caution in an unknown, unassessable venture, it is this one.

79. The reference in the Committee's remit to the possible effects of innovation on industrial efficiency must be recognised as of prime importance now, not recalled with regret if rash, compulsory measures are forced through which alienate those whose day-to-day decisions and skills of implementation are vital to industrial success.

80. At this time, all should be prepared to abandon prejudice, pre-conception and dogma, and to weigh sectional interests against national imperatives. We believe that our proposals represent a basis which deserves careful consideration by the Government and by everyone who has to assess the results of the Committee's deliberations.

N P BIGGS

JACK CALLARD

BARRIE HEATH

14th December, 1976.

MINORITY REPORT: APPENDIX A

Deductions from written submissions to the Committee

1. A list of those who made written submissions to the Committee is included as an Annex to the majority report.

2. It would be unwise to draw too firm conclusions from a purely numerical analysis of the submissions; the sources of the submissions are unevenly balanced, and the varying quality of submissions, and in particular the care which has gone into the reasoning leading to certain conclusions, cannot possibly be reflected in statistical tables. Moreover, some submissions of high quality in fact reached no firm conclusion nor made any specific recommendation.

3. Nevertheless, it cannot be without significance that, of the analysable submissions, two-thirds were opposed to employee elected directors. Only amongst the political and private individual submissions was there a convincing majority in favour of such directors.

4. These statements should perhaps be qualified by the fact that a number of the employers and some others who were against employee directors were, above all, concerned about the possibility of statutory imposition with inadequate preparation.

5. Some, although not all, might therefore be prepared to modify their views in the light of the safeguards contained in the minority report proposals.

6. Other arrangements which gained widespread support were:
   Employee Councils,
   A Code of Practice,
   A Monitoring Agency,
   (the latter two were frequently coupled).
Of these, Employee Councils gained significant support in every category of submission.

7. A relatively small number of submissions declared a preference for the type of board which they felt would be appropriate for the introduction of employee representatives, and many of these made such a statement only after stressing that board representation was not, in their view, likely to be an effective way of meeting the real requirement for extending employee participation. However, of those making a choice, over two-thirds opted for a Supervisory Board arrangement.

Unitary and Supervisory Boards

1. The principal objections to a two-tier structure are that the system would involve two separate Company Law structures; that it would involve detailed legal definition of functions which would cut across the flexible traditions of United Kingdom Company Law; and that it would be detrimental to operational efficiency. It has also been argued that the adoption of the two-tier system in European countries has either formed part of an historical tradition (as in Germany), or has created a source of conflict (as in France), and that experience elsewhere shows that attempts to modify the system are unsatisfactory. Finally, it has been suggested that its adoption in the United Kingdom might result in frustrating employee participation at Board level and thus perpetuate the dominance of management.

2. We believe the supposed difficulties of legal definition have been over-estimated. British Company Law has provided since 1908 for different types of company—public, private and, between 1948 and 1967, exempt private—as well as legislating for companies engaged in certain activities such as Insurance and Banking; regulations of the Stock Exchange and the City Panel on take-overs and mergers have, to all intents and purposes, the force of law governing one special category of company, ie quoted companies. All Western European systems accept the existence of different types of legal corporation and proposals are in train for the creation of yet another type of company—an EEC company. We would not expect the task of legislating in the United Kingdom for a special category of company with a two-tier Board structure to be any more difficult than that of defining in statutory terms the respective functions of the Board and Management under a unitary system.

3. Evidence has been adduced of over-formalism under certain European systems—for example, in relation to the qualification of members entitled to sit on the Supervisory Board. This, however, appears to us to be irrelevant to the merits of the argument. As regards the more general argument that a two-tier system would require detailed treatment in the law, we believe that it could be shown that the legal definition of the type of supervisory control necessary to establish a workable system for British companies would be no more difficult than defining the regulations devised in many known instances, well established by precedent, for exercising supervisory control within the existing UK company structure, for example, when two companies, in partnership, set up a joint enterprise.

4. It has been maintained, however, that the aim of a two-tier Board could not be properly fulfilled in a statutory system unless legislation defined the respective functions and membership of the Board and management. The definition of functions may indeed cause some problems, but these will exist whether a Supervisory or a Unitary Board solution is favoured and there seems to us to be no significant difference in this respect.

5. On the question of membership, it is difficult to believe that a satisfactory legal definition to accord with the minority proposals would present any real difficulty or in any way militate against flexibility in the conduct of a company's business operations.

6. However, more important than any supposed difficulty in defining the legal functions and membership of the Supervisory Board would be the statutory provisions governing the relationship between a Unitary Board and senior management. The terms in which the functions to be reserved to the Board might be defined (and are defined, for instance, in the Majority Report) appear to us, particularly in relation to large and diverse companies, to open up a field so complex and wide-ranging that any attempt at statutory definition would inevitably give rise to an area of detailed rules and regulations equivalent to a written constitution which might well put management in the thrall of company lawyers, involve the possibility of delays, and legal disputes, and seriously frustate the dynamic of company management.

7. If, for example, the Board of a large and diverse company had to deal with all matters relating to the appointment, removal, control and remuneration of management throughout its many divisions, this would be an intolerable burden unless management was defined in such restricted terms as merely to apply to the type of executive whose terms of remuneration would be referred to the Board under the existing system.

8. If all matters as mentioned in the last two paragraphs had to be decided through the Board, it would result, in our view, in a rigidity of structure worse than the adverse effects on the present flexible system which is advanced as an objection to a two-tier system. On the other hand, we doubt whether a general delegation of powers would in the long run be likely to be acceptable to the employee representatives on a Unitary Board.

9. If then there is to be a legal definition of powers as between Board and management, the question of sanctions inevitably arises. Third parties could no doubt be protected in relation to their dealings with the company, but it would be quite unacceptable to impose sole responsibility on the management and to subject certain individuals to dismissal if they exceeded their powers. Management should not be put in the position of having to determine whether each decision taken at any level is constitutional or to face dismissal. Any such system would require a series of statutory safeguards equivalent to those now appertaining to employment protection and unfair dismissal. Nor would delegation of authority necessarily resolve the problem; it would be an equally onerous burden to determine whether or not any given matter fell within a specific delegation. In practice, management might be forced to refer all decisions, even comparatively minor ones, to the central Board with a consequent overloading and slowing up of the decision-making process.

10. It has been pointed out that one of the virtues of UK law, unlike Continental law, is that it allows companies to define for themselves the role of their Boards in relation to management. Thus the Articles of Association of companies invariably provide, as in Table A of the first Schedule to the Companies Act 1948 that the Directors of the company shall have power to manage the business of the company and to exercise all such powers as are not required by the Companies Acts to be exercised by the company in General Meeting. A two-tier system would leave this position unaffected except that the Directors' authority to exercise the powers of the company would be subject both to the powers reserved by the Companies Act to the shareholders and also to those requiring the approval or confirmation of the Supervisory Board. Since the only additional matters we propose to those requiring the approval of shareholders under the existing system are those relating to exceptionally large expansion or contractions and substantial disposals (which would probably already require approval of shareholders or debenture holders under Stock Exchange or other regulations and which would certainly require notification to them), the approval of a Supervisory Board would give rise to no restriction on existing flexibility as between Board and management; it would merely extend the relationship which now exists between Board and shareholders, in appropriate cases, to that which would arise between Board and Supervisory Board.

11. To draw on the experience in Europe requires, in our opinion, a review of the available evidence at least as exhaustive as that undertaken in the reports made to the Committee by Eric Batstone and P L Davies. We do not consider that selected citations from these reports are justifiable without at the same time drawing attention to the general conclusion of one of the authors that 'in practice the difference (ie in relation to the significance of worker directors) between the two-tier and unitary board system is often marginal' (Eric Batstone, p 39).

12. The broad conclusion which we derive from the existing European experience is that there is certainly no weight of evidence to suggest that the two-tier system is any less effective in achieving a degree of employee participation at Board level than a unitary system. The decisive considerations are (a) the objectives aimed at, and (b) the system most suited to the conditions already prevailing. In determining objectives, the concept of 'democracy' is paramount. If this means direct involvement in the affairs of the enterprise at the highest level, in common with the owners (shareholders) and the management, the evidence from the most successful of European economies indicates a two-tier Supervisory Board structure as the most effective. If it is taken to mean a wider measure of worker control, then the concepts of 'the company's best interests' and market considerations must be radically revised, there must be a fundamental change in the pattern of investment in industry and 'worker directors' must be regarded as a means of achieving a major change in the structure of industry and society. This must be a matter for the electorate and not for this Committee.

13. The terms of reference of the Committee require it to have regard to the interests of the national economy, employers, investors and consumers as well as the efficient management of companies. The first and last of these factors, as well as the interests of consumers, dictate that the company's best interests and market considerations must remain paramount. The interest of investors requires that they retain adequate representation on the ultimate controlling body. In no sense, therefore, would a two-tier system offend against the terms of reference of the Committee; it would cause the minimum of dislocation to the existing system of management while affording each of the parties interested a practical, and, in our view, adequate, degree of participation; and it would equate with the best available European experience and with the current proposals of the EEC Commission. By contrast, a unitary board system would cause a fundamental change in the pattern of company direction; by interposing a defined range of reserved functions as between Board and management it would open a wide area of constitutional legality and potential disagreement and friction at a time when the national interest demands clear and decisive action; and the European experience shows that in positive terms it would, at the best, lead to little significant increase in the effectiveness of 'worker directors.'

14. We repeat, therefore, our opinion that a two-tier structure would be less likely to be restrictive than a unitary board structure. A further and more general criticism, however, has been brought against the two-tier structure. It has been suggested that it might be used, or even designed, to frustrate worker participation, and to perpetuate the dominance of management. This is not so. If indutsry is to be efficient, management should indeed be given freedom to manage, but subject to such supervisory control as is required to protect the rights of those concerned with the enterprise. The task of anyone legislating in this field, certainly anyone taking into account the interests to which we are to have regard by our terms of reference, is to strike the right balance. We believe that, if the practical problems are analysed, it will be seen that the Supervisory Board structure is the one best fitted to achieve this balance and that it will be for those charged with implementing the policy to give Supervisory Boards the power required which will prevent the system being abused or frustrated.

Subsidiary companies

1. It is common ground that the application of employee representation on Boards of subsidiary companies, particularly subsidiaries of foreign multinationals, presents special and difficult problems. It is clear that if any subsidiary is to qualify, the group itself will be substantial; it is equally probable that it will be a group with more than one, and possibly many, subsidiaries.

2. We consider that it is first necessary to appreciate the practical position within groups such as these, particularly in relation to their wholly owned subsidiaries. Here the practical situation is that a large number of the powers of the Boards of the subsidiaries are, and indeed must be, abrogated to the central group management, eg in relation to capital expenditure, control of finances, allocation of profits, executive appointments, pensions, etc.

3. While this might be argued in theoretical terms to militate against the interests of the employees of the particular subsidiary regarded as a separate body, our experience is that there are likely to be substantial compensatory benefits derived from the employees being members of a group which is both more powerful and financially stable than their own particular unit on its own. This is especially true in regard to employees of UK subsidiaries of North American multinational corporations where terms and conditions of working are usually at least as favourable as for employees of UK controlled companies.

4. Secondly, many subsidiaries exist as legal entities only because of historical accident or other special tactical reasons; there are many anomalous situations where in one group a large plant may be a separate company. Any statutory regulations could be negated by the simple expedient of divisionalising within a group and bringing separate trading activities within the ambit of a single company; or alternatively by hiving off separate plants into separate companies. In consequence, a complex structure of anti-avoidance legislation might have to be enacted. Until some method could be devised of dealing with these problems, the Supervisory Board of the ultimate holding company should, in our opinion, be the only Board within the group on which employees are represented.

5. We recognise, however, that in any legislation providing for employee representation at Board level this might not be found acceptable and we must, therefore, consider as an alternative the adaptation of the two-tier structure recommended by us to 'large subsidiaries' as defined in the Majority Report. If, regardless of the particular circumstances ruling in any given case, these subsidiaries are to be regarded as separate companies within the proposed legislation, we would advocate that the provision under which the appointment of members of the Management Board is subject to the approval of the Supervisory Board, together with the provision under which the Supervisory Board might by a unanimous vote dismiss the Management Board, should not apply to the Supervisory Boards of subsidiary companies. The power to appoint senior management is the one fundamental power which a holding company must have if it is to run a large and diverse group, and we believe that it is a power which should not be taken away from the Management Board of the holding company as the top managing body of the group. This should not, of course, prevent the Supervisory Board of a subsidiary company from making recommendations about its Management Board to the Management Board of the holding company, and that body would frequently be ill-advised not to take note of such recommendations.

6. In considering large subsidiaries controlled by foreign multinationals, we have to bear in mind that, although the companies involved at the moment are largely controlled from North America, our recommendations must be such as to be applicable to companies controlled from other territories such as other European countries and Japan. In our opinion, subsidiaries of foreign holding companies should for the time being be excluded altogether from any legislation. Our experience of North American controlled companies, as indeed is the case as regards overseas subsidiaries of United Kingdom companies, is that the question of employees' interests is sufficiently crucial to the success of the operations to command at least as high a degree of priority as employee participation at Board level could achieve. By contrast, we doubt very much whether overseas investors would develop their operations in the United Kingdom if their plans could be frustrated at any time by their being outvoted by a majority of employee elected representatives and co-directors who might have been appointed by a United Kingdom Government Agency.

7. We consider, therefore, that such a solution would be both impracticable and unwise; also, it represents, in our view, far too rigid and legalistic an answer to the problem. If, for the sake of consistency, employee representation at Board level has to be extended to foreign controlled subsidiaries, it should only be through a minority representation on a Supervisory Board and the shareholders should be entitled to appoint the co-opted members, subject perhaps to a proviso that the majority of them should be UK residents. This, together with the involvement of employees and management at plant level, should ensure an adequate degree of employee participation until an international solution emerged.

The special case of major financial institutions, clearing banks and insurance companies

1. We have considered how far the proposals and recommendations in the Minority Report, as they relate to companies employing 2,000 or more persons, could and should be applied to institutions in the financial sector of which the London & Scottish Clearing Banks and major Life Assurance Companies are most obviously concerned.

2. To the extent that substructures, as defined, are shown to be less than satisfactory to meet the reasonable expectations about pay and conditions of service, opening and closing of branches, mechanisation plans, etc, we recommend they should be revised and if necessary expanded with due regard for the collective bargaining procedures already in force or to be established.

3. Employee participation in decision taking which relates to the banks' operations for their customers already exists in considerable depth. Indeed the Clearing Banks could not operate without such participation at various levels involving employees with a wide variety of skills. It is simply not practical, however, to envisage collective decision taking in relation to the multitudinous complex and highly confidential affairs of the banks' customers in the private, corporate and public sectors.

4. In considering the scope for the appointment of employee representatives, the nature and responsibilities of bank Boards must be recognised. Clearing Bank Boards include executives recruited from career staff and a large number of outside directors chosen for their judgment of men and affairs and for their wide experience of business and industrial conditions. The directors as a body share in the assessment by the executives of highly sensitive information relating to their principal customers while determining the banks' policies in the light of current economic conditions and monetary policy and with proper regard for the interests of depositors. By their composition, the Boards in fact combine in a very real sense both executive and monitoring functions. The confidential nature of their work must preclude any appointments of a representative character implying an obligation to report back to either shareholders or employee organisations of individual customer affairs or of sensitive market information.

5. The Clearing Banks are, moreover, closely monitored by the Bank of England. In helping to implement the Authorities' wishes in regard to monetary policy, they are guided both formally and informally by views expressed to them from time to time by the Bank of England. Such views and the impact which they must have on Clearing Bank operations cannot be other than strictly confidential.

6. It is our view that in the case of a Clearing Bank the appointment of a Supervisory Board would in effect create an additional and superfluous layer of supervision, and that no such Board could work effectively unless the Chairman and Senior Directors participated in the existing top level contacts with the Bank of England; without this much information bearing on important policy matters would have to be withheld.

7. Similar considerations apply to the large Life Assurance Companies. Their Boards of Directors are directly concerned with the protection of policy holders and with the prudent investment of the savings entrusted to them. The investment policies of the companies are highly confidential, being market sensitive, and are effectively monitored by the Department of Trade. In this instance also no appointments of a representational character implying an obligation to report back to any outside body other than through the Annual Report and Accounts seems desirable, and it

must be remembered that the Industrial Assurance Act, 1923 specifically contained prohibitions against allowing certain categories of employee to sit on Boards or Committees of Management. Moreover, Mutual Companies established by individual Acts of Parliament and others formed under a Royal Charter do not come within the scope of the Companies Acts.

8. We conclude that there is a very strong case for specific exclusion of financial Institutions from any provisions relating to employee representation on Boards. We have in mind not only the Clearing Banks and Life Assurance Companies but generally speaking all Insurance Companies and those undertakings which take deposits from the public and which will in future be subject to licensing by the Bank of England or exempted from such licensing procedure. This opinion is reinforced by consideration of the importance attaching to the City's still dominant role in banking, insurance and financial services generally.

ANNEX A

LIST OF THOSE WHO SUBMITTED EVIDENCE

(*denotes those who gave both oral and written evidence)
(**denotes those who gave oral evidence only)

Abel Morrall Ltd
Mr David Abel Smith
Dr Peter Abell, Dr Frank Heller and Professor Malcolm Warner
Mr E K Abrahall
Acrow Ltd
Mr J C Adams, FCA, ACMA
Mr Kenneth Adams
Advisory, Conciliation and Arbitration Service
Aims for Freedom and Enterprise
Airflow Developments Ltd
Albright & Wilson Ltd
Allen & Caswell Ltd
Allied Breweries Ltd
All-Party Parliamentary Group for Common Ownership
Amalgamated Union of Engineering Workers
APV Holdings Ltd
Ash & Lacy Ltd
Associated Portland Cement Manufacturers Ltd
Association of British Chambers of Commerce
Association of Independent Businesses
Association of Investment Trust Companies
Association of Jute Spinners and Manufacturers
Association of Professional, Executive, Clerical and Computer Staff
Association of Professional Scientists and Technologists
Mr Bedford Attwood
Mr Harry Ball-Wilson
Bar Association for Commerce, Finance & Industry
Mr J W Barber
Bass Charrington Ltd
Mr S P Bate and Professor I L Mangham
Richard Baxendale & Sons Ltd
Beecham Group Ltd
Mr T Bentley
Professor Paul Bernstein
Biggs Wall & Co Ltd
Mr J R Birds, LL M, and Mr B A K Rider
Birmingham and West Midlands Productivity Association
Birmingham Chamber of Industry and Commerce
Blackfriars Consultative Council of Unilever Ltd
Board for Social Responsibility of the General Synod of the Church of England
Bodycote International Ltd

Mr N I Bond-Williams
Bonser Engineering Ltd
Boots Ltd
Bovis Civil Engineering Ltd
Members of the Bow Group
A E Boyman & Son
Mr Jeremy Bray, MP and Mr Nicholas Falk
Brewers' Society
Bristol Channel Ship Repairers Ltd
British-American Tobacco Company Ltd
British and Irish Communist Organisation
British Footwear Manufacturers Federation
British Independent Steel Producers Association
*British Institute of Management: Sir Frederick Catherwood
                                              Mr Bernard Cotton
                                              Mr Roy Close CBE, MSC
                                                Mr William Bree
British Insurance Association
British Insurance Brokers' Council
British Leyland Ltd
British Oxygen Co Ltd
British Paper and Board Industry Federation
British Petroleum Group
British Plastics Federation
British Poultry Federation Ltd
British Printing Industries Federation
British Textile Employers' Association
Mr Richard Britton MBA, MBCS
Mr John R Brockhouse
Lord (Wilfred) Brown PC
Mr Peter J Buckingham and Mr Bruce Lloyd
James Burrough Ltd
Commander Hyde C Burton FCA
Business Equipment Trade Association
Business Planning and Development
Mr Francis Bywater ACIS
Cadbury Schweppes Ltd
Lt Col A E H Campbell
Dr Charles Carter and Mr George Goyder
Mr Peter Chadwick and 7 others under the auspices of the Oldham
    Chamber of Commerce
Chemical Industries Association Ltd
Chloride Group Ltd
Christian Association of Business Executives
City Company Law Committee
Clarke Chapman Ltd
Cocoa, Chocolate and Confectionery Alliance
Mr A J Colman and Mr David Tench
Combine Trade Union Conveners of British Leyland Ltd
**Commission of the European Communities: Commissioner Finn Gundelach
                                                     Mr Robert Colman

Committee of London Clearing Bankers
Committee of Scottish Clearing Bankers
Communist Party of Great Britain
Company Council of Ransomes Sims and Jefferies Ltd
Compen Management Consultants
*Confederation of British Industry: Viscount Watkinson PC, CH
                                     Sir Campbell Adamson
                                     Sir James Barker
                                     Mr H G DeVille
Confederation of Employee Organisations
Consolidated Gold Fields Ltd
Mr Neville J Cooper
Co-operative Productive Federation Ltd
Council of Bank Staff Associations
Council of Engineering Institutions
Courage Ltd
Coventry & District Engineering Employers' Association
Coverdale Organisation
Mr Jim Craigen MP
Mr D B Crawford
Delta Metal Company Ltd
Department of Education and Science
Department of Manpower Services, Northern Ireland Office
Val de Travers Asphalte Ltd
Mr A Drinkwater
Dunlop Ltd
Professor Samuel Eilon
Eldridge, Pope & Co Ltd
Electrical Contractors' Association
Electrical, Electronic, Telecommunication & Plumbing Union
Electrical & Musical Industries Ltd
*Embassy of the Federal Republic of Germany: Dr R J Vollmer, Labour
    Attaché
Engineering Employers' Federation
Engineering Section of the Amalgamated Union of Engineering Workers
English Clays Lovering Pochin & Co Ltd
Esso Petroleum Company Ltd
Esso Research Centre Group of the Association of Scientific, Technical and
    Managerial Staffs
European Institute for Industrial Relations
European Management Association
Evans Adlard & Co Ltd
Members of the Executive and Management Staff Committee of the British
    Aircraft Corporation, Bristol
Fabian Society
Fairbairn Lawson Ltd
Mr David Farnham
**Sir Eric Faulkner: Chairman of Lloyds Bank Ltd
Federation of Civil Engineering Contractors
Ferguson Industrial Holdings Ltd
Mr R J Fletcher

198

Mr T Fletcher
Professor Michael P Fogarty
Ford Motor Company Ltd
Foundation for Management Education
**Mr Ian Fraser: Deputy Chairman of Lazard Brothers & Company Ltd
Freshfields
Mr John Garnett
Professor L C B Gower
Mr George Goyder   (a joint submission)
Sir Bernard Miller
Mr Trevor Owen
Gauge and Tool Makers' Association
General and Municipal Workers' Union
General Council of British Shipping
General Electric Company Ltd
Gestetner Holdings Ltd
Grand Metropolitan Ltd
Mr John Gratwick
Greenall Whitley & Co Ltd
Grubb Institute
Grundy & Partners Ltd
Guest Keen & Nettlefolds Ltd
Arthur Guinness Son and Co Ltd
Dr Bjorn Gustavsen
Mr Tom Hadden LL B, PhD
Mr C G Hanson
Harris & Sheldon Group Ltd
Mr W J Hart
Mr N A Hawkins BA, LL B
Mr E R Holton
Imperial Chemical Industries Ltd
Inbucon/AIC Management Consultants Ltd
Industrial Common Ownership Movement
Industrial Participation Association
Industrial Society
Institute for Workers' Control
Institute of Chartered Secretaries and Administrators
Institute of Directors
Institute of Management Consultants & Management Consultants
   Association
Institute of Personnel Management
Institution of Mechanical Engineers
Institution of Production Engineers
Institution of Works Managers
International Harvester Company of Great Britain Ltd
Mr Greville Janner QC, MP
Professor Elliott Jaques
Mr T Kempner
Mr Tom Kilcourse
Kleeneze Holdings Ltd
Ms Lisl Klein

199

Richard Klinger Ltd
Knight Strip Metals Ltd
Labour Party
Mr Hector Laing
John Laing & Son Ltd
Laity Commission
Law Society
Law Society of Scotland
Mr O R J Lee
John Lewis Partnership Ltd
Liberal Party
Lincolnshire Standard Group
Peter Lind & Co Ltd
London Factories Works Council of the Glacier Metal Co Ltd
London Young Managers of the British Institute of Management
Mr A L Louden
LRC International Ltd
Manchester Branch of the British Institute of Management
Market Research Society
Marks and Spencer Ltd
Mr Hugh Marlow
Mars Ltd
Mr David F Marshall
Mr Edward Matchett
Mr Alexander Matejko
Mather & Platt
Mr J Matthews
Sir Robert McAlpine & Sons Ltd
McKinsey & Co Ltd
Mersey Docks and Harbour Company
Metra Oxford Consulting Ltd
M & G Investment Management Ltd
Mr P A J Milligan
**Mr Peter Moody: Joint Secretary and Investment Manager of the Prudential
    Insurance Company Ltd
Moyle Castings & Marine
MQS (Drilling) Ltd
Multiple Shops Federation
MWP Incentives Ltd
*National Consumer Council: Mr Michael Young
National Federation of Building Trades Employers
National Opinion Poll Market Research Ltd
National Ports Council
National Union of Bank Employees
National Union of Licensed Victuallers
Sir Leonard Neal and a group of Industrial Relations Specialists
Newspaper Society
1972 Industry Group
Nottinghamshire Chamber of Commerce and Industry
Mr Robert Oakeshott
Ocean Transport & Trading Ltd

Opinion Research Centre
Mr Richard N Ottaway
Robert Owen Association
Mr S R Parker
Parliamentary Committee of the Co-operative Union Ltd
Petroleum Employers' Advisory Council on Employee Relations
Philips Electronic and Associated Industries Ltd
Professor Sir Henry Phelps Brown
Pilkington Brothers Ltd
Plaid Cymru
J & F Pool Ltd
Mr Arthur Priest
Prudential Section of the National Union of Insurance Workers
Mr W K Purdie
Rank Hovis McDougall Ltd
Reckitt & Colman Ltd
Sir Brandon Rhys Williams Bt MP
Mr C P Richards
Mr P J Ridley
Rock Services (Midlands) Ltd
Rohm and Haas (UK) Ltd
Dr Donald Roy and members of the Young Fabian Group
Royal Insurance Co Ltd
**Royal Swedish Embassy: Mr I Janerus, Labour Attaché
John Sacher Industrial Group
Sand and Gravel Association Ltd
Scott Bader Co Ltd
Scottish Council Development and Industry
Scottish & Newcastle Breweries Ltd
Seagram Distillers Ltd
Selsdon Group
Mr W J Shaw
Shellabear Price Contractors Ltd
Shell Petroleum Co Ltd
Shephard, Hill & Co Ltd
Shipbuilders and Repairers National Association
James Sim Ltd
Sketchley Ltd
Smiths Industries Ltd
Society of Industrial Tutors
A member of the South Western Printers Alliance
Spencer Stuart & Associates
SPW (Civil Engineering) Ltd
Staff Committee of the British Oxygen Company Ltd
Staff Council of the London Service of the Shell Petroleum Co Ltd
Mr D L Stebbings
Mr D W H Steeds
Steel Industry Management Association
Sir Iain M Stewart LL D, BSC
Stock Exchange
Storey Brothers and Company Ltd

Mr Geoffrey Stuttard and members of an industrial relations seminar, Department of Extra Mural Studies, London University

Mr Geoffrey Stuttard and 16 trade union members of an adult education seminar on industrial relations, Department of Extra Mural Studies, London University

Tarmac Ltd

Tate & Lyle Ltd

Staff Members of the Tavistock Institute of Human Relations

Taylor Woodrow Ltd

Technical, Administrative and Supervisory Section of the Amalgamated Union of Engineering Workers

Thomas Tilling Ltd

Thornton & Ross Ltd

Tobacco Industry Employers' Association

Tootal Ltd

*Trades Union Congress: Rt Hon Lionel Murray PC, OBE

Mr D McGarvey CBE

Mr C H Urwin

Mr A W Fisher

Trebor Sharps Ltd

Tube Investments Ltd

Unicorn Industries Ltd

Unilever Ltd

United Kingdom Association of Professional Engineers

Unit Trust Association

Unquoted Companies' Group

Urwick, Orr & Partners Ltd

Urwick Technology Management Ltd

Vallance & Davison Ltd

L M Van Moppes & Sons Ltd

Mr John Verdin Davies

Vickers Ltd

Wakefield and District Trades Council

Warne, Wright & Rowland Ltd

Mr R Warren Evans

Mr M Warwick-Smith

Mr Michael Wedge

Weir Group of Companies

Mr John Wellens

Mr David Wheeler

Whitbread & Co Ltd

Mr M D Wibberley

Wider Share Ownership Council

Professor A T M Wilson

Robert Wilson & Sons Ltd

George Wimpey & Co Ltd

Wool (and Allied) Textile Employers' Council

Work Research Unit of the Department of Employment

Working Together Campaign Ltd

Mr W L Wright

Mr Dennis Wyke

LIST OF THOSE WITH WHOM DISCUSSIONS WERE HELD OVERSEAS

A SWEDEN

Atlas Kopco Group

Mr Tom Wachmeister, Managing Director
Mr R Lahnkagen, Personnel Director
Mr K Modig, Production Director
Mr P E Nyholm, Worker Director (Metal Workers' Union)
Mr Sigreid Landin, Worker Director (Supervisors' and Foremen's Union)

Central Organisation of Salaried Employees (TCO)

Mr Lennart Bodström, President
Mr Jan-Erik Nyberg
Mr Karl Erik Nilsson
Mr Stig Gustafsson
Ms Birgitte Isaksson
Mr Nils Ellebring

Electrolux

Mr H Werthén, Managing Director

Factory Workers' Union

Mr Nils Christofferson
Mr Jan Odhnoff

Ministry of Industry

Mr Lindquist

Ministry of Labour

Mr Allan Larsson, Secretary
Mr Olaf Bergquist, Legal Department

Skandinaviska Enskilda Banken

Mr Jacob Palmstierna, Deputy Managing Director
Mr Runé Barneus, Personnel Director

State Enterprise Board

Mr Bertil Olsson, Chairman
Per Sköld, Managing Director

Swedish Association of Supervisors and Foremen (SALF)

Mr Sune Tidefelt, Chairman
Mr Björn Bergman, First Secretary

Swedish Bank Employees' Union

Mr Hilding Sjoberg
Ms Birgitta Persson, Worker Director

Dr Karl-Olof Faxén, Director of Research
Mr Rolf Lindholm, Director of Technical Department
Mr Lennart Grafström, Assistant Director, Industrial Democracy

SWEDISH TRADE UNION CONFEDERATION (LO)

Mr Claes-Erik Odner, Economic Adviser
Mr Anders Wetterberg
Mr Lindbohm

UNIVERSITY OF STOCKHOLM

Professor Folke Schmidt
Professor T Sigeman
Professor S Edlund
Professor A Vicktorin
Professor W Korpi
Mr A C Neal

OTHERS

Mr Sven Hilding, Statskonsult AB
Mr Bertil Höglund, G P Personnel AGA/AB
Mr Ake Nordlander, Engineering Employers' Association
Mr Erik Pettersson, General Director, National Industrial Board
Mr Peter Stare, Chief Negotiator, State Enterprises Negotiating Board
Professor Gösta Rehn, Director, Social Research Institute

B FEDERAL REPUBLIC OF GERMANY

GERMAN EMPLOYERS' ASSOCIATION (BDA)

Dr Hanns Martin Schleyer, President
Dr Ernst-Gerhard Erdmann, Director-General
Dr Wolf Dieter Lindner, International Secretary
Dr Rolf Thüsing, Head of Economic and Social Department

GERMAN TRADE UNION FEDERATION (DGB)

Herr Gerhard Schmidt, Member of Executive
Herr Pfeiffer, Member of Executive
Frau Bode, International Section
Herr Walter Jung, Head of Department of Social Policy
Dr Gerd Liminsky, Economic and Social Science Institute

IG METALL

Herr Eugen Loderer, President
Dr Schunk, International Secretary
Herr Friedrichs
Dr Hans Adam Fromm
Herr Gunther
Herr Dieter Hennig
Herr Kattenhom

BANKERS

Dr Robert Ehret, Management Board Member, Deutsche Bank AG
Dr Ernst Plesser, Assistant General Manager, Deutsche Bank AG
Dr Werner, Legal expert, Deutsche Bank AG
Dr Hans A Wuttke, Management Board Member, Dresdner Bank AG
Dr Henkel, Dresdner Bank AG
Dr Hans-Georg Gottheiner, Partner, Berliner Handelsgesellschaft-Frankfurter Bank (BHF Bank)
Dr Wind, BHF Bank
Dr Jürgen Terrahe, Member of Management Board, Commer AG

BRITISH–GERMAN TRADE COUNCIL

Mr I R G Ferguson, Industrial Consultant and Vice-President of the Council
Dr K J Malchow, Industrial Relations Manager, Deutsche Unilever
Dr Helmuth Schwesinger, Personnel Director, Deutsche Shell
Herr Wontorra, Joint Manager, Lingner und Fisher
Mr E B Wootten, Manager (France and Germany), Girling Bremsen

MANNESMANN AG

Dr Marcus Bierich, Member of the Management Board
Herr Hans Otto Christiansen, Worker Director
Herr Peter Keller, Labour Director
Dr Schundler, Public Relations Executive

OTHERS

Herr Bartels, Chairman, Blohm und Voss
Professor Wolfgang Däubler, Professor of Labour Law and Commercial Law, University of Bremen
Herr Gelhorn, Deputy Chairman of Mineworkers' Union
Herr Jakob Hurtz, President of Works Council, Gebrüder Böhler
Herr Kluncker, Chairman, ÖTV (Public Services & Transport Workers' Union)
Dr Walther Kolvenback, Chief Legal Adviser, Henkel & Co AG
Dr Heinz Lecorek, Labour Director, Gebrüder Böhler
Herr Englebert van de Loo, Director, Metallgesellschaft AG
Mr Tom Lossius, Director, ICI Europa
Herr Lutz, Chairman, Ford Germany
Professor Dr Reuter, Rector of Düsseldorf University
Dr Walter Schlotfeld, Member of Management Board, Adam Opel AG
Herr Adolf Schmidt, Chairman, IG Bergbau (Mineworkers' Union)

Printed in England for Her Majesty's Stationery Office by Oyez Press Limited
Dd. 294245   K80   1/77